A Design

for Social Work Practice

FELICE DAVIDSON PERLMUTTER

Editor

A Design for Social Work Practice

Columbia University Press
New York and London

1974

Library of Congress Cataloging in Publication Data

Perlmutter, Felice Davidson, 1931–
   A design for social work practice.
   Includes bibliographies.
   1. Social service—Addresses,
   essays, lectures. I. Title.
HV40.P39   361   74–1200
   ISBN 0–231–03808–9

To my parents,
Helen and Samuel Davidson,
who coupled personal caring
with social concerns

Foreword

As its title indicates, this book represents an attempt at achieving a redefinition of social work practice. This particular attempt deserves an especially sympathetic and attentive reading because of its stated objective of integrating those old adversaries in the social work profession, cause and function. The achievement of this integration has long been one of the major challenges of the profession. By focusing as it does on an institutionally defined conception of social work practice as the means of achieving the integration of cause and function, this book extends its potential importance well beyond the confines of social work itself. In taking an institutionally defined approach this book implicitly requires new thinking about cooperation and integration within institutions but across disciplines and across professions. Thus this work, while ostensibly suggesting an integrated model of social work practice using institutions as the practice unit, is really suggesting a new concept for the practice orientation of all human service professions.

This is a bold undertaking, but social work's current dilemmas, which can be attributed at least in part to the inadequately defined boundaries of all of the human service professions, can only be approached by such boldness.

Our professional practice will always require examination, and this requirement will probably always be fueled by pressures from both within and without the profession. The strength of the efforts represented in this volume lies in the recognition of an immediate set of problems and in the attempt to deal with these problems through proposals of long-term relevance rather than short-term convenience. Attempts like those within this volume to stimulate the evolution of our conception of social work practice by relating short-term pressures to possible long-term solutions are critically important to the successful evolution of the profession. Whether the directions described in this volume generate agreement or not, the debates that they will encourage are essential to the strength of our future work.

HAROLD A. RICHMAN
Dean, the School of Social
Service Administration,
the University of Chicago

Preface

THE PROFESSION of social work is in a period of self-examination and change; this book offers a model for that change. It proposes that social work practice be considered in its institutional context. Thus the book is not organized around issues in practice, as many social work books have been in the past, but instead according to issues within selected, relevant fields.

In Part I the various functional fields are presented as they relate to social work practice. Part II discusses the implications of this new approach for social work practice; specifically, the dilemmas of professionalism and the areas where a different expertise is needed. And finally, an educational model is presented which aims to prepare social workers for the various functions and roles they will perform in the social welfare sector.

The contributing authors have been chosen on the basis of their expertise in specific functional fields; many are not social workers and approach the issues for social work from their particular perspective. The contributions were written by invitation and are all original in this volume, designed to meet the editor's objectives. Consequently, the volume presents diverse points of view as well as diverse styles of presentation, on the assumption that the argument can best be presented from these different vantage points.

The book is directed to planners, practitioners, and educators in social work and social welfare; it is also intended for use as a textbook for introductory courses in graduate school programs. The bibliographical references from each field provide an overview of the relevant materials available in this broad spectrum for social work practice.

Formulation of the philosophy of practice presented here was made possible through a summer faculty fellowship in 1970, provided by the University of Pennsylvania. Continuing curriculum reorganization at the School of Social Work of the University of Pennsylvania reinforced the editor's conviction of its worth. The interest and cooperation of the contributors were invaluable throughout. Miss Barbara Branham and Mrs. Dee Bristow who provided the secretarial support made the entire project feasible.

The synthesis of professional and wife/mother roles was made possible by my husband, Daniel, and our children, Shira, Saul, and Tova.

FELICE DAVIDSON PERLMUTTER

Contents

Part Two. New Directions for Social Work Practice

Contributors

Shirley M. Buttrick, Associate Director and Professor, School of Social Work, University of Minnesota, Minneapolis

William Gellman, Executive Director, Jewish Vocational Service, Chicago; Past Chairman, Chicago Chapter, National Association of Social Workers

Toby Golick, Senior Attorney, Legal Services for the Elderly Poor, New York

Elsbeth Kahn, Associate Professor, Department of Community Medicine and Public Health, and Adjunct Associate Professor, School of Social Work, University of Southern California, Los Angeles

Alan Keith-Lucas, Professor, School of Social Work, University of North Carolina, Chapel Hill, N.C.

Theodore Levine, Executive Director, Youth Service, Inc., Philadelphia; former Chief, Community Services Administration, Region III, Social and Rehabilitation Service, HEW.

Felice Davidson Perlmutter, Associate Professor, School of Social Administration, Temple University, Philadelphia

Eugen Pusić, Professor, Faculty of Law, University of Zagreb, Yugoslavia; Past President, International Conference on Social Welfare

Gordon Rose, Reader, Department of Social Administration, University of Manchester, England

Richard Scobie, Executive Director, Unitarian-Universalist Service Committee, Boston; former Director, Department of Tenant and Community Relations, Boston Housing Authority

Simon Slavin, Dean, School of Social Administration, Temple University, Philadelphia

Neilson F. Smith, Chief, Community and Group Services Section, Social Work Training Branch, National Institute of Mental Health, Rockville, Md.

Jonathan M. Stein, Chief of Law Reform, Community Legal Services, Inc., Philadelphia

Louis G. Tornatzky, Associate Professor, Department of Urban and Metropolitan Studies and the Department of Psychology, Michigan State University, East Lansing, Mich.

Elaine Werby, Housing Consultant, Arthur D. Little, Inc., Boston; former Chief of Social Planning, Boston Housing Authority

Milton Wittman, Chief, Social Work Training Branch, National Institute of Mental Health, Rockville, Md.

A Design

for Social Work Practice

FELICE DAVIDSON PERLMUTTER

A Philosophy for Social Work Practice

THE PROFESSION of social work is in a critical period of examination and change. This period differs from other periods of the profession's development in that the examination is occurring not only within the profession but simultaneously without—by the government, the consumer, the university, and even by other professions (law, medicine, for example). This very difference raises the process to the level of "a critical decision" (Selznick, 1957)—critical in regard to the future directions and possibly the survival of social work as a profession.

Earlier periods of examination and change were largely internally motivated and inner-directed, albeit in response to external phenomena. This is illustrated in Gordon Hamilton's Foreword to Stein and Cloward, *Social Perspectives on Behavior* (1958):

The preoccupation of social work was first with economic phenomena—relief of poverty, then, gradually, income maintenance and standard of living. The next swing was to an understanding of personality and the development of a psychosocial approach to all problems. For over a quarter century social workers have been familiar with a theory of personality which enabled them, as never before, to understand the individual and his behavior in certain important respects. The advent of dynamic psychology, chiefly due to the creative genius of Freud, changed the whole approach of the profession toward relationships, especially those of the family, children, and worker-client. It was not as possible, however, to derive comparable insights from the social sciences whose concepts, problems, and even terminology remained obscure to social work. The current revolution of which we are slowly becoming aware lies in this very area of social and cultural insights for which social workers require a new sophistication in social science (p. xi).

By contrast, the present analysis, from the many vantage points suggested above, raises questions involving external processes: the government's focus is on efficiency; the consumer's is on effectiveness; the university's is on excellence; the professions' on their own expanding and competing welfare functions. It is therefore important to examine what is unique and useful about social work which justifies society's support.

The seriousness of the situation is further evidenced by the observation that social workers are marginal even to those programs which are central to our professional concern. Thus Gilbert Steiner's trenchant analysis (1971) exposes the basic dilemmas of the social work profession: first, we are not translating our important values and goals into program realities; second, we are in fact primarily, though marginally, involved in the implementation of punitive and restrictive procedures in public welfare. Morris (1972) suggests that the Steiner volume demonstrates "(1) the misleading mythology with which social work has surrounded itself; and (2) the limitations of our present education" (p. 75).

The purpose of this volume is to provide a philosophy for practice and a program for change. Not only does it deal with new content areas essential for social work practice, it also provides a context within which the practice should be framed. The issues are of long-term interest. While hopefully these discussions can contribute to a more effective response to present short-term and shifting realities, they aim to offer fundamental proposals of long-term relevance for this changing profession.

Two principles shape the philosophical underpinnings of this endeavor, and both are viewed as inextricably linked. First, this volume is designed to provide a conceptual framework to handle with an integrated approach the dilemma and duality in social work practice. This dilemma has been discussed in numerous writings as cause and function (Lee, 1937) or social action vs. service delivery (Rein, 1970). Generally, the dichotomy has been operationalized in practice to support service delivery (function) in one's professional job while supporting social action (cause) through one's professional association apart from work (Heffernan, 1964). This dichotomous response has been sharply questioned (Briar, 1972; Gill, 1973); not only is it harmful to the profession to have in-house fighting but ultimately, and more importantly, it harms the clients being served by the welfare system.

The intent of this book is to stimulate the application of new knowledge, functions, and roles so that social work practice need not be divided, but rather can be viewed as an integrated totality involving service provision, service development and systems change within clearly defined areas directly related to social work competence and responsibility. The participation in social change will thus flow from practice and be supported by clear-cut knowledge from professional involvement at the proper level in the social system. It will not be directed toward those broader areas of change with which we must concern ourselves as informed citizens but which are not our sole and special prerogative as professionals.

The second organizing principle is that social work must be placed in an institutional context and that practice can no longer be viewed from a methodological framework. While the theoretical base for social work practice has, to date, focused primarily on technical aspects (skill and method), as evidenced throughout the literature of the profession (Hamilton, 1951; Konopka, 1963; Smalley, 1967), we propose that social work must be viewed in an institutional context within those contexts which are socially sanctioned and accepted by society. Thus, for example, health, education, rehabilitation, and correctional systems are illustrative of the programs which demonstrate society's mandate.

The English definition of social policy and social administration (Marshall, 1965; Titmuss, 1959) provides an analytic framework within which the functional fields can be defined and within which the profession of social work can responsibly perform. It includes all those functions in health, education, and welfare which are designed to improve the life of the individual and hence the life of the nation.

The problem before a society which desires to turn its income to the best account does not differ, therefore, save in magnitude, from that confronting a private individual. What concerns it is not to maintain any fixed proportion between private and public expenditure, but to ensure that its limited resources shall be applied, not capriciously, but to meet its requirements in the order of their relative urgency. It is to reduce expenditure which neither raises the quality of individual life nor promotes social efficiency, and to augment expenditure which heightens them.

In reality, of course, the greater part of the expenditure upon the social services is not a liability, but an investment, the dividends of which are not the less substantial because they are paid, not in cash, but in strengthened individual energies and an increased capacity for co-operative effort. The manufacturer or mine-owner, whose establishment is staffed with workers who, after being prevented from dying in infancy by the public health service, educated in public elementary schools, and taught their craft in the municipal college of technology, are housed in buildings erected with the aid of a subsidy from the State, maintained during sickness and unemployment from funds to which it contributes, and paid their old-age pensions through the Post Office when they can no longer be useful to him, may continue to believe, with the romanticism of his kind, that his profits are created solely by his personal intelligence, initiative, thrift, and foresight. But, as a mere matter of prosaic fact, the State is a partner in his enterprise, whose contribution to its success is at least as important as his own. It is able to take for social purposes part of the wealth which he, as he thinks, produces, because it plays itself, through the social services, no small part in producing it (Marshall, p. 154).

It is thus evident that health, education, and housing are as central in the English idea of welfare as are social insurance and the more delimited social services generally included in discussions of welfare in the United States.

Furthermore, the English argue for a universal system of services for all, as opposed to selective programs for the needy, for the integration of insurance and assistance in the discussion of income maintenance, for partnership between public (statutory) and private (voluntary) agencies, and for the integration of social policy with economic policy (Marshall, 1965). This approach sharply contrasts with the issue that earlier concerned Hamilton and serves to point up the difference in emphasis and direction which frames the context of social work practice in the United States and in Great Britain. It is the English approach which provides a useful framework for the selection of relevant functional fields for social work practice.

It should be noted that our use of functional fields as the organizing framework for practice is different from the typical earlier focus on "fields of practice"; the social work role formulated in that period was that of service provider (Fink, Wilson, and Conover, 1955; Friedlander,

1955). Contrast Fink's description of the social worker in the medical setting with Kahn's discussion in this volume. According to Fink, regardless of setting (in hospitals or outside hospitals in public health, vocational rehabilitation, and health and welfare organizations), the basic function of the social worker was to "use the knowledge and skill of medical social work in such a way that a more effective service is ultimately available to more patients and in more places" (p. 303). Furthermore:

> . . . medical social work . . . involves the practice of social casework, and sometimes group work, in a hospital, a clinic or another medical setting to make it possible for the patient to use the available health service most effectively. Medical social work is characterized by emphasis on help in the social and emotional problems which affect the patient in his illness and his cure (Friedlander, 1955, p. 389).

Kahn's approach is dramatically different for it encompasses service delivery, advocacy, administration, and policy formation.

The link between the two fundamental principles which underpin this philosophy of practice is that social work can best perform its integrated functions of service delivery, service development, and systems change within specific socially sanctioned programs. Thus social work has a vital role in helping the institutions to meet the needs of their consumers effectively, and its expertise is viewed in relation to these systems and their objectives. Furthermore, activity in service provision, service development, and systems change has a logical boundary, specified and delimited by the particular system of service, here defined as functional field.

We are concerned with all forms of service in the functional fields regardless of auspice. Thus this book includes both the public and the voluntary sector in its focus on differential roles in social service systems, as exemplified by Pusic's discussion of administration and Keith-Lucas's discussion of an integrated and coordinated child welfare system which links public and private agencies. This approach facilitates the collaboration of social work with other professions within the functional fields to meet the interests of the consumers and society in a broader and more integrated manner.

References

Briar, Scott. "Means, Ends and Confusions," *Social Work*, XVII, No. 5 (1972), 2.

Fink, Arthur E., Everett E. Wilson, and Merrill B. Conover. *The Fields of Social Work*, New York, Holt, Rinehart, and Winston, Inc., 1955.

Friedlander, Walter A. *Introduction to Social Welfare*. Englewood Cliffs, N.J., Prentice-Hall, Inc., 1955.

Gill, David G. *Unravelling Social Policy*. Cambridge, Mass., Schenkman Publishing Co., 1973.

Hamilton, Gordon. *Theory and Practice of Social Case Work*. 2d ed., New York, Columbia University Press, 1951.

—— "Foreword," Herman D. Stein and Richard A. Cloward, eds., in *Social Perspectives on Behavior*. New York, Free Press of Glencoe, 1958.

Heffernan, Joseph W., Jr. "Political Activity and Social Work Executives," *Social Work*, IX, No. 2 (1964), 18-23.

Konopka, Gisela. *Social Group Work: a Helping Process*. Englewood Cliffs, N.J., Prentice-Hall, Inc., 1963.

Lee, Porter R. *Social Work as Cause and Function, and Other Papers*. New York, Columbia University Press, 1937.

Marshall, Thomas H. *Social Policy*. London, England, Hutchinson and Co., Ltd., 1965.

Morris, Robert. "Book Review," *Education for Social Work*, VIII, No. 2 (1972), 74-78.

Rein, Martin. "Social Work in Search of a Radical Profession," *Social Work*, XV, No. 2 (1970), 13-28.

Selznick, Philip. *Leadership in Administration*. New York, Harper and Row, 1957.

Smalley, Ruth E. *Theory for Social Work Practice*. New York, Columbia University Press, 1967.

Steiner, Gilbert. *The State of Welfare*. Washington, D.C., the Brookings Institution, 1971.

Titmuss, Richard M. *Essays on "The Welfare State"*. New Haven, Conn., Yale University Press, 1959.

PART
ONE

Functional Fields

for Social Work Practice

ALAN KEITH-LUCAS

Co-planning and Advocacy in Child Welfare Services

CHILD WELFARE, in part perhaps because the term indicates a cause or an objective rather than an operation, is not only hard to define, it suffers in many instances from an emotional involvement or partisanship which needs to be understood before programs and the role of social work in them can be intelligently discussed.

Family or Child Welfare

On the one hand, it is very difficult to distinguish any set of operations under the name of child welfare that do not overlap with general family welfare. Children are members of a family, and it is obvious that the greatest impact on the greatest number of children will always be realized in those programs that benefit the family as a whole. What is not quite so obvious is that even those services that are thought of as primarily child-centered, such as protective services and foster care placement, must be envisaged in a family context, so that even children's institutions, normally the most child-centered of all agencies, can, as some are beginning to do, justifiably describe themselves as family agencies. In this view there is little that can be claimed to be specifically a "child welfare" operation, and child welfare services can perhaps only be defined loosely as those social services in which attainment of a primary, or a distinct, or even a recognizable subgoal will bring improvement in a child's or children's living conditions, experience, functioning, or behavior.

Yet there is at the same time a traditional yet ever-present strain of thinking in the field that sees the purpose of child welfare as basically that of rescuing the child from unfavorable living conditions or mistreatment, which often means his family life and which therefore opposes the child's "rights" to those of his parents. The social worker and, increasingly, the lawyer are envisaged as the advocates of the child. He or she "speaks for him" or "represents his interest" in protective, adoptive, divorce, or delinquency proceedings and in all types of family counseling.

While there are undoubtedly many situations in which a child's basic rights are violated by his parents, or he needs someone to be concerned for his interests when these might otherwise be ignored, many such "advocates" make the implicit assumption that they have in some way been commissioned by the child, or would have been if the child had been able to express himself. Their relationship to the child is that of a lawyer with his client, despite the fact that the child has little actual say in the process. What they have done is simply to assume that their perception of the child's needs and rights is superior to that of his natural parents. They understand children's needs and the parent either does not or is blind to them. But so far from actually "speaking" for the child the fact is, as anyone who has worked with children in foster care can testify, that the majority of children, if free to choose, would prefer their parents to speak for them and see their self-appointed "advocates" for what they actually are: "parental interveners" who are competing with their parents for control over their lives.

This does not mean that the parental intervener may not be right and may not be acting in the child's best interest. It does mean that he cannot claim a special authority conferred, however indirectly, by the child, and therefore to be preferred to the parent's wishes, which are all too often in contrast considered to be selfish or insensitive. The situation is further confused when the worker or the agency begins with the assumption that opens a famous child welfare book of the

1940s (Emma Lundberg, *Unto the Least of These*), namely, that a child's needs (which can only mean a social worker's perception of his needs) and his rights are synonymous. Such an advocacy, however well-meaning or informed, reinforced with the conviction that one is speaking for children, can and does lead to attempts to deal with children out of the context of their families and philosophically to elitism and at least quasi-totalitarianism. Indeed, Mandell (1971, Part 1, p. 22) includes the power to remove or even to threaten to remove children from their parents as one of the totalitarian features of the present welfare system.

Such attitudes have also contributed to the national scandal of long-term, rootless foster care. The problem is often, and with some partial justification, laid to overindulgent treatment of parents and an unrealistic belief in the value of any kind of parental contact, remnants perhaps of self-determinatory and Bowlbian concepts of the 1950s and early 1960s. McCrae (1960, p. 5) expresses the belief, which he says is supported by many child welfare specialists, that parental rights have been overstressed and have prevented adoption planning for children whose parents might have been helped to release them, and that a rash of laws at that time made it more possible to force this result. The evidence is clear, however, as Maas had found out even earlier, that most parents of children in foster care had not been indulged but rather were left to a "self-healing process" (Maas and Engler, 1959, p. 5). The literature is full of complaints that no help is given to parents of children in foster care (McAdams, a parent of foster children herself, 1972; Stone, 1970, p. 7), that they too need advocates (Bryce and Ehlert, 1971, p. 503), and have not been studied or shown concern for. Real question has also been raised (Jenkins, 1969, pp. 339–40; Stone, p. 7) as to what such intervention and neglect of the parent do both to the child's ability to return to his family and to his success if he does return there. Yet as Taylor (1972), Williams (1972), the Chapel Hill Workshops (1971), and much more material have shown, parents can and indeed need to be constructively involved in their children's lives before, after and during placement if placement is not to become a limbo of "professional foster children."

Advocacy and Intervention

Yet the feelings that lie behind such thinking and practice are natural
and are shared by many community persons—a fact of great significance if the welfare program of the future is to be more community-
based, and if the child advocacy movement, which in general is ad-
mirable, is really to contribute to the welfare of children. The feelings
are maternal, or perhaps more properly parental, inspired by the apparent helplessness of children; protective, arising in part from an
underestimation of a child's ability to cope with his situation; and in
many cases, the probable result of an unresolved conflict on the part of
both professionals and lay persons with their own parents. They are fed
by the somewhat alarming increase of at least detected cases of child
abuse, and by the generally accepted psychological theories of the past
half century, which ascribe all of a child's problems to the lack of love or
some other inadequacy of his parents, and have been made more tenable
due to the fragility of the nuclear family. They are based on a modicum
of truth: children are, as Rubin (1972, p. 502) says, "nonpersons" in
several respects. But by and large, such advocacy is emotional rather
than rational, and often places blame in the wrong places, or refuses
to help those who, even if they have temporarily violated the rights
of a child—even abusive parents can be helped, as shown by Brown
and Daniels (1968)—still mean much to their children and may be
the principal sources of help to them in the future. Yet juvenile courts
in some jurisdictions in the United States today include on their printed
legal forms the statement that in the event that a child is found to be
neglected, there is an automatic termination of all parental rights; this is
a legal and psychological horror that agencies must either ignore or else
find themselves dealing with a child who is disturbed, confused, and
resentful principally because of what his so-called "advocates" have
done to him.

A useful sidelight to the problem of intervention and advocacy is
provided by Gill (1960, p. 3) when he comments that the court's "power
to assist a child" stems not from a child's so-called "needs" but from
the self-interest of the state and that "'the best interests of the child'
is the concluding determinant . . . and not the beginning of a neglect
hearing." In other words, although the state must intervene when chil-

dren are in danger, it does so only when a family ceases to exercise its function in a minimally adequate manner, and not from its generally greater wisdom about what would be good for children.

It therefore seems incumbent on the profession to arrive at some basic concept of child welfare practice that is neither "child-centered" nor "parent-centered" but truly family-centered, that will protect children, where necessary, but at the same time enhance their possibilities for family life as well as for a good life in general. Such a program not only must deal with the general and community conditions of family life; it must also help families who are faced with disintegration or disaster cope with what is threatening them and come to the best possible plan to overcome or accommodate to what has happened to them.

Co-planning in Child Welfare

The key to such a program would appear to lie in the concept of co-planning between the parents, the child, the community, and the agency for family enhancement. It begins not with one client, the child, but with the pooled interest of everyone concerned (including the child) in conditions for growth. In individual situations the parent, as the child's natural guardian, is the primary decision-maker, in so far as he is not constrained by law or unwilling to perform his role. Agency and community stand ready to help him as best he can. Protective services and foster care are therefore seen not as means to rescue children from their families but as possible resources in family planning to meet difficult situations, just as are counseling, day care, and recreation. They are, however, resources applicable in general at a stage in which a family is undergoing considerable strain. Separation for longer or shorter periods may be the best possible plan for the time being and may be legally required if the parent does not choose it himself. At no time, however, is the parent considered anything less than a partner in this co-planning until he himself breaks off the partnership, and even then, every effort is made to help this be, if it must, part of a plan in which he has a part.

The concept of co-planning is an important one for social work. It represents perhaps as nearly as possible the spirit of a new partnership between consumers and providers of service (Keith-Lucas, 1973). It can be contrasted with the basically "therapeutic" stance that social agencies have more or less adopted in the past, which carries inevitably the implication that those seeking social services are, if not sick, at least in some way inadequate. Under a co-planning concept no such assumption is made. All that is recognized is man's mutual dependence in the complexities of life today—a logical extension from the fact that anyone may need help with some area of personal planning, be it travel, or income tax, or academic program, with no implication of inadequacy.

Co-planning is also the most satisfactory and the most easily understood explanation of what a social worker does. He co-plans with people, or groups, or communities in relation to social services, social institutions, or social conditions. It is, in fact, his primary skill, backed by his knowledge, and is perhaps his primary value.

It is also a systems concept; that is, it must take into account all parts of a system in order to be valid. It is co-planning in relation to something, the system in which an individual, a family, or a community operates.

At the base, then, of a public child welfare system there needs to be a co-planning service. For administrative reasons this may be partially differentiated into a co-planning unit with the community, with the individual family, and in relation to the law, reinforced with a research unit, and this model will be assumed in envisaging what a public child welfare service might be.

Co-planning on a community level starts with both the potential consumers of service and those who provide service. Ideally, perhaps, these should be one and the same, and with the inclusion of clients on agency boards they may become closer. At the moment, however, there may be some difficulty in treating the two as identical, although there may be overlappings. Yet a child-advocacy group or, more properly, a family-advocacy group is perhaps the logical consumer group to begin with not only to ensure that child care facilities are adequate, but to determine needs and spearhead the development of new resources. One such group would act, perhaps officially, as an advisory body to the whole public child welfare system, and there should be representatives of client interests on any governing board. Community workers with both grass-roots organizing and planning skills are needed, and there will have to be, too, an educational process so that citizen groups operate with the knowledge necessary really to assess what an agency is doing or what services might be needed. Co-planning involves putting together the perceived needs of the community with the expertise of those who know how services can be made to work, and this is fundamentally a social work skill. This is also the group that should act in the political sphere to obtain what is needed for family life. "Child welfare" is an illusion so long as there is inadequate housing, widespread unemployment, niggardly income-maintenance measures, pollution, and lack of medical care. Social workers may not be principals in influencing measures to correct these ills, but they can and will be involved in testifying to the need for them and helping groups organize to obtain them.

This discussion, however, is directed more to those services that meet the needs of individual families and children within the framework of such general measures, not because such measures are unimportant—they are supremely important—but because the problems are so vast and involve so much more than social work, and so much more than children, that the specifics of the necessary and particular segment of work with which we are here concerned would be lost.

Co-planning with the providers of service will also require considerable skill. America has a long tradition of pluralism. In New York City, for example, according to the Citizens' Committee for Children of New York (1971, p. 28), 80 percent of what are now classified as child welfare services are provided by private organizations. The job will be to co-plan so that neither are these organizations stifled in making what can be a unique contribution to children and families, or to the field, nor is there unnecessary duplication of service, or real gaps in a comprehensive plan which an existing agency could fill.

This is a difficult area. While many so-called "private" agencies can exist only by virtue of purchase-of-care payments from the public purse, and are thus in a sense controlled by the public, much of what a private or a church-sponsored agency has to give is derived from its private or church-sponsored nature—its freedom, for instance, to select its clientele or to do something different and experimental. In many parts of the country such agencies are not only stronger than the public agencies but have been responsible for some of the more progressive social work concepts. It will be important to work with these agencies in such a way that the government is clearly not planning *for* them but rather *with* them, as colleague and consultant rather than as governmental force. Tradition, religious convictions, and relationships with regional and national bodies are factors that cannot be overlooked and may be sources of strength as well as of weakness. A co-planner who cannot recognize what these mean to agencies will be lost in trying to work with them.

The Citizens' Committee for Children of New York (1971, p. 28) proposes a "clearly defined relationship to a publicly accountable, family-centered service system" in which "responsibility for case accountability and service integration will be located in the public department." Care would have to be taken that the public department really knows what it is doing. Public agencies have not been notable for the quality of their planning with families and are all too often so overburdened that they can do little more than meet emergencies.

There are also other services which vitally affect children and family life: the basic income-maintenance service, the schools, the police, the juvenile or family court system, public recreation, the health services, and perhaps others, according to how the community is organized. These need to be interwoven with the planning done by the other groups. General agreements need to be made in terms of the needs of each, the referrals that are made between them, and the cooperation each is able and willing to offer to the others. These must be tied in both with a child-advocacy organization and with planning with providers of service. A primary social work skill here will be that of consultation, a specialized form of co-planning for which social workers today get perhaps an inadequate preparation. All too often it is seen as simply related to expertise, with little attention to the helping skills involved.

Research Needs

Another most important tool in the co-planning process will be adequate research. While in many ways the field is wide open, there is particular need for research on the results of social work intervention of various kinds. Studies of the results of foster care such as Maas (1969), Bryce and Ehlert (1971), Fanshel (1971), Hoopes *et al.* (1969), Kadushin (1966, 1967), and Maas and Engler (1959), and of institutional care such as Jaffe (1969), and Wolins (1969) have been of real importance in recasting programs and have challenged many comfortable illusions. Research is also needed in the characteristics of a population served. So far, this has probably been done best in the area of neglect and abuse, in such studies as those of Gil (1971), Giovannoni and Billingsley (1970), and Mulford and Cohen (1967), and in relation to foster parents by Babcock (1965) and Madison and Shapiro (1969). There is, however, little research in the area of prediction—Kraus (1971) is an exception—and in practice variables. The question of what brings people to a social agency and what are considered problems capable of being helped by social workers badly needs researching. There has been little evaluative research on social work settings or on the use of various helping procedures or principles.

Still more research is needed in intra-agency operation. Few agencies are willing to subject themselves to a thorough systems analysis, even in making important decisions about structure or future directions. Indeed, one of the functions of the public child welfare agency might well be not only general research but consultation to agencies wishing to use research methods in their own decision-making.

The Basic Family Service

For individual families there needs to be, first of all, a basic family service (BFS), co-planning in nature, entirely voluntary, and clearly a "public utility" existing with no implication that its use implies insufficiency. The New York Citizens' Committee "dreams" of such a service. Its beginning point might be something akin to the British Citizens' Advice Bureaus (Zucker, 1965), but it would provide much more than a referral service. It might, in fact, have four major functions. These would not, however, be separate bureaus but would all be actions of the BFS.

1. Co-planning or consideration of directions in which a family might want to go: This could be at a fairly general level and not involve prob-

lem-solving at any very high level of expertise. It would probably be staffed, as the New York Citizens Committee suggests, by today's public assistance staff. Its role would be more a tentative identification of problems and likely ways to meet them.

2. A crisis intervention service: This would include a twenty-four-hour telephone "hot line" (Schreiber, 1971) both for troubled parents and for children in difficulty, and a staff able to take over in emergencies. In this respect BFS would have immediate access to, or administer, both an emergency homemaker service and shelter-care facilities for children whose parents cannot immediately be located and for runaways.

3. An advocacy service: This would use both the family worker and legal advocacy channels, and deal with problems as various as failure to get service from a hospital, tenants' rights, applications for benefits, or, as one public welfare service manual puts it, "helping the client obtain relief from social injustices such as discrimination and public discourtesy suffered on the basis of age, sex, race, background, physical condition or socio-economic background" (Forsyth County, 1971, p. 5). But it would be presumptuous to believe that all advocacy would start in the public agency, or even in a "child advocacy" group. As much advocacy is likely to come from private agencies.

4. A referral service: This term needs defining and perhaps modifying. What is *not* meant is an informational bureau, or the use of a referral slip, or even the kind of struggling with a client's plans and fears that should precede any referral, but a consistent, followed-through activation of the system in the client's behalf. Perhaps "maintained referral" would be a better phrase. The concept is that around the BFS, for most people the entry point into the system, there would be a cluster of more specialized services. These might include at a minimum, marriage counseling; child guidance (including behavior-modification agencies and agencies concerned with developmental and learning disorders); adoption; direct child care, through homemakers, day care, foster family care, group homes, and institutions; various educational opportunities, such as parent groups; and protective services staffed with specialists. Some of these agencies would be private and some would be units within a public welfare system. The public agency is likely to maintain foster family care, homemaker ser-

vice, possibly some day care and shelter service, though such direct services, except in the case of foster family care, which involves as it were a vendor service, appear in general to be tending in the direction of purchase of care from nonpublic agencies. The BFS worker would follow through and if necessary or desirable represent the family in working with these agencies. They would become accountable to BFS, at least to the point of periodic reports, inclusion in replanning, and in agreeing not to close service without the family worker knowing of it and being able to offer further support.

To what extent the BFS should remain an active counselor while the family is using one of these services is a moot point. The experience of one agency holding custody of a child while another agency cares for him has often proved difficult. In practice, it has frequently meant decisions being made on visiting, or case plans, by an agency that does not really know what is happening between parent and child, and in many instances—perhaps because of the role the custodial agency has played in the removal of the child—tends to have a negative effect and support separation. Family service rendered to the parents of a placed child by a worker who is not part of the caring agency has often lacked direction. Parents need to be involved directly with the agency over visiting, support, vacations, and therapeutic plans for the child, and to plan with the agency, often with the child being present. Work with separated "part-time" parents is itself a specialized area of skill and knowledge, nor does one "rehabilitate" parents in a vacuum, but around their exercise of part-time parental functions while their children are in care (Aptekar, 1953). This would seem to suggest a role for the family worker, in some cases, of being informed and on call rather than being continuously involved. One must also remember that BFS would be a purely voluntary service. Some may not want the continuous involvement of a base agency when they are actively engaged with another agency on, say, adoption or a more or less parent-managed service, such as day care.

This also raises the question of the client who knows what he wants and goes first to the agency offering that service. Any attempt to channel all intake through a central planning agency is a denial of the service's voluntary nature. A church-related person who sees the church as his extended family may turn naturally to an agency of his church;

most people would not think it necessary to enroll a child in a day-care center through some other agency. Yet clearly if there is to be accountability of some sort and elimination of the present inappropriate placement of some children by agencies having only a caring function, the BFS needs to be involved. A law forbidding separation without public agency approval would cause much resentment and evasion; what might be done is to agree to include a member of the basic planning agency as well as, perhaps, a specific child-advocate on the admissions committee of all agencies accepting children into care away from their parents, or to require such agencies to report and clear plans before accepting a child. When a child is without parents, the BFS worker might possibly fill the role of "parental force" suggested by Barnes (1967), but there are even stronger arguments for a properly appointed guardian of the person (Appelberg, 1970; Weissman, 1964).

Protective Services

It will be noticed that in the cluster of services to which the family has access through the BFS, protective services were included. This may seem a denial of the voluntary principle and one that sets up an adversary relationship. Yet actually, despite a great deal of social work discussion of authority in protective services, and attempts to justify this on the basis of "community concern" (Mulford, 1969, p. 15) or "inherent authority" (de Schweinitz and de Schweinitz, 1964, p. 289), both rather questionable in terms of a truly consumer-based service, examination of the actual authority involved shows it to lie in the law and not in the social worker. If it were otherwise, social work would become once again a matter of values imposed by an elite group. The state most certainly has the right and the responsibility to intervene when a child is neglected or abused. That it should do so only for reasons clearly supported by evidence, weighing with great care the present and likely future damage to the child and keeping in mind the need to maintain "the delicate balance which presently exists between the interest of the state in the welfare of its children and the integrity of the family" (Gill, 1960, p. 5), does not deny its responsibility to act. It must also have the police power to investigate alleged cases of neglect and abuse. To this end it must employ or commission investigators of some kind, either police, social workers, or citizen groups (which is, in effect, what a private protective agency is).

The offering of a protective service is, however, something quite different. It is essentially a service; that is, something designed to be helpful, offered to a family potentially or actually in danger of state intervention which may require at least temporary separation of child and parent. It may be a service that places certain restrictions on a parent's activities, much as probation does on a probationer, but these are part of the conditions of any service offered as an alternative to a purely legal solution to the problem; that is, either contesting the case in court or accepting the court's ruling. There is no need for Bellucci (1972, p. 111), for example, to apologize for setting a condition in a protective service that the parent join a parents' group with the alternative being placement of the child, for this is the realistic choice that one has when one neglects one's child. One can either accept a service that is offered or take one's chance with the law. The only thing that is important to a kind of social work that frees people from arbitrary judgments on them is that this choice is a real one. Some parents have been forced in the past to abandon or neglect children in order to force a social worker bent on rehabilitation to consider the need for separation. Protective service, whether of the structured, time-limited-holding-to-requirements type long practiced by the Baltimore protective services unit, or conceived of as aggressive intervention, as in Herre (1972) or undertaking the role of the "extended family" (Barnes, 1967), and however it may combine casework and group work methodologies (Bean, 1971; Bellucci, 1972) can be offered either before or after the child is found to be legally neglected. It is simply a service offered to families who are in trouble or are likely to be in trouble with the law's insistence on at least "prudent" parenting, the term used in Gill's legal definition of neglect (1960, p. 6). It can be chosen by a parent who recognizes his own inadequacy, or offered by whoever wields the investigatory power in lieu of a petition to the court, or be itself the disposition of the court; always, however, with the understanding that the court retains the right to reopen the case and recommend separation.

Structurally, it would seem wise to separate the protective service from the BFS because a protective service does need one piece of authority—the authority not to bring a case to court, but to offer the service instead. Also, working with people in conflict with the law is perhaps a specialty, not too easy for the basic family worker. When the service is a public one it might suggest a second unit, the protective-probation unit (PP). This unit would need to work very closely with BFS, and indeed might obtain through BFS the auxiliary services needed for its job. It would not necessarily be the investigative unit, although it might be so.

A difficult situation is here raised if the BFS working voluntarily with the family becomes aware of neglect, or even abuse. Can such a voluntary advocate and co-planning agency become the informant that invokes the police power of the state? This dilemma occurred all too often when the public assistance worker of the past "offered" a "child welfare" service that often resulted in court action when voluntary methods "failed." The argument for such a responsibility is that the family worker is much more likely than neighbors, or the police, or even the school, to know that a child is being neglected. Recent child-abuse laws place responsibility even on a family doctor to report suspected abuse. Yet knowing that the BFS could misinterpret one's problems and initiate investigation and even court action would keep many troubled families away. It would seem that it should be clear that such action should only be taken by the BFS in the sort of situation that calls for immediate emergency action—a child desperately ill, or beaten so severely that he needs medical care, or left alone in an immediately threatening situation—situations in which all control has been lost and any citizen would intervene. Normally, neglect allegations should come from the community, and the investigatory unit be distinct from general family service.

OUTREACH

Another difficult problem is raised by the need for outreach. Outreach is a concept based on the experience that many families will not or cannot ask help with problems for which they actually need help and are, indeed, relieved to be able to get it. It has perhaps best been described by Overton as long ago as 1953. It has its dangers. It can all too easily become a disguised form of protective service carrying the persuasive power of self-appointed child advocates, yet outreach of some kind is needed.

Some outreach would be provided by the investigatory unit when actual neglect was not established but the family was clearly in trouble. Referral to BFS could be suggested, but if this is to remain a purely voluntary service it could hardly do its own outreach. This might, however, be a function of a child advocacy group or a special team of neighborhood indigenous workers—ethnicity would be important here—not formally attached to BFS but acting to identify families in trouble and to make the services of BFS known, including its wholly voluntary nature; supporting families in approaching and using it; and acting as their advocates in seeing that they get the service they want.

RELATIONSHIPS TO THE COURTS

The role of the courts in this system and the social worker's relation to them should be clear. Family and juvenile courts should be recognized as exclusively courts of law. They are not, or should not be, social agencies with the power to enforce their plans. As Rubin points out (1972, p. 6), *parens patriae* is an "archaic notion." The business of the courts is to consider the evidence and determine whether the situation is such that the state is empowered to overrule the parents' plan for a child, and in what way, and for how long. They are not surrogate parents or even personal advocates for children. The most interesting and helpful work described by Dohen (1971) in interpreting an ethnic culture to the court and to other agencies, as well as vice versa, belongs in a BFS or an outreach unit and not in a court. There should be no such thing as a "ward of the court." If a child needs guardianship, and many children are in need of a personal representative to make major decisions for them, the court should appoint one. But chiefly a court should be in the business of adjudicating rights. It must act by law and not by virtue of a vague power of supposedly superior wisdom, as Judge Woodward pointed out so ably (1944), and both the Gault decision and Rubin (1972) confirm. It must act by due process—it is good to see consideration of due process in protective situations (Decker, 1972)—

and basically, since it is concerned with rights, it must be an adversary process and allow for advocacy of two potentially different points of view.

In protective proceedings this may result in social workers functioning in both adversary and advocacy roles, although not necessarily opposed to each other. A protective worker may have to present material contrary to the parent's wishes. At the same time, working with a family which has been brought into court a BFS worker may need to help that same family plan how to present their side of the story or to refute unfair evidence. Both owe the family absolute frankness about what has been found. The day of the "confidential report" is long gone.

The court may assign custody—that is, the physical, day-to-day care of the child—but should be empowered to do so only for a limited period with renewals only after further hearings. This should be true of both "neglected" and "delinquent" children. It should make clear the rights and the responsibilities of the parent in either case, and should be empowered to terminate parental guardianship and residual rights only on clear evidence either of abandonment, failure to exercise guardianship rights in planning for a child when aware of this responsibility and being given every assistance in doing so, or on the parents' own petition, as recommended by the U.S. Children's Bureau (1954), whose definition of the difference between custodial and guardianship rights is here adopted.

To whom the court should grant custody is an important question. Despite the difficulties inherent in custody held by an agency that is not caring for the child, there would be some value in assigning it to a joint protective-probation unit which would then confer with the BFS worker in selecting a caring facility and enter into a formal plan of delegation with the facility that empowers the latter to make its own decisions as to visiting, vacations, and so forth. Neither courts nor the protective-probation unit should have the power to limit visiting on their own motion. The BFS worker would act as advocate for both parents and child with the PP unit and the caring facility. If the caring facility has to give up caring for the child this would involve a joint plan between the three units involved.

The court may also offer to parents the opportunity of using a protective service, or to a child the alternative of probation, in lieu of reassignment of custody. In fact, probation and protective services might well be combined. They often deal with the same underlying problem although in one situation it is the parent and in the other the child who is in trouble with the law. But neither probation nor protective service should be part of the court, although the former often is so today. A court should not be put in the position of evaluating evidence presented by its own employees.

The whole question of delinquency and correctional services needs careful consideration. As Rubin (1972), Sheridan (1967), and others point out, it is an anomaly in our society that a child can be confined for doing something that would not be a crime if he were an adult, or for a far longer time than if he were an adult. Sheridan recommends (p. 29) that no petitions alleging "incorrigibility," "beyond control," "runaway," or violation of ordinances referring only to children, such as truancy or curfews, be made by anyone other than school officials or representatives of public or private agencies. It might be even better to restrict this to the protective-probation unit.

To arrive at a proper balance between the "just" and the rehabilitatory function in juvenile justice is no easy thing. Too much emphasis on the just reduces the court to a dispenser of punishment, the point of view inherent in the Gault decision (in *re* Gault, 387 U.S. 1, 1967), the logical conclusion being that equal "crimes" deserve equal punishment. Too much emphasis on rehabilitation can keep a child in semiconfinement for years because of his general or even potential behavior although his actual offense has been trivial. It would make more sense to take a stand on the family's responsibility for a child up to an agreed-on age, and make the committing of a delinquent act by a child one form of evidence of a family's need for state intervention in the same way that neglect is such evidence. The two would be handled the same way, with child-care facilities of different kinds, from foster homes to group homes to "security" institutions with behavior modification programs available if protective services do not help. The focus would then be on the family system, although the principal target in any one case might be the child, or the parents, or some other overlapping or impinging system, such as the schools. Certainly it does not make sense to put all the onus of delinquency onto the child, to relieve the parents of all responsibility, even financial, as the present system does, and to label some children as delinquents to be placed in a "correctional system" and others as neglected or dependent and deal with them as part of their family's problems. Some states are already moving toward the elimination of their juvenile correction institutions.

Whether it would be necessary to reduce the age at which children can be brought to the juvenile court or to declare some children emancipated minors if they were, in fact, involved somewhat autonomously in organized crime and deal with them in a youth court but on an adult level might have to be considered; but the present anomaly whereby the more a child needs protection because of the seriousness of an (often impulsive) act such as rape or murder, the less protection he receives, should certainly be reversed. The child of sixteen today may be far more mature and more involved in actual crime than was the eighteen-year-old at the time most juvenile court laws were enacted, nor is there any reason that a humane and rehabilitative correctional system for youth and young adults should not be developed.

The basic plan for child welfare services in a community could therefore be drawn somewhat as in the accompanying Figure. It would, of course, vary from community to community in terms of the sponsorship of certain services. One important factor, however, is that of community size. All too often, states have organized their child welfare programs in relation to too small a region to be served (in some states, the county), which does not provide sufficiently flexible resources to serve families and children. Such a system would require a level of cooperation between social agencies not at present implemented, and present a tremendous challenge to keep operating efficiently. The quality of leadership in the public agency would need to be exceptional.

Involvement of Social Work

Social work's involvement in these programs is to some extent conditioned by changes that have been taking place in the field as a whole, as well as by the experience of what is needed in each program. First, social work has been constantly expanding its boundaries, so that there are social work roles in teaching, consultation, planning of service systems, administration, and research, as well as in community work

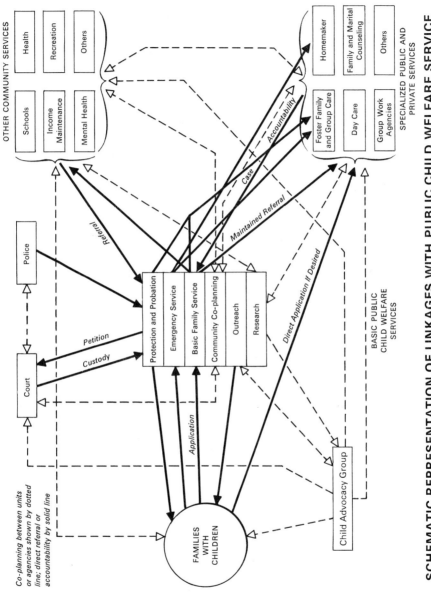

SCHEMATIC REPRESENTATION OF LINKAGES WITH PUBLIC CHILD WELFARE SERVICE

and direct services to groups and to families and children. The one thing that seems important, however, if social work is to retain any identity, is that it hold to a co-planning stance and not become, however subtly, an instrument of the culture acting to change people in the interests of those who hold power in that culture. Thus, there will be need in child welfare for many different social work skills, all of them, however, exercised with full participation by the consumers of service.

Secondly, social work is not only abandoning a therapeutic stance toward people in trouble, but it is paying much more attention to the content of day-to-day living and the small, practical, but important affairs of managing one's life. This is obvious in children's homes, according to such books as *The Other 23 Hours* (Treischman, Whittaker, and Bendtro, 1969), and in the increasing number of social workers who are directors of group care, a role with no clinical component. It is also obvious in newer concepts of protective and preventive services (Taylor 1972, p. 83) and in the increase of parent education groups, where the emphasis is on practical handling of children's problems. There still is room for the therapist in child care work, but it is no longer true that therapy is seen as the primary service even in the residential treatment center, and in an analysis of the social work role in institutions the Group Child Care Consultant Services (1970, p. 5) puts therapy in fourth place among social work functions, behind planning, evaluation, and advocacy.

Concurrently, social work is making far more use than formerly of both paraprofessionals and volunteers. This is not only a matter of establishing linkages with a consumer group by the employment of "indigenous" personnel—a move that sometimes has about it an air of confession of one's inability to accept or understand a culturally different group, as in Dohen's ethnically controlled court (1971)—but an upgrading of certain skills in what might be called the eoprofessional, or "dawning" professional rather than the paraprofessional role. Children's workers (houseparents) in children's institutions are an example. Increasingly, they are being considered counselors or even therapists (Diggles, 1970), and recognition as full-fledged social workers, as in Great Britain, cannot be far off. Similarly, social work is turning toward both an interdisciplinary and an intradiscipline team approach to problems and the use of a variety of methods even in meeting a single problem. But the greatest change of all lies in the willingness to include the consumer of social work service not only in plans for himself but in plans for the service itself. Young people in children's homes are being brought into decision-making, and parents are serving on advisory committees or on boards. The whole concept of co-planning demands the inclusion of those served in creating and implementing the service.

The role, then, of social workers with a Master of Social Work degree is rapidly changing. They are being seen either in policy-making or leadership roles as supervisors, administrators, specialists in staff development, program planners, consultants, or as entrusted with highly complex clinical practice. More and more service delivery is passing into the hands of the worker who has only the Bachelor's degree. There are, however, two areas in which more extensive and intensive training that can be given at the undergraduate level still seems very necessary.

One is the choice of models of practice and the ability to use them fitly. Social work has vastly expanded the ways in which it works with people, from more or less conventional analytic psychology to behavior-modification to encounter groups to neo-Rogerian counseling or reality therapy. The B.A. worker or the volunteer or the paraprofessional may be trained in one or more of these models; he is rarely competent to decide which one or what combination of models a situation may require. Enthusiasts for a particular model can be quite dangerous in a program.

The other is knowledge and experience in the actual working of a service, in the kind of relationships it engenders, and the structure needed to carry it out. Much of the problem, for instance, with the foster family care program today is not a lack of knowledge and skill about human beings and their feelings. It is a lack of understanding of the way in which such a system can work, the role of the worker, the agency, the foster parent, and the own parent; the parts of the parental power each needs to exercise—the providing of clothing, for instance; and the enormous difference between a "caring" and a "placement" program (Keith-Lucas, 1959), between foster family care and adoption, in its purpose, structure, feeling, and the kind of person who is needed to do the job. It is not true that any social worker can implement a good foster home program merely by using general social work principles, and too many mistakes are due to the fact that many have tried to do so and that the pioneer work done in the late 1940s and 1950s by such writers as Baker and Hutchinson has been ignored. Similarly, to work effectively in an institutional setting needs a knowledge of institutional systems that most social workers acquire slowly.

Trends and development in individual specialized programs can only be given somewhat cursory mention here. In many fields there is no recognizable trend but rather a searching out of new methods to deal with problems as experience or research suggests new approaches. Nor is it possible to record all the significant literature in each field. Rather a sample has been selected, from *Child Welfare* and other current resources, as some indication of what is being discussed or attempted.

Developments in Protective Services

In protective services perhaps the greatest change that is coming about is due to the greater realization that neglect and abuse are not so much individual problems of psychopathology as they are cultural and environmental problems. Both Gil (1971) and Rubin (1972) hold that abuse is endemic in our society and correlate it with the growing violence of society in general. Neglecting parents are seen as persons with very low self-image and, among other things, subject to a high rate of residential mobility (Mulford and Cohen, 1967, pp. 8, 9), perhaps to some extent victims of "future shock." Giovannoni and Billingsley accept the general identification with lower socioeconomic status but suggest that the predisposing factor is stress (often the number of children in the family). They comment on the impoverishment of relationships with the extended family but find little correlation with the parents' own familial pattern (1970, pp. 201, 203). Brown and Daniels give more credence to unresolved conflicts in the parent's own childhood in abuse situations (1968, p. 90), but stress the need to treat the parent as a client capable of overcoming the problem. In general, the trends in the field seem to favor more of a parenting or nurturing role with reliance at times on group methods. If so, the co-planning role must not be forgotten.

Social workers frequently speak of preventive as well as protective services. Yet it is hard to identify specific preventive services, and one needs to ask what is one specifically preventing. Projects such as the "detached" worker program of the New York Youth Authority are or were specifically preventive of antisocial gang activity. Parents' groups and the very existence of a BFS can be said to be preventive of family breakdown in some respects; homemaker service can be a preventive of unwise child-parent separation; but the basic preventive services are not those directed toward specific problems but those that affect the quality of life of the family as a whole: income maintenance, health services, schools, recreation, and community betterment programs.

GROUP CARE FOR CHILDREN

The children's home field offers almost unlimited possibilities. Since the revulsion against the old-time institution and the perhaps unreal expectations placed on foster family care in the 1930s it has almost been assumed that the only respectable role for the children's institution has been that of the residential treatment center. Indeed, the First National Survey of Children's Residential Institutions discussed institutions largely in terms of the psychiatric and casework service provided although the directors of these same institutions list as their first need raising the quality of their child care staff (Papppenfort and Kilpatrick, 1969, p. 458).

Yet there has been growing evidence, as for instance in the work of Wolins (1969), that group care may be advantageous to some children as a living experience and in any case is not necessarily as harmful to human relationships as was believed. Although most of Wolins' arguments are drawn from Europe and the *kibbutzim* experience in Israel, this has long been apparent in the better children's homes of the South and Southwest, where similar groups, less regimentation, better-trained child care workers, and above all an intensive and well-structured planning process with parents and children are showing what can be done even for quite disturbed children through a living experience that is not necessarily clinical in nature (Konopka, 1969, p. 31; Whittaker, 1972, p. 56). Indeed a number of these institutions have developed techniques of planning with families that are beyond anything that has been developed elsewhere, and look not to a specific goal of family

reunion so much as to the best possible family plan, whether this be
reunion, family support of a group placement not unlike the boarding
schools used by certain middle-class groups, adoption, or the assumption of a parental role by relatives or often self-selected foster parents
(Chapel Hill Workshop Reports 1968–1971: Keith-Lucas, 1963). Plans
for children are also becoming more flexible. Not all plans are for the
child to spend 168 hours a week in the institution; some children need
care by the day, or for weekends, or for every day except the weekend
(Gula, 1969).

At the same time, the trend is obviously toward decentralization of
the large institution, either into "colleges" or units on the campus, with
families either living together or within the same unit, or toward group
homes, "detached" cottages in the community, not essentially different
from Pratt's "assembled families." For three years, now, the most
sought-after workshop at the Chapel Hill Workshops has been one on
counseling techniques for child care workers, and many problems that
were previously referred to social workers are being taken care of in the
cottage setting. At the same time, there has been a growth of an entirely
different form of group care that relies on the group itself to act as a
modifier of behavior. This takes various forms, from "positive peer
culture" groups to camps in which the children are virtually self-sus-
taining. There is not so much a disillusionment with traditional forms
of child care as an opening up of a wide range of alternatives.

If these recommendations are accepted and "delinquent" children
are no longer cared for in separate institutions but in group homes and
institutions, as well as in foster care, the number of acting-out children
in institutions is likely to rise. This will accelerate the move to smaller
units, particularly group homes, and probably also lead to more use of
sociobehavioral techniques. It will also challenge the institution to open
its doors to even more children whom at present it rejects as beyond its
capacity to treat. The findings of the First National Survey reported,
however, that in the opinion of the staff more than half the children in
"institutions for the care of dependent and neglected children" were
"disturbed" to some extent, and these contained 29 percent of all
"disturbed" children in care in all types of institutions (Pappenfort
and Kilpatrick, 1969, p. 451).

The group home, a development largely of the 1960s, has been used for a large number of different functions, including a "halfway house," an intake unit, a specialized setting for disturbed children, a place for long-term family units, and simply as a form of group care in itself. It appears to avoid the major disadvantages of both institutional care (regimentation or institutionalization) and of foster care (impermanence) and may become the most typical form of care in the 1970s.

FOSTER FAMILY CARE

Foster family care is still the major way of caring for the neglected or dependent child. De Fries, Jenkins, and Williams (1965, p. 82) trace the belief in it to its being "an antidote to the evils of congregate care" and suggest that it has been used uncritically and sentimentally. Certainly it has not lived up to expectations, and this is reflected in such article titles as "Foster Care in Question" (Stone, 1970) and "Foster-Family Care—Has It Fulfilled Its Promise?" (Lewis, 1964). While considerable research has been expended on the program since Maas and Engler's 1959 study, the whole program appears to have generated few new ideas in the past thirty to forty years. Two recent exceptions seem to be a move toward including the foster parent in plans for the child, in much the same way the child care worker has been included in many children's homes today (Reistoffer, 1972) and the attempt to get away from the parenting image and recast the foster parent as a "family life counselor" (Bigley, 1968). In the meantime there have been some important studies on foster parents as a group, suggesting that they tend to share certain common characteristics, such as coming from a fairly large family, early marriage to a person from their childhood area, clear differentiation in sex roles, with female domination exercised through "their rights and prerogatives as mothers," and relatively isolated from the community (Babcock, 1965) and, in terms of their possessiveness and tendency to use the child as a weapon against men, not unlike the unmarried mother (Miller, 1968). This suggests not only a somewhat unusual group but also a group whose particular patterns are unlikely to be favored by emerging new patterns of society.

It seems clear that on the whole agencies cannot rely indefinitely on a foster care program that depends on meeting the personal needs of foster parents. The present "voluntary" foster home with minimum board rates and little status belongs to a vanishing culture and, coupled with the greater disturbance of children coming into care, has led to an alarming rate of replacement. Indeed, De Fries, Jenkins, and Williams hold (1965, p. 82) that to "simulate a family for the disturbed foster child is an unrealistic and outdated concept."

It is not surprising that the field has been turning both to the subsidized or agency-owned foster home, the "assembled family," in which the foster parents are full staff members, and to long-term, assured placements, often with guardianship assigned to the foster family to take care of children whose need for fostering is long-term (Madison and Shapiro, 1970).

ADOPTION

Adoption is a service that is undergoing great change. It has passed in the last ten years from a "seller's market" where there were many more applicants than children available to a "buyer's," with few families risking adoption. It now faces a new situation due to the use of abortion and the growing acceptability of illegitimate birth, so that a "seller's" market is again a possibility. One cannot but comment, however, that the lot of the "less desirable" (older children, those with medical problems, children of mixed race, and even black children as a whole) has always been hard. They have always been difficult to find homes for. This has led in general to three moves: the subsidized adoption, the quasi-adoptive foster home, and transracial adoption.

Adoption as a field has probably been as fully researched as any area of child welfare, particularly as to outcome (Elonen and Schwartz, 1969, Hoopes et al, 1969, Kadushin, 1966). The results have in general been favorable and have tended to negate earlier studies showing a disproportionate number of adopted children brought to psychiatric clinics. In terms of practice one theme that is being more clearly stated is the recognition that adoption is much more than finding a home for a child. It is the creation of a special "artificial" relationship which is subject to many stresses, putting emphasis on the need for post-adoption counseling (Lawder, 1958; Watson, 1972, p. 229) and for helping the adoptive parents understand the relationship (Biskind, 1966). Again the need for a social worker thoroughly versed in the service itself is apparent.

DAY CARE

Day care stands out from other services because of two unique characteristics. It is first a service that is by way of becoming a true social utility. People moving to a new neighborhood expect day care to be available in much the same way they expect to find churches and schools. The emphasis in the federal government on "workfare" has approved day care as an acceptable way of rearing children, at least for the poor, despite President Nixon's veto of a day care bill on the grounds that day care was weakening family life. Secondly, it is a service that is provided primarily on a commercial basis, with little or no professional concern for the family and, by and large, a suspicion of social work, due in part to concern about licensing. Professional day care agencies are clearly in the minority.

As a result, day care has rarely been seen as a resource that can be integrated into a continuum of services, as an alternative, precursor, or postscript to foster care, nor have the separation elements and the need for family planning in day care received the kind of attention they deserve. Social work has largely been restricted to problems uncovered by the service. A recent pamphlet from the Child Welfare League explains that "parents of day care children generally are able to carry out their responsibilities," but "still, there are problems posed by day care" (Child Welfare League of America, 1972, pp. 20–21), and consultation and educative services to day care personnel (Pisapia and Hanwell, 1969), although Chazin (1969) suggests the use of the therapeutic milieu of day care to help disturbed children. There would seem to be wide opportunities in this field for community organization, advocacy, and co-planning with families under stress.

Homemaker service is a program integral to all family co-planning. It can be used in emergencies to hold a family together during a period of planning to meet a crisis, in lieu of temporary placement to relieve stress for a while, or even for long-time care (Brodsky, 1958), though many would question this as establishing too intrusive a service in a family. One agency regularly uses a homemaker by implicit agreement in one family situation where pressures rise to the point that the normally adequate mother feels herself compelled to desert for short periods—a fine example of trustful co-planning. Many agencies, however, use the service not so much as a caring as an educational service, using both individual and group approaches (McDowell, 1964).

To bring these services into a continuum as resources for the family, to make them available to those who need them, to keep them sensitive to needs, to remove from them the stigma of the implication of failure, and to ensure that they are provided with knowledge and skill is the task of social work in public child welfare today.

References

Appelberg, Esther. "Significance of Personal Guardianship for Children in Casework," *Child Welfare*, XLIX (1970), 6–14.

Aptekar, Herbert. "Casework with the Child's Own Family in Child Placing Agencies," in *Six Papers on Child Welfare Problems*, pp. 41–45. New York, Child Welfare League of America, 1953.

Babcock, Charlotte. "Some Psychodynamic Factors in Foster Parenthood," *Child Welfare*, XLIV (1965), 485–93, and XLIV, No. 10 (1965), 570–76.

Barnes, Milford. "The Concept of Parental Force," *Child Welfare*, XLVI (1967), 89–93.

Bean, Shirley M. "The Parents' Center Project: a Multiservice Approach to the Prevention of Child Abuse," *Child Welfare*, L (1971), 277–82.

Bellucci, Matilda. "Group Treatment of Mothers in Child Protection Cases," *Child Welfare*, LI (1972), 110–16.

Bigley, Ronald J. "What Direction for Children in Limbo—Foster Home or Family Life Home?" *Child Welfare*, XLVII (1968), 212–15.

Biskind, Sylvia E. "Helping Adoptive Families Meet the Issues in Adoption," *Child Welfare*, XLV (1966), 145–50.

Brodsky, Rose. "Philosophy and Practices in Homemaker Service," *Child Welfare*, XXXVII (1958), 10–15.

Brown, John A., and Robert Daniels. "Some Observations on Abusive Parents," *Child Welfare*, XLVII (1968), 89–94.

Bryce, Marvin E., and Roger C. Ehlert. "144 Foster Children," *Child Welfare*, L (1971), 499–503.

Chapel Hill Workshop Reports, Group Child Care Consultant Services, University of North Carolina, Chapel Hill: "Specifics of Planning with Families and Children," 1968, Part II, pp. 7–11; "Helping Parents Become More Responsible," 1969, Part II, pp. 17–22. "Social Work with the Whole Family," 1970, Part II, pp. 13–17. "Panels of Parents and Staff," 1971, Part II, pp. 52–77.

Chazin, Robert M. "Day Treatment of Emotionally Disturbed Children," *Child Welfare*, XLVIII (1969), 212–18.

Child Welfare League of America. *Guidelines for Day Care Service.* New York, the League, 1972.

———— *On Fostering.* New York, the League, 1972.

Citizens' Committee for Children of New York. "A Dream Deferred," 1971; mimeographed. Excerpted in *Child Welfare*, L (1971), 448–59, under title, "Toward a New Social Service System."

Decker, Thomas T. *Due Process in Child Protection Proceedings.* Denver, American Humane Society, 1972.

De Fries, Zira, Shirley Jenkins, and Ethelyn C. Williams. "Foster Family Care for Disturbed Children: a Non-sentimental View," *Child Welfare*, XLIV (1965), 73–84.

de Schweinitz, Karl, and Elizabeth de Schweinitz. "The Place of Authority in the Protective Function of the Public Welfare Agency," *Child Welfare*, XLIII (1964), 286–91, 315, reprinted from the *Child Welfare League of Bulletin*, August, 1946.

Diggles, Mary C. "The Child Care Counsellor: New Therapist in Children's Institutions," *Child Welfare*, XLIX (1970), 509–13.

Dohen, Dorothy. A New Juvenile Court Role in an Ethnically Controlled Community Agency, *Social Work* XVI, No. 2 (1971), 25–30.

Elonen, Anna S., and Edward M. Schwartz. "A Longitudinal Study of the Emotional, Social and Academic Functioning of Adopted Children," *Child Welfare*, XLVIII (1969), 72–78.

Fanshel, David. "The Exit of Children from Foster Care; an Interim Research Report," *Child Welfare*, L (1971), 65–81.

Forsyth County (N.C.) Department of Social Services. "Descriptive Model for Social Services." Mimeographed; n.d. [1971].

Gil, David G. "A Sociocultural Perspective on Physical Child Abuse," *Child Welfare*, L (1971), 389–94.

Gill, Thomas. "The Legal Nature of Neglect," *NPPA Journal*, VI, No. 1 (1960), 1–16.

Giovannoni, Jean, and Andrew Billingsley, "Child Neglect Among the Poor,"ᵛ *Child Welfare*, XLIX (1970), 196–204.

Group Child Care Consultant Services, University of North Carolina. *The Social Worker in Group Child Care: Proceedings of the First Winter Seminar for Social Workers.* Chapel Hill, 1970.

Gula, Martin, "Group Child Care in the World of Tomorrow," in *Chapel Hill Workshop Reports*, Part II, pp. 37–42. Group Child Care Consultant Services, University of North Carolina, Chapel Hill, N.C., 1969.

Herre, Ernest. "Aggressive Casework in a Protective Services Unit," in Tony Tripodi, Philip Fellin, Irwin Epstein and Roger Lind, eds., *Social Workers at Work: an Introduction to Social Work Practice*, pp. 12–18. Itasca, Ill., F. E. Peacock, 1972.

Hoopes, Janet L., *A Follow-up Study of Adoptions.* New York, Child Welfare League of America, 1969.

Jaffe, Eliezer. "Effects of Institutionalization on Adolescent Dependent Children," *Child Welfare*, XLVIII (1969), 64–71.

Jenkins, Shirley. "Separation Experiences of Parents Whose Children are in Foster Care," *Child Welfare*, XLVIII (1969), 334–339.

Kadushin, Alfred. "Adoptive Parenthood: a Hazardous Adventure?" *Social Work*, XI, No. 3 (1966), 30–38.

——"Reversibility of Trauma: a Follow-up Study of Children Adopted When Older," *Social Work*, XII, No. 4 (1967), 22–33.

Keith-Lucas, Alan. "Care or Placement?" *Child Welfare*, XVI (1959), 19–22.

—— *The Church Children's Home in a Changing World.* Chapel Hill, N.C., University of North Carolina Press, 1963.

—— "Philosophies of Public Social Service," *Public Welfare*, XXXI, No. 1 (1973), 21–24.

Konopka, Gisela. "Re-thinking from the Beginning What Is Absolutely Essential in a Child Care Program Today," in *Chapel Hill Workshop Reports*, Part II, pp. 26–37. Group Child Care Consultant Services, University of North Carolina, Chapel Hill, N.C., 1969.

Kraus, Jonathan. "Predicting Success of Foster Placements for School Age Children," *Social Work*, XVI, No. 1 (1971), 63–72.

Lawder, Elizabeth. "A Limited Number of Older Children in Adoption," *Child Welfare*, XLIX (1958), 435–42.

Lewis, Mary. "Foster Family Care—Has It Fulfilled Its Promise?" in Alan Keith-Lucas, ed., *Programs and Problems in Child Welfare. (Annals of the American Academy of Political and Social Science*, CCLV) [1964], 31–41.

Maas, Henry. "Children in Long-Term Foster Care," *Child Welfare*, XLVIII (1969), 321–33.

Maas, Henry, and Richard F. Engler. *Children in Need of Parents.* New York, Columbia University Press, 1959.

McAdams, Phyllis Johnson. "The Parent in the Shadows," *Child Welfare*, LI (1972), 51–55.

McCrae, Robert H. "Jane Addams and Our Unfinished Business," *Child Welfare*, XXXIX (1960), 1–5.

McDowell, John T. "A Community Approach to the Home: Homemaker Service," in Alan Keith-Lucas, ed., *Programs and Problems in Child Welfare (Annals of the American Academy of Political and Social Science*, CCCLV [1964], 62–68)

Madison, Bernice, and Michael Shapiro. "Long-Term Foster Family Care: What Is Its Potential for Minority Group Children? *Public Welfare*, XVII, No. 2 (1969), 167–91.

—— "Permanent and Long-Term Foster Family Care as a Planned Service," *Child Welfare*, XLIX (1970), 131–36.

Mandell, Betty. "Welfare and Totalitarianism," *Social Work*, XVI, No. 1 (1971), 17–26, and XVI, No. 2 (1971), 89–96.

Miller, James. "Some Similarities between Foster Mothers and Unmarried Mothers and Their Significance for Foster Parenting," *Child Welfare*, XLVII (1968), 216–19.

Mulford, Robert. *Protective-preventive Services—Are They Synonymous?* Denver, American Humane Association, n.d. [c 1969].

Mulford, Robert and Morton I. Cohen. "Psychosocial Characteristics of Neglecting Parents," in *Neglecting Parents*, pp. 1–10. Denver, American Humane Society, 1967.

Overton, Alice. "Serving Families 'Who Don't Want Help,'" *Social Casework*, XXXIV, No. 7 (1953), 304–9.

Pappenfort, Donnell M., and Dee Morgan Kilpatrick, "Child Caring Institutions, 1966: Selected Findings from the First National Survey of Children's Residential Institutions," *Social Service Review*, XLIII (1969), 448–59.

Pisapia, Matthew and Albert F. Hanwell. "Social Work in Day Care," *Child Welfare*, XLVIII (1969), 268–72.

Reistroffer, Mary E. "Participation of Foster Parents in Decision Making: the Concept of Collegiality," *Child Welfare*, LI (1972), 25–29.

Rubin, Sol. "Children as Victims of Institutionalization," *Child Welfare*, LI (1972), 6–18.

Schreiber, Leona E. "The Help Line for Parents—a Demonstration Project," *Child Welfare*, L (1971), 164–67.

Sheridan, William H. "Juveniles Who Commit Non-criminal Acts: Why Treat in a Correctional System?" *Federal Probation*, XXX, No. 1 (1967), 26–30.

Stone, Helen D. "An Orientation to Foster Care Theory and Values," in Helen Stone, ed., *Foster Care in Question*, pp. 3–10. New York, Child Welfare League of America, 1970.

Taylor, Joseph L. "The Child Welfare Agency as the Extended Family," *Child Welfare*, LI (1972), 74–83.

Treischman, Albert E., James K. Whittaker, and Larry K. Bendtro. *The Other 23 Hours*. Chicago, Aldine Publishing House, 1969.

United States Children's Bureau. *Standards for Specialized Courts Dealing with Children*, Children's Bureau Publication 346–1954. Washington, D.C. 1954; revised as *Standards for Juvenile and Family Courts*, Children's Bureau Publication 437–1966, Washington, D.C., 1966.

Watson, Kenneth. "Subsidized Adoption: a Crucial Investment," *Child Welfare*, LI (1972), 220–30.

Weissman, Irving. "Guardianship: Every Child's Right," in Alan Keith-Lucas, ed., *Programs and Problems in Child Welfare (Annals of the American Academy of Political and Social Science*, CCCLV (1964), 134–39).

Whittaker, James K. "Group Care for Children: Guidelines for Planning," *Social Work*, XVII, No. 1 (1972), 51–61.

Williams, Carol J. "Helping Parents to Help Their Children in Placement," *Social Work*, XVII, No. 1 (1972), 297–303.

Wolins, Martin. "Young Children in Institutions: Some Additional Evidence," *Developmental Psychology*, II, No. 1 (1969), 90–109.

Woodward, Marion C. "Letters to the Editor," *Social Service Review*, XXVIII (1944), 367–68.

Zucker, Mildred. "Citizens' Advice Bureaus: the British Way," *Social Work*, X, No. 4 (1965), 85–91.

JONATHAN M. STEIN

AND

TOBY GOLICK

Public Legal Programs: a Team Approach

LAWYERS AND social workers are having more to do with each other than ever before. There are a number of reasons for this, of which one of the most important is the establishment of a nationwide "legal services" program, a program without precedent in this or any other Western country. While there have been legal aid societies and some experimental programs providing free legal services on a limited basis for a number of years, the funding of the legal services program in 1965 by the federal government's Office of Economic Opportunity (OEO) vastly increased the number of lawyers available to the poor (Cahn and Cahn, 1966; Lowenstein and Waggoner, 1967). OEO Legal Services established "storefront" or neighborhood law offices in hundreds of communities across the country; close to twenty-five hundred lawyers are actively practicing law for the indigent clients served by these offices.

On a smaller scale, law schools and other private organizations have established numerous legal assistance clinics and public interest law firms, and some private law firms permit their members to do a limited amount of so-called *pro bono* legal work for poor clients (Borosage *et al.*, 1970). In addition (and frequently because of cases brought by legal services lawyers), there are an ever increasing number of judicial decisions allowing or requiring lawyers at proceedings where lawyers formerly were never involved, such as juvenile court hearings on child neglect and delinquency, school suspensions, and welfare hearings.

The result of the proliferation of lawyers for the poor has been that lawyers are now intruding into arenas formerly dominated by social workers, such as welfare centers and juvenile courts. Social workers are being forced to deal not only with their cases but also with their cases' lawyers, who are often more than willing to rock the boat to get what their clients want. At the same time, a parallel development has been taking place in the social work profession. Many social workers have been questioning the old assumptions about their profession and have been moving toward a new view of the social worker as an advocate, concerned less with changing the poor person and more with changing the institutions and circumstances (including the laws) which make him poor. Some of these social workers have found working along with lawyers for the poor compatible with their philosophy. In addition, lawyers working for the poor quickly discover a fact known to all social workers—poor people often have extremely complex problems which require more than legal help.

Unfortunately, little attention has been paid to the difficulties and problems faced by social workers in legal services offices (Smith and Curran, 1968). The basis of the problem is the difference in approach used by lawyers and social workers. The social worker's approach is therapeutic and framed by considering the "best interests" of the client and of society as a whole. This sometimes may result in a social worker determining that what should be done is not what the client himself wants (or says he wants), and makes the social worker into a judge who determines what is wrong with the client that needs adjustment (Ryan, 1971).

In contrast, the lawyer is trained to be an advocate on behalf of his client and is bound by the canons of ethics which govern the profession to use every legal technique and device to fulfill his client's lawful wishes. This means that on some occasions a lawyer will use what seems to be a technicality to achieve a result which seems unjust to the nonlawyer.

But the lawyer's or advocate's approach is not necessarily inconsistent with the social worker's philosophy. For it is often (or, in the author's view, always) in a poor person's "best interest" to have someone representing him who is trying to obtain what the poor person himself wants. The availability of aggressive advocates to stand up on behalf of a poor person can be crucial in ending feelings of uselessness and dependency, as many studies have shown (Perlman, 1957; Weiss, 1970).

Individual and aggressive advocacy can become a process which results in new pride and dignity for the poor who see advocacy work for them. Instead of resignation to his unfortunate lot, the poor person develops a new self-assertiveness and consciousness of the possibility of opposition and protest to improve his situation. The doctrine and rhetoric of legal rights (a right to welfare, decent health care, a habitable dwelling, or the converse right to withhold rent) become internalized by the individual and are passed on to those who have contact with him (Mathews and Weiss, 1967). This result comes in part from the institutional framework in which the lawyer operates:

He must treat his clients as equals and conceive of himself as an agent to effectuate their, the principals', desires in the legal framework and the practical world. . . . Mouthpiece can be an honorable word. The activity of advocacy can bring the clichés of equal access to the law and the best interests of the child, welfare of the family, etc. . . . closer to the facts (Weiss, 1970, p. 67).

The individual self-respect and worth generated by the equality of position of attorney and client and the totally client-oriented approach give a more fundamental psychological support to a client than a palliative adjustment process founded on someone's judgment of the social value or worth of the client's desires and needs.

Finally, it is somewhat arrogant to assume that the professional's view of his client's "best interests" is more accurate than the client's own perception of these interests.

Four Fields of Practice

WELFARE ADVOCACY

Most poor people are eligible for public assistance under one or more programs, yet for every person on assistance there is at least one other eligible person not receiving the benefits to which he is entitled. Because of the number of public assistance programs, the complex eligibility and means tests, and the arbitrariness of administration, many poor persons have welfare problems (Stein, 1967). The social worker, working closely with a lawyer, can play an important part in solving these problems and preventing their recurrence. This is true despite the fact that many social workers will often be working under the very real institutional constraints of a public welfare agency. In recent years younger social workers in public agencies have demonstrated that they still can maintain an advocacy posture notwithstanding the pressures of the bureaucracy.

One valuable thing social workers can do is to identify welfare problems in the first place. Because welfare regulations are complicated and frequently changed, many welfare recipients are not aware of their rights under the law. The welfare regulations themselves are often not published and appear only in "internal" state or county welfare manuals, and in the past, individuals asking to see these regulations have in some cases been refused permission to do so. (After considerable pressure was put on the U.S. Department of Health, Education, and Welfare (HEW) a regulation was enacted recognizing the federal right to have copies of manuals of welfare regulations.) In addition, many poor people (particularly older persons) attach stigma to the receipt of benefits and even when receiving them do not consider themselves to be citizens with rights in this regard (Briar, 1966).

Social workers can learn the eligibility requirements and benefits available under the different welfare programs by reviewing welfare manuals and consulting with lawyers to enable them to ask the right questions and spot the problems. It is very common for there to be an underlying welfare problem at the root of another problem which can be uncovered through careful questioning, as illustrated by case material from the author's files:

The client, a poorly educated woman in her twenties, came to the Legal Services office to which she had been referred by the New York City Family Court. Her child, age one, had been removed from the home under a state law permitting emergency removals, and placed in a shelter. The client was charged with neglect, based on a complaint by a neighbor that she hit the child. A physical examination revealed that the child was not injured, but was ill-nourished. The client told the attorney who interviewed her that she did hit the child but only to prevent him from eating the chips of paint constantly peeling off the walls of her apartment.

The social worker employed by the Legal Services office visited the apartment and found it to be in very deteriorated condition. The social worker discovered that the woman wanted to move, but could not find an apartment she could afford. She also discovered that the woman's welfare grant was twenty dollars less than she was entitled to receive.

The social worker contacted the welfare department and obtained the following information. The father of the child had originally been sending support money for the child, and the client's grant was reduced by this amount, as New York law requires. The client had never informed the welfare department that the father stopped sending money, and the welfare caseworker had not discovered this on her own. The social worker was able, after several telephone calls, to get the welfare department to correct the grant. The social worker was also able to explain to the client the procedure to get a higher rent allowance from the welfare department, and helped get the higher rent approved when a better apartment was found. Because of the change in circumstances, the child was returned to his mother before trial, and eventually the child neglect case was dismissed.

The social worker can also work with the client to put together the evidence to establish entitlement to particular benefits and can prepare a report giving the worker's expert opinion on the situation, which is often quite effective. As the example illustrates, one of the most important functions of the social worker in a legal services office is to adjust welfare problems at the welfare center. What is required is a knowledge of the law (and consequently, of the client's rights), aggressiveness, and enormous persistence. Here, social workers may find that their status as social workers is of assistance in getting results since, rightly or wrongly, they will be treated as fellow professionals.

A number of welfare benefits are available at the discretion of the welfare center, and a social worker's report demonstrating that a client should get the benefits to which she is entitled will be effective, especially if accompanied by persistent prodding. In addition, by working with a client to solve an individual welfare problem, the social worker may teach the client how to deal with the welfare center himself. If clients do not acquire this skill at asserting themselves, a new dependency on the social worker is created which precludes the client from being able to deal with the next grievance that arises.

Nearly all public welfare programs provide for an administrative hearing for aggrieved persons. Here the social worker's proper role is more problematical. Ideally, every person who so desires should be represented by an attorney. Nonetheless, many legal services offices, because of the shortage of lawyers or other reasons, are not able to represent all clients at such hearings. Should a social worker represent a client at a hearing if a lawyer is not available. Legally, it is permitted at most welfare hearings, including public assistance "fair hearings," unemployment compensation referee hearings, and at Social Security hearings. It is often helpful for a client to have another person present; the presence of another person may deter the hearing officer from the blatant misconduct which often occurs when a client is unaware of his rights and unrepresented. In addition, the social worker can assist the client, at the prehearing stage, in marshaling evidence and witnesses helpful to his cause. But there are many disadvantages to such representation which result from the fact that a hearing is a legal proceeding, and often the last step before a court will subject the hearing decision and record made there to judicial review. Of course, social workers are not trained in law, and ordinarily will not know how or when to make technical objections to hearsay or other improper evidence, for example. Yet, failure to do so may badly prejudice the client's case. As a result of extensive experience, some social workers are alert to possible legal complications at hearings and request adjournments in order to have counsel present when problems arise. The fact remains, however, that the use of social workers as paraprofessional lawyers is not a good use of their special training and expertise and may be misleading to a client who may think he has been represented by a lawyer when in fact he has not. Furthermore, for a nonlawyer to give "legal" advice is not only illegal but dangerous.

Ideally, the proper role of the social worker in preparing for a welfare hearing is to work with the lawyer on the case in obtaining evidence and particularly in evaluating (for completeness and accuracy) the case records made by the welfare department, which are now supposed to be available as a matter of right to the lawyer before the hearing.

The social worker can also play a helpful part in welfare litigation. By working with community groups, the social worker will frequently discover important welfare problems which can be referred to legal services. For example, a social worker working for a New York legal services office accidentally discovered that the welfare department was releasing confidential information from welfare clients' files in order to help the city department of public housing determine whether to accept them for public housing. The release of confidential information violates state and federal law and, on the basis of information supplied by the social worker, attorneys filed a suit in federal court which led to the welfare department's promise to cease this practice.

But another role for social workers remains; without intensive follow-up and monitoring of welfare department practices, such victories can become pyrrhic. Because of the cumbersome nature of much welfare bureaucracy, and the bureaucrats' dislike of court decisions adverse to their practices, there are frequent instances of noncompliance with court decisions ordering changes in welfare practices. Unfortunately, many lawyers lose interest in the problem after the case is decided; the result is a good case decision but no real change. Social workers can educate client groups on the existence of the decisions, and can help implement the decisions by pressure on the administrators of the welfare department in the form of telephone calls, letters, and, in cases of blatant noncompliance, by collecting affidavits from aggrieved persons for use in a motion to hold the welfare department in contempt of court. In a 1972 case in Illinois (*Rodriguez v. Weaver*, No. 69 C 2615 N.D. Ill.) a federal court held that because of the welfare department's repeated failure to comply with the court's ruling on prompt processing of welfare applications, the welfare department would have to pay all eligible applicants whose applications were not processed back benefits *plus* compensatory damages of $100 each. But such orders are only obtained when a court is presented with considerable evidence of misconduct by the welfare department. Social workers can be crucial in collecting such evidence.

Much of the preceding section on welfare advocacy is applicable to caseworkers employed by public welfare departments. Such caseworkers also have as their goal the solving of welfare problems, and must know what their clients need and are entitled to under law.

But public welfare caseworkers are in many ways not in as easy a position as social workers who can devote their entire loyalties to their clients. Public caseworkers also have imposed on them obligations to the welfare agency which employs them. When there are conflicts between agency policy and the client's needs, the caseworker is in the middle. In such cases, the most desirable course is to refer the client to independent welfare rights organizations and legal services programs. Welfare departments receiving federal funds are required by federal law to advise welfare clients of their right to a hearing when they are aggrieved by agency decisions and of the availability of legal services to represent them.

˙ When confronted with a client or his advocate insisting (perhaps impolitely) on what he perceives to be his rights, the public welfare caseworker should resist the perhaps natural impulse to take an adversary role in opposition to the client, and to do whatever is possible to defeat the client's claim. The caseworker must always remember the importance of even a few dollars to a welfare recipient and be aware of, and resist, the temptation to cover mistakes or to "punish" difficult clients by refusing to provide service.

THE FAMILY COURT

The family court (in some states called "juvenile court") has unfortunately become something of a battleground for social workers and lawyers. There is enormous misunderstanding of the proper role of lawyers who represent children brought before the family court (charged with juvenile delinquency, truancy, incorrigibility) and adults (charged with child neglect or abuse and a variety of other offenses, such as nonsupport). Because of this misunderstanding, social workers employed by the court or by agencies associated with the court are often extremely hostile to lawyers working for clients brought before the court, and the social workers who are employed by legal services offices to work with the lawyers and for the clients are often confused about their role (Schultz, 1968).

The misunderstanding also comes from the view that the family court is a benevolent institution designed not to punish but to do what is best for the individuals brought before it. Because of this, lawyers are often criticized for interfering with the court's functioning by insisting on time-consuming legal procedures, technical rules, and/or evidence and the like.

There are a number of responses to this criticism. First, it must be kept in mind that the family court, however benevolent in intention, is also a coercive institution—coercive in very sensitive areas of family life and personal freedoms. The court has grave powers, such as the power to take away a mother's children, to direct how parents should bring up children, and to put children in institutions. In addition, the court has very limited resources. Most of the institutions where children may be placed are sadly inadequate, as is well known, especially by those in the court system.

It is particularly important that the family court's dispositions be based on accurate facts. Both the historic and the actual justification of the adversary system of justice and the advocacy approach it entails is that this is the best means of discovering the facts. Most of the technicalities that a competent lawyer must insist on in a family court proceeding are actually constitutional rights which are necessary to accurate fact-finding. For the lawyer this means the use of the traditional lawyers' tools for fact-finding, including pretrial knowledge of the records and evidence to be used against the client, subpoenaing witnesses, and insisting on competent, legally probative evidence. For the social worker, this means investigating the facts completely and treating reports by others, no matter how professional, with the utmost skepticism.

The social worker who makes an independent investigation of the facts will often discover that written reports by social workers, psychiatrists, and others, have little or no relationship to the actual facts. Such thorough fact-finding procedures take time and slow down the work of the court. But they remain essential to protect against injustice.

Similarly, both lawyers and social workers should insist upon orderly procedures by the police, the agencies, and the courts. This too is time-consuming, but again it is necessary for the family court to do its job of helping people properly. There is nothing therapeutic about procedures which seem to the client arbitrary, confusing, and unfair. Such procedures simply reinforce the client's preexisting and justified feelings of being constantly ordered about by an autocratic and oppressive system. Social workers can be especially helpful in this regard by explaining what is happening to the persons involved (since frequently the courts fail to do this), and by urging persons brought before the court to get lawyers.

There are a number of other important uses for social workers in family courts. One is to adjust cases in order to avoid formal proceedings. It is of course desirable to have charges withdrawn. This is usually permitted when the complainant consents. For example, in a delinquency case the social worker can speak to the complaining witness and the police officer involved in the case. Without admitting the child's guilt, the social worker can explain, for example, that the child was never involved in any criminal activity before, or can promise that remedial steps will be taken, such as the social worker working with the child, or the child being put into another school, or being sent to a drug clinic, or whatever mitigating facts exist. If the problem is being taken care of, it is possible to convince a complaining witness that it is not worth his time to make repeated appearances in the family court. Sometimes "incorrigibility" proceedings are brought by the child's parents, when they find themselves unable to control their child. Frequently, the parents are unaware of all the consequences of such a proceeding (such as jail for the child, or a neglect case against them). The social worker can explain these consequences and alternatives to family court proceedings, such as family counseling or psychiatric help.

The social worker is most helpful at the dispositional stages of family court proceedings. Usually, the court relies heavily on the advice of probation officers employed by the court, who have many cases to handle; consequently, their recommendations are often based on inadequate investigation of the problem and of the facilities available. Seldom do they consult the persons whose lives are to be affected. The courts know this, and also know that they need all the help they can get; therefore a dispositional plan arranged by the client's own social worker is very influential and frequently followed. A large and prestigious private law firm in Washington, D.C., has taken a social worker on its staff largely for this purpose. In addition to seeking the best placement possibilities the social worker must also find out what his client wants and explain the options available and techniques for obtaining them. It is a paramount consideration of the social worker to take seriously the dictates of client self-determination.

COMMUNITY ORGANIZING

One of the most promising areas for mutual cooperation between lawyers and social workers is that of community organization and group representation (Morris and Rothwax, 1968). If the problems of poverty, inequality, and injustice are to be confronted successfully, it must be by the exploited individuals organizing themselves, making allies in other social and economic classes, and using the tools and strategies at their disposal.

The first major area of cooperation is in attempts to open up government programs to community input and control. The 1960s have left a legacy of law which gives community groups support for the right to participate in governmental decision-making, supported by statutes, regulations, and administrative policies.

Requirements for community participation exist in a number of substantive areas affecting the poor. For example, the federal government requires community participation in various housing programs. When this opportunity is used by community groups, it can lead to real improvements in the lives of the intended beneficiaries of the programs.

In 1968 the federal department of Housing and Urban Development (HUD) mandated a right of tenant participation in new public housing modernization grants to local housing authorities. In Philadelphia, an administrative complaint was filed against the local housing authority to block the $2.5 million grant unless the participation requirements were met. With the threat of holding up this money as bargaining leverage, and with encouragement from HUD, an agreement was reached recognizing a public housing tenants' group, called the Residents' Advisory Board, as the spokesman for the tenants. The existence of this organization led directly to a tremendous increase in the number of public housing tenants employed by the housing authority—from 35 to over 1,000. Other improvements, such as reduction in crimes and rent defaults, were attributed to active tenant organizations participating in the running of the housing authority (Hirschen and Brown, 1972).

In the health area there are also broad participation requirements in many programs, such as community health centers and mental health centers. Since these requirements are frequently circumscribed by the sponsoring health service providers, it takes a combination of legal expertise and an alert, organized community to make use of the right to participate. The results of such participation have included changing the composition of hospital boards, and challenging the

Joint Commission of Accreditation of Hospitals for its failure to consult with communities served by hospitals evaluated by the Commission.

There is a second newly recognized right of community groups: to intervene in the administrative process when their interests are affected. This occurred, for example, when the National Welfare Rights Organization (NWRO) was allowed to intervene in a "conformity" hearing held by HEW to determine if a state was obeying federal law in the administration of its federally reimbursed welfare system. These hearings were rarely held, and welfare rights groups feared the hearings would be ineffective because of lack of information on the actual working of the state's welfare plan and because HEW has tended to avoid controversy and antagonizing local officials. Despite HEW's vigorous opposition, the D.C. Court of Appeals in a case called *NWRO* v. *Finch*, ordered that NWRO had a right to participate in the conformity hearings and could examine and cross-examine witnesses. Such intervention gives poor people some control over the administrative agencies which exert such great influence on their lives (Bonfield, 1969; O'Donnell and Chilman, 1969).

A third major area for lawyer-social worker cooperation is in group representation and grass-roots organizing, especially with groups of individuals who are not currently organized but whose potential when organized to affect the decisions that control their lives is great. There has been relatively little of this in legal services programs because of tight budgeting and the feeling that lawyers already representing many groups should not divert resources to encourage new groups to organize. But there are groups of individuals, such as drug addicts, prisoners, and the elderly, who are discrete minorites isolated from advocacy agencies, with limited internal resources to organize themselves to change their environment.

For example, in the Philadelphia Office of Community Legal Services, Inc., an organizer has worked for two years with a group she helped organize, the Addicts Rights Organization (ARO). The group of former addicts and addicts in treatment programs helped attune legal services lawyers to addicts' health issues of which they were unaware because of lack of contact with this formerly isolated group of clients. Through a process of meetings and discussions, the ARO

established agenda for action which included challenging the dis-
criminatory treatment addicts received at hospitals by either being
rejected for treatment of nondrug diseases or being denied treatment
of their addiction; challenging the treatment of addicts detained in
city prisons who were forced to undergo "cold-turkey" withdrawal;
and challenging the administration of methadone clinics. With a legal
services lawyer providing legal consultation and, in the case of the
prison problem, bringing a lawsuit against the city prisons, the activities of the group led to an Addicts' Bill of Rights of fair and equal
treatment signed by most of the large hospitals in the area—a precedent-
making court decision establishing a right to adequate medical treatment (including medical detoxification to replace "cold-turkey" withdrawal), and various actions to save and improve treatment facilities.

Professionals though, and especially lawyers, must be careful to
avoid manipulating their clients by, for example, limiting their advice
to a single option. Both the lawyer and the social work organizer must
avoid the usual professional role of telling the poor and relatively
powerless client what is to be done.

One further caveat relates to the community organizer's and the
community's view of, and reliance on the law, particularly the courts,
to achieve social reform. A community organizing activity that uses
the law should be predicated on a full and objective understanding
of the limits of the legal system. The maxim attributed to Saul Alinsky
that once you have to go to court you have lost, has much truth in it
(Naison, 1970).

STUDENT RIGHTS

Many legal services offices have found that school suspension cases
constitute a significant part of their caseload. Not surprisingly, students
attending the problem-beset schools in poverty neighborhoods frequently have difficulties with teachers and administrators which
lead to expulsion or suspension from the school. Daily absenteeism
rates of 30 percent of high school student populations appear in urban
areas, such as Philadelphia, and suspensions or expulsions contribute
substantially to these statistics, according to Mark Shedd, former superintendent of the Philadelphia school system (Philadelphia *Inquirer*,
Feb. 8, 1972).

School suspensions are usually of great concern to the students' parents, who view education as a way for their children to break out of poverty. Students are usually more realistic about the value of their schooling but still may wish to contest this disciplinary action (among a host of other autocratic shool practices) to vindicate themselves when they feel they have been unjustly treated.

In response to these incidents, legal services and civil liberties lawyers have brought cases in several states which have had the result of obtaining at least minimal procedural safeguards for students to prevent them from being arbitrarily suspended indefinitely (Nussbaum, 1970). While the exact procedures required vary, it is generally held that students may not be suspended (except for very short temporary suspensions) without some kind of hearing.

While the decisions obtained in student rights test cases have been important, individual cases going to court on behalf of a student are not that effective. Even at their fastest, court proceedings are time-consuming; for this reason, individual cases are best solved through advocacy at the school as illustrated below:

A young boy from an impoversihed family recently arrived from Puerto Rico achieves his "break": in his last year of junior high school, as a result of his unusual music talent, he is accepted into the High School of Music and Art, one of New York's finest institutions. During his last week in junior high school, an incident occurs with a teacher. The teacher alleges the boy assaulted him; the boy alleges the opposite. Delinquency charges are filed, and, but a few days before his junior high school graduation in June, he is suspended from school. In court, the delinquency charges are dismissed. But the suspension is not removed; the boy does not graduate; he is informed that no hearing will be held until the following fall after school begins. The High School of Music and Art informs the boy that he cannot be admitted until he graduates and that he will have to forego admittance during the coming year—and perhaps altogether. The boy turns sullen and angry; the community prepares for a new delinquent in its midst. Fortunately, however, a lawyer and a social worker join the boy's cause. While the lawyer prepares a court action, the social worker seeks out the acting school superintendent and argues the boy's cause. Before the lawyer files his papers, the suspension is lifted and the boy graduates (Sparer, Thorkelson, and Weiss, 1966, p. 502).

Like many welfare workers, school authorities are often hostile to intervention from lawyers. Social workers, even when they advocate the student's cause as strongly as any lawyer, do not arouse the same suspicion, and their views are treated with more respect because they are better equipped to discuss the problem in terms of what is best for the student rather than in terms of the student's constitutional rights, which school officials view as impeding the function of the school. For these reasons, social workers are particularly effective at this type of advocacy.

Social workers can be especially helpful in the school area where broad-based student and parent action is often necessary as an organized countervailing force to the two groups which until now have had a monopoly in education decision-making—the school administration and the teachers, often organized into a trade union. For example, social workers can assist students in organizing vigorous student unions that can select and train student ombudsmen to do lay advocacy on behalf of fellow students, and they can also assist in the organization of parents either to supplement or to replace passive P.T.A.'s of home and school associations (Lurie, 1971). Recent HEW Title I regulations under the Elementary and Secondary Education Act have given poor parents the legal right to participate in planning and monitoring the expenditure of hundreds of millions of dollars of federal funds intended to benefit low-income children. Social workers and lawyers can work together to assist parents to exercise these rights (Lurie, 1971).

Conclusion

At a time when many social work agencies and schools of social work are reevaluating their role in attempting to meet the social problems that they have been struggling with for decades, the opportunities for community organization in conjunction with independent, aggressive lawyers should not be overlooked. Such organization offers the possibility of getting beyond the casework quagmire which does not improve the lives of those who will never see a professional or who will always need professional services to eke out an existence among institutions and social forces that will still be around to exploit or oppress them irrespective of the fact that the best casework services have been offered them. Such collaboration does mean, though, that there must be major shifts in the curricula of social work schools both in teaching the techniques of organizing and the legal and political know-how to be able to influence policies and institutions (Schottland, 1968; Sparer, 1968).

One key role for the social workers of the 1970s and beyond will be advocacy. As the Cahns remind us, the rights and grievances explosion of the 1960s created a demand not so much for legal services as for justice and redress through the legal system. Recognizing the limitations of a judicially oriented legal services program to provide justice on the mass basis required, the Cahns (1966) call for new methods to complement a legal system that is incapable of meeting the demand for services that the 1960s made apparent to everyone. Developing this "extra-judicial, institutionally oriented law reform" includes expanding the legal manpower supply through new forms of legal education, developing new justice dispensing institutions and forms of group representation to enfranchise the powerless (Cahn and Cahn, 1970).

Social workers are ideal professionals (given changes in their education, skills, and attitudes) for these extrajudicial efforts at law reform. Avoiding courts can often be a healthy alternative. Lawyers who do have a profession-created monopoly on access to courts do not have a monopoly on justice attainment, and other professionals should be involved in the act of advocacy. Work with the law and legal problems is neither beyond the competence of trained social workers nor new to them (Brickman, 1971; Sparer, Thorkelson, and Weiss, 1966).

The extent and quality of advocacy will be a function of the institutional and job restraints on the social worker as well as his ethics, skill, and courage. But wherever a social worker works, whether with a private or a public agency, or in the freedom of an independent advocacy institution, he can still be sensitive and active in achieving justice for clients. He must continually be aware, however, that this is the goal, whatever may be the agency's policies, directives, or practice.

References

Bonfield, Arthur E. "Representation of the Poor in Federal Rulemaking," *Michigan Law Review*, LXVII (1969), 511–58.

Borosage, Robert, *et al.* "The New Public Interest Lawyers," *Yale Law Journal*, LXXIX (1970), 1069–1152.

Briar, Scott, "Welfare from Below: Recipients' Views of the Public Welfare System," in J. Tenbrock, ed., *Law of the Poor*, pp. 46–61. San Francisco, Chandler Publishing Co., 1966.

Brickman, Lester. "Expansion of the Lawyering Process through a new Delivery System: the Emergence and State of Legal Paraprofessionalism," *Columbia Law Review*, LXXI (1971), 1153–1255.

Cahn, Edgar S., and Jean C. Cahn. "What Price Justice: the Civilian Perspective Revisited," *Notre Dame Laywer*, XLI (1966), 927–60.

—— "Power to the People or the Profession? — the Public Interest in the Public Interest Law," *Yale Law Journal*, LXXIX (1970), 1005–48.

Hirschen, Al, and Vivian Brown. "Public Housing's Neglected Resource: the Tenants," *City*, V (1972), 15–21.

Lowenstein, Daniel H., and Michael J. Waggoner. "Neighborhood Law Offices: the New Wave in Legal Services for the Poor," *Harvard Law Review*, LXXX (1967), 805–50.

Lurie, Ellen. *How To Change The Schools: a Parent's Action Handbook on How to Fight the System*. New York, Random House, 1971.

Mathews, Arthur R., Jr., and Jonathan A. Weiss. "What Can Be Done: a Neighborhood Lawyer's Credo," *Boston University Law Review*, XLVII (1967), 231–43.

Morris, Dan, and Harold Rothwax. "Partnership between Social Work and Law: an Essential for Effective Community Organization," in *The Social Welfare Forum*, 1968, pp. 94–104. New York, Columbia University Press, 1968.

Naison, Mark D. "The Rent Strikes in New York," in Fred M. Cox, ed., *Strategies of Community Organization*, pp. 226–38. Itaska, Ill., Peacock Publishers, Inc., 1970.

Nussbaum, Michael. *Student Legal Rights: What They Are and How to Protect Them*. New York, Harper and Row, 1970.

O'Donnell, Edward J., and Catherine S. Chilman. "Poor People on Public Welfare Boards and Committees," *Welfare in Review*, VII, No. 3 (1969), 1–11.

Perlman, Helen H. *Social Casework: a Problem-solving Process*. Chicago, University of Chicago Press, 1957.

Ryan, William. *Blaming the Victim*. New York, Pantheon Books, 1971.

Schottland, Charles I. "Social Work and the Law: Some Curriculum Approaches," *Buffalo Law Review*, XVII (1968), 719–31.

Schultz, LeRoy G. "Adversary Process: the Juvenile Court and the Social Worker," *Kansas City Law Review*, XXXVI (1968), 288–302.

Smith, Audrey D., and Barbara Curran. *A Study of the Lawyer-Social Worker Professional Relationship*, Research Contribution of the American Bar Foundation, Memoranda Series, Pamphlet No. 6, 1968.

Sparer, Edward. "The Place of Law in Social Work Education: a Commentary on Dean Schottland's Article," *Buffalo Law Review*, XVII (1968), 733–40.

Sparer, Edward, Howard Thorkelson, and Jonathan A. Weiss, "The Lay Advocate," *University of Detroit Law Journal*, XLIII (1966), 493–515.

Stein, Jonathan. "Eligibility Determinations in Public Assistance: Selected Problems and Proposals for Reform in Pennsylvania," *University of Pennsylvania Law Review*, CXV (1970), 1307–45.

Weiss Jonathan A. "Law and the Poor," *Journal of Social Issues*, XXVI (1970), 59–68.

ELSBETH KAHN

Social Services in Health Care

THE HISTORY, organization, and structure of practice in the health field have affected the methods used by social workers in order to establish their roles in health settings. There is a difference in the position and role of social work when it functions in a social agency where objectives and goals are primarily related to social health as against a medical setting, such as a hospital, where it exists in essence to contribute to the goals of a health care institution whose mission goes beyond that of social work competence and which does not necessarily share social work's view of social needs or of its own role in the health field.

Historical Perspectives

THE EMERGENCE OF MEDICAL SOCIAL WORK

In the United States medical social work owes its beginnings to Richard C. Cabot, M.D. At the turn of the century social awareness, social goals and policies which affected the development of social welfare programs, and social work were changing. They were shifting from reform, based on individual responsibility, to recognition of the importance of the environment in relation to understanding behavior. Private social agencies, including Boston's Children's Aid Society, were working with ideas of the interrelatedness of social, psychological, and environmental factors in this respect. Dr. Cabot, a member of the

Society's board, became increasingly aware of the consequences of the new approach in relation to planning medical care for children at his clinic. Treatment of children whose medical histories included social, psychological, and environmental data tended to be more successful than that of children whose histories did not include such information.

Cabot concluded that social workers were needed on hospital staffs in order to give adequate consideration to the effect of psychological, social, and economic factors upon the patient's use of medical care. Therefore in 1905, through his efforts and under his direction, the first social service department was established at the Massachusetts General Hospital in Boston. Medical social work, as a specialty within the profession of social work, was created (Rice, 1965). Cabot's formulations regarding the content of social work practice in hospitals reflected his concern with a professional approach to working with patients' feelings and attitudes, with environmental factors which affect individuals' ability to deal with illness, and especially to adapt to changes required due to the consequence of long-term illness. In this respect, continuity of service following hospital care was an important concept to him.

Cabot foresaw the importance of exploring the possibilities of preventive social care to supplement illness- and disability-centered approaches. From his material one may interpret that he saw the role of patient advocate as one of the social worker's roles in the hospital. An additional role which he defined was that of working with community agencies to stimulate the establishment of programs and services in keeping with patients' social needs (Cabot, 1955).

Cabot discussed two issues related to structural and attitudinal aspects of practice which remain partly unresolved. He pointed out that, first, social workers in hospitals must understand what today in sociological terms we would refer to as the social structure and culture of the hospitals in which they practice. Second, Cabot clearly held that social workers, when practicing their own profession, should be viewed as independently practicing colleagues. Only when it comes to direct "medical technique" are social workers to be "subordinate" to physicians. Consequently, he was critical of hospital social workers' tendencies to accept responsibility for work not falling within their province for the sake of incurring approval and finally obtaining acceptance of their services. This way of functioning prevented a clear projection of the professional medical social work function. These issues remain a burden to medical social workers to the present day.

SOCIAL WORK IN THE HEALTH FIELD

Since the early days of medical social work, trends in social awareness and social standards in health and medical care, as well as new psychiatric theory which affected professional social work education, have made an impact upon the field of medical social work.

Bartlett (1957, pp. 15–16) points out that in spite of early problems related to professional status and domain, the first thirty years of medical social work proceeded quite steadily with hospital social work departments being established all over the country. In the absence of psychiatry, which had not yet been sufficiently accepted in the United States, social work was the major voice for the study of social and emotional aspects of illness. Changing societal attitudes in relation to an individual's entitlement to service were also reflected in the changing social work values and practice.

As social philosophy became increasingly concerned with the rights and dignity of individuals over worthiness of service, the time ripened for new knowledge regarding human behavior, particularly in the light of the individual's right to self-direction and self-determination. Of considerable importance next was the influence of psychoanalytic theory on casework which reached its peak in the late 1930s.

The acceptance of this psychological theory as the primary base for practice resulted, among other things, in a new focus upon the client-worker relationship, including the use of authority, a focus on self-direction, the concept of a professional self, and the use of the educational process as part of this process. The influence of Rankian theory led to a focus on the present situation for treatment. The application of these psychiatric theories, and their translation into skills in treatment, soon became popular with medical social workers who were constantly dealing with the effect of psychological and social factors upon health and use of medical care.

Before long, medical social workers began to realize that their "one-to-one" approach in treatment was not adequate to help with the problems of ever-increasing numbers of patients requiring social work services. With the Social Security Act of 1935 and its subsequent amendments came new medical programs for the indigent which were implemented in both the public and the private sector of the health field. Social workers in the health field began to view their total responsibilities much more broadly. They learned that they had contributions to make to the planning, policy formulation, and management of total hospital programs, or of particular services within hospitals, to the establishment of medical care programs in given local areas and at the state and federal levels. Simultaneously, they increased their participation in community work with regard to social services required by persons coping with health-related social functioning problems (Bartlett, 1940, pp. 1–20; 1970, pp. 21–36).

The beginning of social work in public health in 1920, without doubt, provided an impetus for medical social workers to practice in the role of consultants to administrators, physicians, nurses, other health professionals, and government officials. It is important to note that practice in public health also brought a growing awareness of the preventive role of social work.

With the Second World War came new impetus for rehabilitation medicine and with it an ever-increasing demand for competence in team practice. In addition, both interest in the patient as a person and interest in psychological and sociological approaches to understanding behavior and social interaction led to the expansion of the behavioral science base in the generic education and training of all health professionals. Theoretical content from psychiatry, psychology, and social sciences, and to a varying degree the learning of interpersonal skills, became an important part of the basic professional curriculum.

During this period professional societies were central in supporting the development of medical social work. From 1918 until 1955 the American Association of Medical Social Workers was the professional organization spearheading the growth of the new profession (Stites, 1955). Since 1955 the Health Council of the National Association of Social Workers (NASW) has been concerned with advancing the practice of social workers in the health field. In 1966 the American Society for Hospital Social Work Directors was formed, a culmination of years of effort by the American Hospital Association and the American

Association of Medical Social Workers (later NASW) to work in various areas of shared concern in relation to medical care. The Society is particularly concerned with the standard of social work administration in medical and health programs and in increasing communication and exchange of ideas among administrators of these programs.

It is important to note that since 1971 the Joint Commission on Accreditation of Hospitals has required the availability of social work services as a condition for accreditation. This commission represents the American College of Surgeons, the American College of Physicians, the American Medical Association, and the American Hospital Association.

Today many unique opportunities present themselves for the practice of social work in the varied health field. Settings for practice are: general, specialty, and long-term hospitals and their clinics (private, nonprofit, and proprietary; public and federal); clinics of local health departments and neighborhood health centers; home-care programs; vocational rehabilitation programs; the U.S. Public Health Service; the central and regional offices of the U.S. Department of Health, Education, and Welfare; state and local health departments; voluntary health agencies; health divisions of community welfare federations and councils; public social service agencies; and professional schools, including schools of medicine (Bartlett, 1961). Finally, there is a growing trend to use social workers in group practice and in prepaid medical plans.

The Changing Health Field

Forces propelling the health services field toward change are varied and include increasing affluence and a rise in the use of health care, the protest against deprivation and demand for more and better services from socially disadvantaged population groups, as well as population growth and increased longevity. A result of the lengthened life span is the rise in serious chronic and long-term diseases. Many of these are disabling and life threatening. The increase in heart disease, stroke, and cancer has focused national attention on the need for new approaches to their management. Social conditions seem to have contributed considerably to the incidence of alcoholism, drug addiction, and venereal disease.

Finally, it has become apparent that even if more adequate health services were available, not all consumer groups would necessarily be prepared to use them. Investigations indicate that use of services is in part a function of socioeconomic, cultural, and environmental factors (Somers, 1971, p. 19). This is why there is so much emphasis on devising more appropriate systems for the delivery of health care.

Other factors which contributed to the changes in the current federal social welfare programs included the great depression which led to the beginning of the federal Social Security programs, the changing philosophy and role of the government (Schottland, 1971), and labor unions' demands for health insurance as a fringe benefit of employment.

The following discussion of various federal legislation, plans, and programs must be read in relation to present and future trends rather than for precision since the programs and legislation are in a constant state of change and flux.

THE SOCIAL SECURITY AMENDMENTS

The federal government first acted on its awareness of the inequity of health services available to the indigent sick and disabled population under state and local public auspices in the 1950 amendment to the Social Security Act. From that year until 1965 the federal government shared medical care expenses on a formula basis for persons receiving aid under categorical assistance programs eligible for federal participation. The Kerr-Mills Act of 1960 extended this financial assistance to the medically indigent aged.

Title XIX (Medicaid) of the Social Security amendments of 1965 was designed to extend medical aid to all medically indigent persons rather than only to public assistance recipients. The year 1977 was planned as the target year when financial circumstances would no longer keep a person from receiving needed medical care. The alleged cost of such care has led to a considerable variance in services available under Medicaid. In addition, restrictive eligibility criteria limited access to the programs below the federal government's intent and expectation. In regard to social work services for Medicaid, the 1972 amendments to Title II of the Social Security Act assigned responsibility for their provision to public welfare departments.

At the same time, Title XVIII (Medicare) offered the first health insurance program for the elderly, effective July 1, 1966. Coverage under this program is not yet complete. Title XVIII initially established medical social services as an integral part of health services to be provided patients who require posthospital care in an extended facility, regardless of their socioeconomic status. However, according to the 1972 amendments of Title II, medical social work services were no longer mandatory (Sec. 243 D).

HEALTH INSURANCE

A succinct discussion of three major approaches to national health insurance is provided by Somers to include:

1. A federal program, with compulsory coverage of all or most of the civilian population, with broad and explicitly defined benefits, financed by a combination of payroll taxes and federal tax revenues, and administered by the federal government without use of private carriers

2. A federal program of voluntary tax credits to taxpayers and vouchers to nontaxpayers, to help them purchase private health insurance with minimum benefit standards, and financed entirely out of general revenues

3. Various inbetween proposals embodying some characteristics of each of the above (Somers, 1971, pp. 127–48).

Social workers with concern and responsibility for social planning need to study both current federal health legislation and pending health insurance proposals in terms of their compatibility with social goals (Waldman and Peel, 1970). Somers (1971, pp. 136–41) suggests ten criteria which are important in the study of health insurance material: (1) universal coverage; (2) comprehensive care; (3) a pluralistic and competitive insurance carrier system; (4) consumer choice; (5) adequate and stable incomes for health care providers; (6) efficiency and economy; (7) equitable financing; (8) manageable organization and administration; (9) consumer satisfaction; and (10) change and innovation.

COMPREHENSIVE HEALTH CARE PROGRAMS

A number of factors paved the way to more receptivity of the health care system to experiment with new kinds of delivery systems. Among

these were the greater social awareness which had led to public acceptance of the right to health care, growing consumer interest in the
product designed for his use, limited manpower and equipment, and
the rise in combined medical practice and group medical practice
(Somers, 1971, p. 10). Finally, the rehabilitation movement and the
increasing technology of specialized care units (as for intensive and
coronary care) were forces from within pressing toward change.

With wider federal participation in financing health care came
federal concern with quality of care, its distribution, and accessibility.
This, in turn, led to major health legislation designed to promote a
more systematic approach to health care planning throughout the
country.

Thus the Regional Medical Programs Act of 1965 as amended was
designed to encourage state and regional planning. It emphasized
particularly the diagnosis and treatment of heart disease, cancer, and
stroke. As the federal government changed structure for health care
planning by creating a National Cancer Institute, regional medical
programs took on broader responsibilities. Most recently this involved
the development of area health education centers.

The Comprehensive Health Planning and Public Health Service
amendments of 1966 (P.L. 89–749), also known as the Partnership for
Health Act, was the first health legislation which expressed the government's intent to make adequate health services available to all persons,
so that health and health care today are a right rather than a privilege.
This act provided for grants to states for comprehensive health care
planning on a local or area-wide basis. It included funding for projects
for training studies and demonstrations, formula grants for health
services, and project grants for health services development (Burns,
1971, p. 516). Finally, the creation of the National Center for Health
Services Research and Development in 1968 reflected the federal
government's concern with coordinating all efforts to improve and
extend the health services delivery system.

Quality of services, in the government's view, must include the concept of continuity and comprehensiveness. Continuity of care may be
defined as integrated and continuous care as opposed to the fragmenta-
tion of care which so commonly occurs. Comprehensiveness refers to

the availability of the broad range of services which might be required by any given patient without additional cost. (According to the Social Security amendments of 1972, comprehensive health care under Medicare and Medicaid must include health education, preventive maintenance, rehabilitative and restorative care on an in-hospital or out-of-hospital basis, as may be required.) Fiscally speaking, the government favors prepaid health plans which will provide all these services in one package.

To encourage comprehensive systems of health care for the entire population, legislation to amend Title II was first proposed in 1970 to promote the establishment of health maintenance organizations (HMOs). Senate bill 3327 of September 25, 1972, represented a revised version of the originally proposed legislation. One major goal of the Administration with regard to HMOs was to stimulate their formation in areas, particularly rural ones, which were currently lacking in adequate health services. Health maintenance systems which wished to qualify for federal funds under the new law would provide comprehensive inpatient and outpatient services for their enrolled members. Financing would be on the basis of prepaid annual fees. Organizations would have freedom with regard to size, structure (single administration is mandatory however), ownership, and fiscal arrangements with physicians (Ellwood, 1972; U.S. Department of Health, Education, and Welfare, 1971).

The new HMOs would also affect the structure of service. Thus, for example, an organization in an urban center might include several major hospitals, and their clinics and satellites, neighborhood health centers, nursing homes, and home health services. Structurally, social work services might be located in the various facilities of the organization or they might be obtained through contracts with private social work practitioners. Again, needs of geographically isolated consumer groups present opportunities for organization and delivery of social work services involving new models of social work teams and of use of communications technology. An additional dimension involves the relationship of social work to the private practice of medicine, since HMOs may contract with physicians in private practice, group or solo, to provide a variety of services. Generally speaking, private practitioners have made rather limited use of social work services in the health field, but these new service patterns will require functional working relationships between physicians in private practice and social workers.

Social Work Practice Roles

In general, social work students planning to enter the health field have been ill-prepared to cope with the complexities of the social organizations represented by health care systems. They need to know in depth the perspectives of other professionals, including physicians, nurses, and therapists, with their specific professional ethics and culture, their mutualities as well as their differences. They should be knowledgeable about the hospital's social structure, beginning with its goals as compared to those of its staff; its culture versus subcultures of employee groups and of individual employees; the organization of work in terms of role and task assignment and the educational and training requirements for specific role performance; the structure of a variety of services, such as wards, clinics, home-care programs, or satellite programs with emphasis upon organization of work teams, including hierarchies, and resulting status conflicts; value conflicts as they may affect perspectives on patient care; norms for social interaction within and between professional groups; norms for social interaction with patients; the structure for interrelating the variety of services; the nature of rivalry or competition between subsystems; and the communication system.

Finally, in order to evaluate the nature of the patient's and his family's response to the medical problem and its treatment and the quality of their social functioning, these students must understand the nature of the illness or injury and of the required treatment process. Without knowledge in these areas, the best of social workers will not be able to function optimally in the health field, whether in clinical practice, administration, planning, teaching, or research.

THE SOCIAL PLANNING ROLE

Social changes of national scope are indeed reshaping institutional arrangements. Concern for further clarification of the economic, political, legal, social, and psychological dimensions of choices of future health care systems is shared by social work. Social planners have knowledge and skills to apply to the task of bringing about policy change within organizations (Morris and Binstock, 1966). This, of course, is a prerequisite to planning and implementing new programs. From the clinical and social science fields comes information about health practices of individuals and population groups (Freidson, 1961; Lambert and Freeman, 1967; Weinerman *et al.*, 1967) which have applicability to the implications of reorganizing public hospitals. The same material would also provide guidelines for educating potential consumers to use a modified health care system.

Problems related to the distribution of scarce resources in health care will necessitate social workers' thinking in more depth about a variety of ethical and moral concerns in relation to social and psychological consequences of medical care. They are able to contribute social-theoretical points of view, including values and ethics in relation to issues of distribution of resources. In addition to theory, social work has a great deal of information to share from its practice, including characteristics of population groups, which should influence answers to questions regarding the allocation of scarce resources. Some of the questions are: What is to be a minimum standard of acceptable health? What is a minimal level of acceptable health care in relation to this? What are the limitations within which comprehensive services can be provided without further expense to the patient? And more specifically, if highly specialized services such as organ transplants are to be provided on other than a first-come-first-serve basis, or on medical need basis in the strictest sense of the word, what are the criteria for selection? Finally, it would seem that in a national health service system, it would not be reasonable to leave these kinds of decisions to individual HMOs. Rather, some guidelines should be provided in order that scarce resources may be distributed as equitably and ethically as possible throughout the country.

Planning for the effective distribution of scarce social resources is a responsibility which social workers in the health field share with other disciplines and with consumers. From the health maintenance and preventive point of view, two important issues with which social workers must be concerned are: (1) a goal for a minimum standard of social functioning acceptable for the entire population which is compatible with good health; and (2) a level of minimum social care which should be provided for all persons in the nation. Availability of social resources affects the level of social functioning which persons with a physical handicap due to birth defect, a long-term illness, or disabling injury may expect to achieve. Here one thinks of such social requirements as housing, transportation, accessibility of public facilities, educational, vocational, and recreational opportunities, and resources required for independent living.

There are limitations in present federal medical programs and in proposed health insurance plans which have social consequences. Neither one is comprehensive and both place additional financial burdens upon the consumer. Also, little attention is being given to the need for portable health insurance plans in view of the mobility of the population. Inadequate insurance programs and inadequate fiscal planning at the federal level may deprive persons of their basic right to medical care. These programs would continue the dual system for care since the gap would undoubtedly be met through the public hospital and clinic system. Thus they would also deprive the consumer of the freedom to choose providers.

The manpower question is a difficult one for social work as it is for all other health professions. The challenge will be to provide quality service economically, in keeping with the federal mandate, with access for all, and in accordance with accepted standards of social health. As other professions, so has social work been struggling with following through on a systematic approach to the study of deployment of manpower, with emphasis upon the use of staff educated and trained in a variety of ways for a variety of roles and tasks (Dockhorn, 1965; Houston, 1970; Mueller et al., 1971).

Community outreach programs have experimented with training health aides in elementary skills and tasks of several professions, clustering, for example, basic nursing, social work, health education, and nutrition skills. Such programs (Coate and Nordstrom, 1967) have definite merits in terms of economy and appeal to consumers. There is some urgency for social workers to explore the expanded use of this model.

THE ADVOCACY ROLE

According to the professional ethics of social work, advocacy is the responsibility of every social worker. In his role of advocate the social worker is prepared to intervene with institutions which control society's resources and which by their restrictive policies cause grievance and suffering for individuals or groups. Advocacy may also have as its goals the stimulating of changes which have consequences for all of society (Gurin, 1971, p. 1334; Keith-Lucas, 1971, p. 328). There are many opportunities for social workers in the health field to assume the advocacy role with regard to patient needs related to the health care system. Some of the inequities of medical care in relation to the disadvantaged groups have been mentioned.

The quality of long-term custodial care for the aged is another example of serious, unmet need. Clark (1969, pp. 62–67) reports an interesting project which improved posthospital care for elderly patients who required nursing home care in the Boston area. Among other things, the author and the hospital administrator took political action which resulted in standard-setting legislation for nursing home administrators and which ultimately had consequences for federal standards for extended care facilities.

The depersonalization and dehumanizing aspects of hospital care are well-known to many health professionals. They have to do with the entry into the hospital system, the impersonal attitude and seeming lack of concern which are conveyed as fragmented care is delivered. A social worker on a given service may hesitate to assume his ethical obligation in view of the reaction which he may expect from other staff and from administration. Yet it is of particular importance to make an effort to acquaint other health care team members, including the physician, with the problems for which the patient needs help. Enlisting the support of colleagues and, when fitting, their assistance in handling the difficulty, is an important step in the process of advocacy.

The advocacy role is as much the practitioner's as the administrator's or planner's. It may be a shared responsibility in large systems, where several subunits might deal with similar problems, thus requiring a coordinated approach to the advocacy process.

THE CLINICAL ROLE

Prevention and Maintenance. If it is to function more effectively in preventive programs, the structure of social work in health care services necessitates a new look. The first requirement for preventive and health maintenance focused medico-social programs in HMO health care programs is a protocol for social functioning examinations. They are necessary, first, to obtain a base line for evaluation of a person's social functioning status over time, and second, to rule out symptoms of social dysfunctioning which would suggest vulnerability of the general health status and consequent need for preventive and interventive measures.

Professional social work judgment will aid in the development of guidelines for timing, format, and content of social functioning examinations. The goal will be the detection of the earliest symptoms of stressful interaction between physical and psychosocial factors. Following up clues in depth will frequently involve professional social work decision-making. The final diagnostic formulation should be professional responsibility, at least at the present.

For planning treatment measures related to the concept of secondary prevention, except in apparent cases of acute illness, it is essential to explore the person's life situation and social functioning status at the time he first noticed the symptoms related to his present complaint, as compared to when he finally decided to seek care (when he was ready to assume the role of being sick).

There is a need for efficient, economic models for social assessments which will provide a base for prediction of preventive and therapeutic treatment outcomes directed toward the prevention of social dysfunctioning on the one hand and maintenance of given social functioning levels in face of physical and psychosocial stress on the other. This should be a major area of research in social work.

Rehabilitation and Restoration. A generally recognized area for social work practice in health is that of rehabilitation and restoration. This refers to working with persons whose social functioning goals must take into account permanent limitations in physical functioning. Examples of chronic, not necessarily fatal, conditions requiring rehabilitative, restorative care are strokes, spinal cord injuries, arthritis, and diabetes.

In addition, this concept can be applied also to persons with more life-threatening chronic illnesses, such as cancer and heart disease. Once a degree of stability has been established in a given person's health state, medical and social maintenance programs, though on a more time-limited basis, are suitable. Working with persons who must accommodate to lasting changes in physical functioning requires considerable maturity, knowledge, and skill. This must be emphasized in work with patients with life-threatening and terminal illness. Living with uncertainty regarding one's life expectancy, needing to face changes in life style and the consequent emphasis upon readaptation of social functioning patterns, are experiences which would stress any person's coping mechanism. Even with normally adequate inner and outer resources the task of regaining a new balance in social functioning can be overwhelming at times.

Preventing further breakdown of social functioning and offering supportive services to maintain gains made in social readaptation is a major function of social work in the health field. Early social work intervention through direct treatment modalities aimed at optimum social restoration in the face of long-term health problems will keep additional damage from appearing and will serve to maintain a given social functioning state. This is why social functioning examinations are important when a patient first presents himself for care of a catastrophic condition. It is part of social work's unique contribution to help patient and family develop their own new pattern of internal relations and a modified exchange balance with its larger environment.

When applying the concept of social functioning in terms of a balanced exchange relationship between the individual and his environment and rehabilitation or maintenance programs, it is important to recognize that many patients and their families experience social dysfunctioning not because of their inherent inability to cope, but because of lack of supportive devices or "social braces" (Kahn, 1967, p. 692) from community resources. If there were more opportunities for the disabled to invest their energies productively in the home or in the labor market, much of the psychosocial counseling aimed at bending the patient and his family to a passive service system would not need to take place.

Custodial Care. Patients requiring long-term custodial care for health reasons must face the range of problems which confront other patients discussed so far. However, there is added stress. The person in custodial care frequently has suffered loss of significant relationships as well as of role status and independence. Often this is the older person who tends to view his admission to a custodial care facility as coming to the last station in life. Afraid of the illness itself, threatened by feelings of impending death, guilty over being dependent, and ashamed of being deserted by his family, he has little motivation to participate in the maintenance of whatever level of social functioning remains realistic for him. As is well-known by workers in the health field, this group of patients tends to receive least attention by competent professionals and is left to linger often in less than minimally adequate situations.

The greatest need to support the work of health care programs designed for the rehabilitation and/or maintenance of persons with long-term illness and disability is for adequate social utilities and social technologies to enable the disabled person to participate according to his ability and with dignity in the socioeconomic system of the community in which he lives.

THE COMMUNITY ORGANIZATION ROLE

Social workers have a responsibility to work on the development of more adequate social resources which will match medical progress so that life will be worth living even in a state of considerable physical disability. This means that when they encounter these unmet human needs and problems in the community, they must assume the role of community worker in order to initiate the process of achieving community awareness and change.

Traditionally, community workers have been employed by community planning agencies. With the emerging relationships between medical establishments, particularly hospitals and clinics, and consumer and neighborhood groups, community organizers may well have a place not only in hospital social work departments but also on the hospital administrator's staff.

Whether community work originates in the organization's or the consumer's perception of need, the community worker will seek to involve consumer groups in goal definitions and program implementation. He will also plan to bring together representatives from the establishment whose assistance will be required to achieve change in delivery of social services. He will work with groups within the hospital. Ultimately, consumers, community agency representatives, and hospital management may be encouraged to negotiate around alternate choices for program expansion.

THE RESEARCH ROLE

Research needs in relation to social planning, community and clinical work must be mentioned. There is an urgency for research into alternate models of service organization and delivery which should be the product of social work research and collaborative research. Professionals in other fields, like medicine, political science, and economics, may share a specific interest in studying the health care delivery process. Research should include studies of need and feasibility of services, of services vis-à-vis varying cultures and life styles, and designs for models which may be evaluated through controlled experiments. Most importantly, from such research will come findings which will make possible the prediction of outcomes, given alternate choices of service in face of given need conditions. As alternate choices of social utilities are tested successfully the process of achieving translation of innovations into enabling legislation may begin.

Program studies to evaluate quality, effectiveness, and cost are high among research priorities, according to federal mandate. Differential use of staff, career ladder building from an intra- and interprofessional point of view, including consequences for basic professional education, suggest collaborative efforts among social work departments, schools of social work, and other professional departments and their educational counterparts.

The study of the social work role and function on health care teams and in interdisciplinary education is an additional priority for research. Finally, the administrator must encourage his staff to participate in research projects which will advance the standard of practice in a given health care organization.

Implications for Education

The fields of education and practice must collaborate to provide an educational experience which will establish for the graduate professional social worker a central core of social work concern and thus prepare him to practice successfully in the health field in spite of overlap of functions and resulting domain uncertainties.

The field of practice has a major contribution to make to classroom and field learning for generic and more specialized education. For the health care setting provides ample opportunity for the study of human behavior and human needs, especially in face of illness; of the interrelatedness of physical, social, and psychological factors; of complex social organizations, social interaction, the nature of professions, and the organization of the institution of health care itself.

There is an urgent need to come to grips with the fact that the complexity of the health care system requires some added preparation at some point in the educational continuum, whether this is before or after completion of basic professional education. If specialized training is to take place following basic education, then educational systems must offer some consultation to service agencies as the latter develop such programs.

Interdisciplinary education will require all collaborating professions to take a look at the expanding, shared generic curriculum previously discussed. As social work participates more and more in the basic education of other health personnel, clarification of content will continue from its generic base of knowledge, skills, and attitudes which will be taught to students in other health professions. It will also conceptualize with growing clarity its own unique contribution to health care. This, in turn, will make interdisciplinary teaching of social work focus and function more effective.

Last, and for the present, most important, the adequacy of future national standards for social care as reflected in social policy and enabling legislation will to some extent depend upon the ability of social planners to work effectively with those institutions of society which control its resources. Priority must then be given to consider content for generic social work education as well as for specialized education in order to prepare practitioners for these significant planning roles (Zweig, 1969).

Social work in health has made much progress since its beginnings in 1905. This is evident through the great variety of health care and health-related programs in which social workers practice. The challenge for the future is wide open for social work to strengthen its contribution in the health field. It will succeed as it accomplishes the tasks defined for medical social workers by Dr. Cabot long ago, namely, to practice autonomously in clinical settings and to stimulate the social programs required for the maintenance of health.

References

Bartlett, Harriett M. *The Common Base of Social Work Practice.* New York, National Association of Social Workers, 1970.

—— Fifty Years of Social Work in the Medical Setting. New York, National Association of Social Workers, 1957.

—— *Social Work Practice in the Health Field.* New York, National Association of Social Workers, 1961.

—— *Some Aspects of Social Casework in a Medical Setting.* Chicago, George Banta Publishing Co., 1940.

Burns, Eveline M. "Health Care Systems," in *Encyclopedia of Social Work*, pp. 510–23. New York, National Association of Social Workers, 1971.

Cabot, Richard D., M.D. Excerpts from "Hospital and Dispensary Social Work," in Dora Goldstine, ed., *Expanding Horizons in Medical Social Work*, pp. 255–90. Chicago, University of Chicago Press, 1955.

Clark, Eleanor. "Post-Hospital Care for Chronically Ill Elderly Patients," *Social Work*, XIV, No. 1 (1969), 62–67.

Coate, Shirley, and Eugene A. Nordstrom, Jr. "Experiment in Upgrading the Non-professional Worker," *Social Casework*, L (1969), 401–6.

Dockhorn, Jean M. *A Study of the Use of the Social Work Assistant in the Veterans Administration.* Department of Medicine and Surgery, Veterans Administration. Washington, D.C., U.S. Government Printing Office, 1965.

Ellwood, Paul M., Jr., M.D. "Implications of Recent Health Legislation," *American Journal of Public Health*, LXII (1972), pp. 21–23.

Freidson, Eliot. *Patients' Views of Medical Practice.* New York, Russell Sage Foundation, 1961.

Gurin, Arnold. "Social Planning and Community Organization," in *Encyclopedia of Social Work*, pp. 1324–37. New York, National Association of Social Workers, 1971.

Houston, Laura Pires. "Black People, New Careers and Humane Human Services," *Social Casework*, LI (1970), 291–99.

Kahn, Elsbeth. "Social Bracing in Rehabilitation," *Journal of the American Physical Therapy Association*, XLVII, No. 8 (1967), 692–99.

Keith-Lucas, Alan. "Ethics in Social Work," in *Encyclopedia of Social Work*, pp. 325–28. New York, National Association of Social Workers, 1971.

Lambert, Camille, Jr., and Howard E. Freeman. *The Clinic Habit.* New Haven, Conn., College and University Press, 1967.

Morris, Robert and Robert H. Binstock. *Feasible Planning for Social Change.* New York, Columbia University Press, 1966.

Mueller, Jeanne, *et al.* "Community Caretaker or Mental Health Case Finder," *Mental Hygiene*, LV (1971), 214–18.

Rice, Elizabeth P. "Social Work Practice in Medical and Health Services," in *Encyclopedia of Social Work*, pp. 570–76. New York, National Association of Social Workers, 1965.

Schottland, Charles I. "Social Welfare: Governmental Organization," in *Encyclopedia of Social Work*, pp. 1437–46. New York, National Association of Social Workers, 1971.

Somers, Anne R. *Health Care in Transition: New Directions for the Future.* Chicago, Hospital Research and Educational Trust, 1971.

Stites, Mary A. *History of the American Association of Medical Workers.* Washington, D.C., American Association of Medical Social Workers, 1955.

U.S. Department of Health, Education, and Welfare. *Towards a Comprehensive Health Policy for the 1970's*, White Paper. Washington, D.C., U.S. Government Printing Office, 1971.

Waldman, Saul, and Evelyn Peel. "A Comparison of Five Proposals," in *Research and Statistics Notes*, pp. 1–23. Washington, D.C., U.S. Department of Health Education, and Welfare, Social Security Administration, Office of Research and Statistics, 1970.

Weinerman, E. Richard, *et al.* "Yale Studies in Ambulatory Medical Care—Determinants of Use of Hospital Emergency Services," in *Medical Care in Transition*, VIII, 397–416. Washington, D.C., U.S. Government Printing Office, 1967.

Zweig, Franklin M. "The Social Worker or Legislative Ombudsman," *Social Work*, XIV, No. 1 (1969), 25–33.

NEILSON F. SMITH,

AND

MILTON WITTMAN

New Roles and Services in the Community Mental Health Center*

THE MENTAL health service system has undergone an evolutionary series of changes during the first half of the twentieth century. The second half will be devoted to assessing and implementing the significant shifts in philosophy that underpin the provision of mental health services in the United States.

The instrument for delivery of mental health service most likely to emerge as the primary tool for the implementation of social policy as it relates to mental health is the community mental health center, a social invention which has emerged as a means of providing a nuclear structure from which one cluster of people with a wide range of skills and competencies provides services to the wider community. These services are directed toward preventive as well as restorative and curative objectives (Glasscote *et al.*, 1969; Ozarin, Feldman, and Spaner, 1971).

The Historical Context

One of the most significant developments in mental health during the middle of the twentieth century can be said to have been the reversal of the increasing numbers of patients residing in public mental hos-

---

* This chapter reflects the opinions of the writers and does not represent policy of the U.S. Department of Health, Education, and Welfare.

pitals. It is quite conceivable that by the end of the century the large public mental hospital will have been completely abandoned in favor of alternate types of community care, including a wide range of services adapted to the needs of the patient and available within easy reach. The institutional change which brought about this reversal was determined by many factors, not the least of which was the new scientific research resulting in the effective use of drugs to further the accessibility of patients to treatment and to various rehabilitation services (Greenblatt, York, and Brown, 1955). The most significant events of this period were the product of a massive study of mental health and mental illness in the United States launched by the Mental Health Study Act of 1955 and completed in 1959 (Joint Commission on Mental Illness and Health, 1961). One of the direct effects of this study, in addition to publication of its eleven-volume final report, was the introduction of the community mental health centers and mental retardation legislation of 1963 based on the first Presidential message on mental health, delivered by John F. Kennedy.

President Kennedy called for "a bold, new approach." The three major tasks outlined in the message dealt first with the need to "seek out the causes of mental illness and mental retardation and eradicate them." The second major objective was to "strengthen the underlying resources of knowledge and above all of skilled manpower which are necessary to mount and sustain our attack on mental disability for many years to come," and lastly, to "strengthen and improve the programs and facilities serving the mentally ill and the mentally retarded." The direct result of this message was Public Law 88-164, the Community Mental Health and Mental Retardation Centers Act of 1963 (National Institute of Mental Health, 1964).

Concurrently with the passage of the Community Mental Health Centers Act, the fifty states and three territories received planning grants in order to help them move toward long-range planning for the implementation of the new legislation. Each state was able to assess and review its current and planned mental health resources, including the full range of activities intended to serve the mentally ill and provide local mental health services. A group of interdisciplinary state-level planning structures was established in order to accomplish these objectives. The result was the production of comprehensive state plans which formed the basis for implementation of the mental health centers program. While it was originally envisioned that there would be 500 centers established by 1970, the 1974 budget justification revealed that 493 were funded by December, 1972, in all fifty states, Puerto Rico, Guam, and the District of Columbia.

The conception of the comprehensive mental health center emerged from the work of the National Institute of Mental Health work group which undertook the task of following up the publication of the final report of the Joint Commission on Mental Health and Illness. Although this report had recommended substantial expansion and funding of state mental hospital services to include tripling the investment by 1980, the work group did not follow this recommendation. Instead the group evolved an alternative to the state mental hospital as a means of providing care and service for the mentally ill. What was produced was the concept of a comprehensive mental health center which would provide a cluster of ten services as part of a broad program of mental health in a recommended catchment area of from 75,000 to 200,000 in numbers of population. The ten services were listed as: (1) inpatient; (2) outpatient; (3) partial hospitalization; (4) emergency; (5) consultation and education; (6) diagnostic; (7) rehabilitative; (8) pre-care and after-care; (9) training; (10) research and evaluation (Levenson, 1972). The first five were considered as "essential services," and all projects considered for construction and staffing funds were required to offer the five basic services. While it was not perhaps intended in this way, the fact that training and research were listed last tended to give these a low priority in the formation of mental health center programs throughout the United States.

Underlying Concepts

It should be noted that several concepts are central for these community mental health centers. One was that the center should provide a "continuity of care" so that the patient from the time of first entrance, and throughout the rest of his life, if need be, might have access to continuing mental health services either within the center or through follow-up facilities established in the community. It was also understood that the mental health center need not necessarily be set up in a single location but could be based in a complex of services scattered through the community. Because inpatient and outpatient services were listed as core services, the mental health center early on tended to reflect the medical model of a mental hospital under another name. It should also be noted that many services listed for the mental health center were already being provided in some of the public and private mental hospitals and in mental health clinics, many of which had outreach and emergency services functioning as part of their normal activities (Williams, 1972, Chap. 12).

The emergence of the mental health centers movement coincided with a number of social phenomena. One of these was the emergence of the large-scale poverty program of the mid-1960s. The main features of the poverty program provided for community action and outreach intended to mobilize poor people to become involved in the delivery of social and health services. Thus the notion of outreach was one that greatly influenced the planning of some of the mental health services back in urban and in rural settings. Also of moment was the comprehensive health planning legislation (Public Law 749) which projected for each state a movement into comprehensive health planning which would be reflected in area-wide as well as local community health planning to permit the extension of adequate health services to the total population. During this period there were a number of permutations of state structures which involved combinations of health and mental health, mental health and corrections, mental health and welfare, and health and welfare, with mental health subsumed under health administration. The degree to which coordination of local social and health services took place depended in many cases on the type of state leadership and on the pattern for collaborative work which was developed in any given state. The mental health center staff found itself involved in community planning activities which extended far beyond those carried by staff of the conventional system of hospital and mental health clinic services (Panzetta, 1971).

The early literature on the operation of community mental health centers indicates some degree of frustration with the limitations of the medical model and with the new demands thrust on staff to provide a wider range of services than most of them had been trained to provide.

One of the serious problems regarding the delivery of innovative mental health services derived from the fact that most of the mental health staff had received training along the lines of traditional modes of education. This was as true of social work as of the other disciplines. The most successful patterns of mental health center operation required a perceptive use of community organization skills, a knowledge of educational methods, and consultation in a wide range of collateral disciplines and organizational components providing social and health services or engaged in operations which involved work with people who have an important effect on the community (police, clergy, teachers, and lawyers).

It appeared that two main clusters of professional capability were required of the staff. The first was the clinical cluster, which required ability to provide diagnosis, treatment, and rehabilitation services based on the case-by-case approach or through the use of group methods. The second major cluster was the community organization input. This required a knowledge of basic planning, administration, and a high degree of skill in consultation directed toward program coordination and development. The administrators of community mental health centers were called upon for a large input of social as well as medical administration. One of the early controversies developed involved the question of whether the director of a mental health center must necessarily be a psychiatrist or a medical person. The issue was resolved in favor of a more liberal approach, but only after some considerable pressure was brought to bear to increase the latitude of the requirements in this regard.

Scope of Services in Mental Health Centers

The community mental health center represents the culmination of mid-century shifts in philosophy of treatment and service for the mentally ill. Hobbs (1964) refers to the "third revolution" in mental health which he sees as the full application of public health to mental health doctrine. The center is seen by some as a social invention which provides a new and effective means of early diagnosis, treatment, prevention, and consultation service in a community-based organization

fully capable of providing the widest possible range of services. Others
view the center as another medical institution in the community serving
mainly the same caseload as that of standard mental hospitals and mental health clinics—but with another name. What began to emerge from
the early studies of center programs was that centers varied considerably in their functions, depending on staff and structure (Glasscote
et al., 1964; Glasscote et al., 1969). The general projection of centers'
philosophy and orientation has been reviewed by Levenson (1972).
He makes it clear that the public health approach is at the heart of the
center structure and function. Here will be found all three levels of
prevention: primary (consultation and education); secondary (early
detection and treatment through emergency service); and tertiary (rehabilitation through inpatient and outpatient, partial hospitalization,
and outreach services). These dimensions were extended in concept by
Smith and Hobbs (1966), who saw the need for community involvement in center policy formation. The ideal of the community board as
an instrument of policy formation composed of consumers, community
representatives, and professionals in mental health was established at an
early point in the projection of centers operation. This has become a
cardinal issue, particularly in centers serving low-income and minority
populations. The line between community involvement and community
control becomes unclear, with the surfacing of basic dissatisfactions
stemming from the maldistribution of health and medical care benefits
when the income level is used as a base of measurement. The state
mental hospital has traditionally constituted the poor person's main
mental health service. If the center is to replace the hospital, it must
then carry the responsibility for service to the low-income population.

  Brown and Stockdill (1972) assert that "the development and operation of a community mental health center requires that its professional
staff become deeply involved in the political life of the community and
at the same time the center itself is the means for developing this community involvement" (p. 682). This objective is cited because it does
imply that the range of community service expected by the local population in the catchment area far exceeds the simple provision of a psychiatric treatment service. The expectation is that the range of service
will include large components of advocacy (for children, the aged),
specialized areas (alcoholism, drug addiction), consultation and edu-

cation (to courts, schools, police), and policy development (legislators, public officials). The range will depend fully on the charter for the center (objectives described in the authorization) and the staff (professional, technical, and supportive). The public service goals are considered to extend far beyond the normal treatment functions of a psychiatric treatment institution or a social or health agency as commonly conceived. It is the mix of mandates and obligations that tends to be highly frustrating to professional staff prepared along more traditional lines for service in mental health facilities. The internal and external pressures to respond to the challenge to be innovative are difficult to meet when confronted from the first by a heavy treatment caseload for which there invariably will be too little staff.

Innovations, Extensions, and Permutations

Social workers have played a significant part in innovating and implementing creative approaches to the delivery of mental health services in a community mental health context. Many forces, of course, contribute to the generation of new services and ideas for new ways of delivering "old" services. Demographic factors, the unique needs or demands of particular client populations, geographical constraints, the availability of mental health manpower, as well as the talents and commitment of the manpower available, are some of the determinants that may play a part in the design of new services or new modes of service delivery.

NONTRADITIONAL SERVICES

Some of the most fascinating permutations or readaptations of community mental health services are to be found in rural areas. This results in large part from the immense difficulties encountered in attempting to provide services to a widely dispersed, geographically remote population. It is useful, therefore, to report briefly two examples of community mental health centers that have confronted this problem in different but equally creative ways. This will serve to exemplify some of the demands placed on social workers in the community mental health sphere and the roles they are required to assume.

In some states, rural in character and having population groups far removed from urban centers, it is in no way feasible to furnish community mental health facilities that are immediately accessible to all those who need them. One such state, by means of a cooperative venture engaged in by its mental health division and a school of social work, had found a way to provide its remote communities with essential social and mental health services. The basic format consists of organized teams of mental health professionals which are assigned to the most rural, underserved areas. These teams are composed largely of social workers but include representatives from other disciplines on an irregular schedule. Each team, whose members hold other positions in mental health or allied fields, visits its assigned area for a three-day period each month. In the course of these visits, the team participants engage in a wide variety of community mental health activities. While most of their work with individuals and families is carried out on as short-term crisis-intervention, more intensive casework, psychotherapy, or family therapy is offered when it is indicated. Various longer term group programs are provided for children, youth, and adults. Mental health consultation is a particularly important feature of the team effort, and is furnished to school personnel, clergymen, and other caretaker groups. Each team is responsible for engaging in community organization and community education pursuits in its assigned locale. An especially appealing aspect of this program is the expectation that the visiting teams will employ the resources they bring to a rural community in such a way as to advance the capacities of on-site care givers to provide services when professionals are not available.

In another state, the mental health needs of rural people have had to be met in different ways. In one especially remote part of the state, the only mental health professional available to man the area's community mental health center, with the exception of a licensed practical nurse, is a social worker. The community served by this facility is composed of pockets of very poor, very isolated, non-English-speaking people, many of whom are elderly and a high proportion of whom are discharged mental hospital patients. For ethnic reasons, the population tends to be more than usually suspicious and frightened of mental illness and its victims, as well as of those who ordinarily provide mental health services. They prefer to put their trust in lay healers with whom they are ethnically identified.

In this situation, the social worker who administers this rural community mental health center has to rely almost exclusively on nonprofessional personnel for the delivery of mental health services in the facility's catchment area. He is called upon, therefore, to be administrator, supervisor, and teacher, as well as a practitioner, and he must devise the means for mobilizing and utilizing the inherent capacities and talents of untrained people so that they can deliver mental health services to the area. This is accomplished quite successfully. Through the use of individual and group supervision, reinforced by regular teaching seminars led by the center director and outside consultants, mental health workers from very diverse backgrounds are enabled to become deliverers of service of good quality. These workers, selected in part because they speak the language of the population served, are equipped to employ individual and group helping methods, to supervise the use of medication prescribed by local physicians, and to make referrals to the few social and health agencies in the area. They also have the advantage, of course, of being acquainted with the life styles of the people with whom they are working, the part played in their lives by their fears of mental illness, and their reliance upon lay healers.

These two community mental health operations exemplify a number of the concepts and principles that are part of the community mental health approach to service delivery. They demonstrate, clearly, that the social worker best equipped to function in community mental health is one who has been prepared as a generalist, a practitioner possessing the interventive skills enabling him to work with individuals, families, groups, and communities. He must respect and be prepared to exploit the native talents of indigenous people, just as he must also be ready to administer programs and to function as supervisor and as teacher of others who, with a degree of training, may be better able to deliver mental health services to some population groups than are the professionals. The examples proffered also illustrate, among other things, some novel ways of operationalizing the concepts of comprehensiveness of service coverage, community involvement, and the importance of building on the strengths of communities.

The concepts of community involvement and continuity of care, both of which are very central to community mental health, often go unimplemented or inadequately implemented in community mental health settings. An example of another community mental health center will show that these two ideas can be made operational in lively and imaginative ways. This center, located in a rural/urban community, is again manned almost exclusively by social workers, in so far as professional personnel are concerned, and is supported by a large number of indigenous paid and volunteer community workers. The center has been monumentally successful in returning mental hospital patients to their communities and preventing their rehospitalization, a major purpose of community mental health. This is due in large measure to an aggressive insistence that the community take responsibility for its mentally ill members. Intensive engagement of the staff in the community, and of the community in the center, are at the heart of the program's accomplishments. A comprehensive aftercare project, effective local care-giving resources and halfway house arrangements, and the flexible use of basic treatment approaches are some of the ingredients that have enabled this center to be responsive to the mental health needs of its community. Vigorous outreach efforts are also a prominent feature of the center's activities, and these offer reasonable assurance that those in need of help will receive it and that those who have been helped will be sustained. A program such as this clearly demonstrates that community involvement and continuity of care, among other concepts that have emerged from community mental health, are attainable objectives in the provision of mental health services. The activities engaged in by the center staff are an expression of the scope of innovative pursuits in which social workers may become involved as designers and implementers in community mental health centers.

RELEVANCE FOR OTHER PROFESSIONAL SETTINGS

It needs to be noted that a community mental health stance toward service delivery need not be confined to centers per se. The concepts, services, methods, and philosophy of community mental health are readily transferable, in part or in whole, to other forms of service-giving operations. This circumstance is especially relevant to social workers, who are more inclined than the members of other mental health disciplines to find themselves employed in a wide array of settings. In the process of applying and adapting community mental health approaches to noncommunity mental health programs the social worker will be confronted by significant professional challenges and exceedingly rich opportunities for innovation.

A brief example will illustrate the point. A school of social work recently established a field training unit in a very large, very seriously underserved region whose population is characterized by extreme poverty, low employment potential, and racial conflict. The training unit's director had as his first responsibility the obligation to provide comprehensive learning experiences for the eight students for whom he was field instructor. In this instance, however, it was even more apparent than usual that learning and service are inextricably interwoven. It was also apparent that, while the training unit was organized as a community mental health educational program, neither the students nor the community would be benefited by an effort to attend to mental health concerns to the exclusion of other more basic and profound social problems. The elasticity of a community mental health orientation to service, combined with a sensible grasp of what is relevant to the mental health of a given community, enabled the students and their field instructor to carve out a program that at least approximates what is required by the people of the region.

The training unit undertook to assess the needs and resources of the community and to do this in a manner that fully engaged local people in making these determinations. A service/learning program was based on that assessment. A significant part of the unit's obligation is to intercede with, and to make more responsive to, the community the few existing social and health services. The training unit participants are charged with responsibility to work supportively with community and neighborhood organizations, and to work with them and other groups to effect needed social change. The nature of the students' tasks are such that they are obliged to engage actively with the community's political structure. Additionally, of course, the field instructor and the students furnish direct services to individuals, families, and groups, utilizing varied treatment modes according to the circumstances of the community and the resources available to the training unit. They have also taken on the task of developing local service- delivery resources by consulting with and training indigenous caretaker personnel.

It will be apparent that the malleability of the community mental health approach to service delivery has permitted this training unit to construct a program that in many ways simulates a community mental health center operation. It may also be apparent that the program, as it is unfolding, is operationalizing such community mental health in-gredients as continuity of care, prevention, comprehensiveness of ser-vice, concern with all age groups, and community involvement to a degree often not observed in more highly structured community mental health centers.

An especially appealing feature of some modern community mental health centers is the growing use of satellite programs to expand the parameters of their service delivery systems. While no longer new or innovative in themselves, satellite centers offer endless opportunities for variations on a theme for the purpose of reaching out to segments of a catchment area population that are inaccessible to the home base of a community mental health center. Inaccessibility may be because of geographic, socioeconomic, or cultural distance. Satellite programs, seldom complete centers in terms of offering all the required services of a community mental health center, often take the form of neighbor-hood or storefront operations. Their staffs are usually multidisciplinary, replicating on a smaller scale the personnel complement of the parent center. Social workers, in addition to being employed as deliverers of service in satellite centers, often are assigned administrative respon-sibility. A chief virtue of the trend toward satellite programs, of course, is the latter's capacity to bring mental health services to communities whose people would otherwise be disinclined to avail themselves of programs more distantly located. Satellite centers tend frequently to be less formal and more relaxed then centralized organizations, more a part of the community served, and thus less intimidating to those in need of service. Smaller service delivery units such as these have other favorable attributes. While retaining their community mental health orientation, they can be designed, in regard to both location and ser-vices, to emphasize services related to particular social problem areas, such as congregations of drug users, or to disadvantaged barrio or ghetto populations. Satellite centers can also be staffed by professionals or nonprofessionals who, if not indigenous to the areas served, are at least familiar with, and able to function in, their special cultural milieus. Many such centers, too, have community or neighborhood advisory boards composed of local residents who, unlike those serving on larger, more remote boards, have the advantage of being genuinely attuned to their communities and their communities' needs.

Education for Community Mental Health Service

Social work education for service in community mental health, rapidly accelerating in schools of social work, is presently in a state of considerable flux and change. It is particularly taxing, therefore, to undertake to assay what is now occurring in this arena and, especially, to assert what should be happening. A considerable part of the problem rests with the ill-defined, or inconsistently defined, nature of community mental health itself, and of the roles that social workers should play in it. The matter is further confounded by the interdisciplinary character of community mental health service, with the resultant role ambiguity and confusion respecting the roles of social work personnel vis-a-vis those of other mental health professionals and nonprofessionals. An additional complexity is that so much of the basic curricular content of schools of social work, regardless of how labeled, is directly or indirectly relevant to community mental health. It is often difficult to determine, for example, if a school's curriculum in the aggregate offers sufficient classroom preparation for community mental health practice, or if other educational devices are needed such as special courses or seminars specifically focused on community mental health. A further dilemma is posed by the question as to whether training for any field of practice, such as community mental health, is better undertaken in the classroom or in the field.

Perhaps the scope of the task confronting social work education with respect to the community mental health field is best conveyed anecdotally. Not very long ago a major federal funding source received two grant applications for support of social work training ventures in community mental health. One applicant proposed to make a set of videotapes portraying, for purposes of training, the roles and functions of social work personnel in community mental health settings. It was assumed, obviously, that those roles and functions were sufficiently well-comprehended and delineated to be captured on film. The second applicant, who also wanted to undertake a training program for social workers in community mental health, began with a different assumption. He argued that so little was known about social work roles and functions in the community mental health sphere that it was essential first to do research that would define a social work practice model which would become the base for constructing a good training program. A review committee, composed largely of social work educators knowledgeable with regard to community mental health, declined to approve the first application but supported the second with enthusiasm.

A recent publication enables us to move somewhat beyond the dilemmas outlined briefly in the foregoing (Berg, Reid, and Cohen, 1972). The authors undertook a piece of empirical research, one of very few studies in the area, to investigate the consonance between social work education and the realities of community mental health practice as they are confronted by social workers. The findings indicate powerfully that the curricula of schools of social work, at least as perceived by graduates, offer insufficient preparation for the practice demands of community mental health. The study reports that social workers with the master's degree experience much more benefit from "on-the-job experience" than from graduate social work education when it comes to knowledge needed for such practice areas as group treatment, supervision of staff, mental health consultation, working with community boards, working with community groups, interagency collaboration, coordinating mental health resources in the community, and mental health education.

The study suggests that changes will need to be made in graduate professional training programs if their products are to function more adequately as social workers in community mental health. While that study did not concern itself with other phases of training for community mental health service, its results, combined with general observation, make it reasonable to think that similar attention should be paid to training programs in continuing education and faculty development. Continuing efforts to extend or update the competencies of graduate professionals can, according to how they are designed, either enhance or further reduce the consonance between training and practice. Faculty development activities, a form of continuing education, are pursued for the purpose of strengthening the teaching capacities of educators. There is reason to believe that some part of the dissonance between social work education and community mental health service would be reduced if means were found to afford educators opportunities to advance their knowledge in the community mental health sphere.

NEW PATTERNS IN TRAINING

With respect to what is presently happening at the level of graduate social work training for community mental health service, it is useful to take note of a recent major step taken at the National Institute of Mental Health. NIMH, beginning in April, 1972, inaugurated a new program of support for social work education in the mental health sphere. The plan was that all former categorical master's level grants in psychiatric social work, school social work, community organization, administration, and so on, would be consolidated into a single grant category. While there were obvious administrative advantages to this, the primary intent of the new program was to reemphasize the NIMH mission to prepare personnel for the community mental health field. Thus, it was required that schools of social work with multiple categorical grants from NIMH submit proposals for consolidating them under the rubric of "Social Work Training for Community Mental Health." It was permissible for grantees to continue training in fields of practice formerly supported by categorical grants, but these forms of training had to be brought into meaningful relationships with community mental health* (NIMH, 1972).

In the course of the first phase of implementing this new approach to federal support of social work education, prior to realization that it would have to be abandoned because of massive cutbacks in governmental funding of all professional training, some thirty schools of social work were engaged in redesigning their NIMH-supported training efforts. Despite the ill-fate of the consolidation program, it is useful to

---

* At the time of this writing, it had become apparent that this new NIMH program in relation to social work education was in serious jeopardy due to unforeseen fiscal constraints and was likely not to go forward.

review briefly some of the ideas that emerged as schools of social work struggled to recast training activities into a community mental health context.

The faculty members involved in devising social work training in community mental health programs were required to reexamine their classroom and field components, and to inquire regarding the goodness of fit between them and the community mental health service delivery scene. In regard to existing curricular offerings, it was not enough to claim that all social work content is relevant to community mental health. It became necessary to look in depth into what content really did bear upon community mental health, and with what degree of proximity. When lacunae were identified, decisions had to be made regarding whether these could be filled by strengthening courses and seminars or whether new courses were needed. In many cases it was determined that the latter option was essential if community mental health conceptual content was to be conveyed to students in an integrated and coherent fashion. It is noteworthy that the reexamination of curricula from a community mental health perspective had several important effects: (1) accelerating the movement of formal course provisions out of the school and into the field; (2) focusing on the preparation of professionals to work with nonprofessionals on a cooperative, collegial basis in addition to a supervisory or educational relationship; and (3) attaching the issue of interdisciplinary training as essential for the interdisciplinary practice inherent in community mental health.

In many respects, it was the reformulation of field training components under the consolidation plan that brought the more exciting and potentially rewarding departures from previous patterns. Here, again, consolidation fostered the further development of an educational innovation that had already begun in social work by offering an opportunity for extending and refining the notion of the teaching/learning center as an ideal vehicle for field practica (Cassidy, 1969; Jones, 1969). The teaching/learning center approach to field education was found by many schools to be an excellent mechanism for restructuring previously disparate categorical grant-supported training programs into cohesive practicums organized around community mental health. Creation of field teaching centers, because they involve large numbers of students, made field-based courses or seminars economically and educationally feasible as an important means of offering core community mental health curricular content. Teaching/learning centers, typically embracing a range of loosely associated service delivery settings, were particularly advantageous for implementing the expectation that the varieties of social work training programs supported by NIMH be "brought into meaningful relationship with community mental health."

Some of the resultant teaching/learning centers were so designed as to conform geographically with previously established catchment areas. This permitted students and field faculty to have direct exposure to community mental health center programs, while also devising training strategies that allowed affiliation with many other types of service agencies. Where community mental health centers per se did not exist, the teaching center approach permitted the use of simulated community mental health opportunities. Thus, by the use of multiple, diverse, service delivery operations, it was possible to approximate the reality of a community mental health program and to provide a learning environment in which central community mental health concepts and principles could be acquired. The multiplicity of varying learning opportunities in teaching/learning centers of this sort enabled students with quite different educational interests, such as those who wanted to specialize in one or another basic social work method or some combination of them, to be brought together for shared learning experiences while at the same time satisfying their individual learning needs. It is apparent, also, that trainees preparing for social work roles in, for example, school settings, work with the aging, narcotics addiction, or children's services, could advantageously undertake field practice in teaching/learning centers of the sort proposed, and that their specialized educational experiences would be enriched by occurring in a community mental health context.

THE NONPROFESSIONAL IN COMMUNITY MENTAL HEALTH

In recent years, substantial discussion has taken place relative to the place and use of nonprofessionals—or paraprofessionals, new careerists, indigenous workers, and so forth—in the helping services, and perhaps especially in community mental health. A considerable literature has emerged concerned with the nature of the training such personnel should have, the kinds of work that can legitimately be expected of them, their relationships with professionals, with what clientele they can most productively work, and so forth (Grosser, Henry, and Kelley, 1969; Southern Regional Education Board, 1970). While much rhetoric and many dilemmas characterize the so-called "era of the nonprofessional," there is little question that he is here to stay and, as was suggested earlier, has a vitally useful role to play in community mental health service delivery. The issues here, however, are what bearing the existence of the nonprofessional has upon social work education for community mental health and, more particularly, how the graduate student's professional training should be oriented to this new type of mental health worker.

Very few graduate social work educational programs make provision for preparing community mental health professionals to work with nonprofessionals. Many graduate students, of course, especially as they pursue field assignments, engage with nonprofessionals in one way or another. As a result, they acquire experience in associating with them, but such experiences are largely fortuitous and unplanned. Also, these associations are more often than not fraught with tension, competition, and role ambiguity. It is seldom that one sees an organized, systematic effort to train social workers to make effective use of themselves in their interactions with paraprofessionals. Until there are such programs, modern social work education is incomplete.

Some efforts are being made to equip social workers to train personnel who have less than full professional training, but these are few in number. The better programs provide for field practice in which students design and carry out training activities for nonprofessionals, in the course of which they acquire knowledge of curriculum building and skills in teaching. A scattering of other graduate educational curricula offers occasional courses or seminars concerned with preparing students for supervisory and consultant roles with lesser trained personnel. For the most part, however, educational components of this type are lacking in schools of social work and are greatly needed. Equally as important, more must be invested in preparing social workers not only as trainers of nonprofessionals, but as service delivery collaborators and colleagues who are ready to learn from them.

A New Knowledge Base

A significant feature of community mental health service, and presumably of education for it, has been virtually ignored in the literature and in educational programming. This is the reality that an outstanding characteristic of community mental health is its interdisciplinary nature. In community mental health settings, typically the four core mental health disciplines of social work—psychology, psychiatry, and psychiatric nursing—are required to work together, and frequently other disciplines and nonprofessionals are also part of the staffing pattern. If service delivery is to be effective, the several disciplines must be equipped to function collaboratively and harmoniously in environments characterized by professional tensions and overlapping roles and responsibilities. And yet the educational programs that prepare for community mental health, with few exceptions, are undisciplinary in structure.*

A recent article by Bandler treats the issue of interdisciplinary training by discussing the boundaries that have set the mental health professions apart and the consequences this has had for service delivery (Bandler, 1972).

Another paper focuses directly on interdisciplinary training as a recommended approach to professional education by arguing, among other things, that programs in which the mental health professionals share common learning experiences offer educational values that are not otherwise realizable (Smith, 1972). There are a number of assertions that can reasonably be made to support the desirability of interdisciplinary training vis-à-vis community mental health. Professionals who are trained together, it can fairly be assumed, will be better prepared to work together productively and with a minimum of misperceptions of one another's roles and capacities. The mental health professions, moreover, share a common body of knowledge in the behavioral

* Social work education, of course, is not devoid of interdisciplinary training activities. A small number of post-master's programs, some designed specifically to train for community mental health, are organized along interdisciplinary lines. A few schools of social work offer master's and doctoral programs that have interdisciplinary features. Some master's programs are clearly interdisciplinary in that social work students are trained in both class and field with students from other schools or departments.

sciences, permitting the ready development of interdisciplinary courses. Courses of this type, as well as interdisciplinary field provisions, enable trainees from the various professions to come to know one another in a common learning environment. Community mental health as a field of service has its own body of knowledges, skills, and methods, and those, too, are amenable to interdisciplinary training. Contrary to the fears expressed by some, professional identity is likely to be enhanced and sharpened by interdisciplinary educational pursuits in which students have opportunities to perceive the similarities and uniqueness of the several disciplines.

Some final observations remain to be made regarding the training aspects of continuing education and faculty development and the implications for community mental health. In view of what has been said with respect to the adequacy of graduate community mental health programs, it will be clear that many of their products are entering community mental health practice deficient in the knowledge and skills required for that specialized service. Substantial support for this assertion is found in the study prepared by Berg and his associates (Berg, Reid, and Cohen, 1972). Until such time as community mental health training programs are sufficient in number and kind to produce the type of personnel needed, it is incumbent upon service delivery studies to provide the curricula for continuing education programs in order to extend staff capabilities in community mental health. Subsequently, of course, even as professional education changes to conform more clearly to the needs of community mental health, continuing education will still be required in order to expand and update practitioners' knowledge and skills in the field.

The quality of the education obviously rests on the availability of teaching personnel who are thoroughly acquainted with the substantive content associated with the training endeavor. Community mental health training programs are often staffed by faculty who have only a peripheral acquaintance with community mental health and so have been inadequately prepared for their roles. There is a critical need, therefore, for faculty training programs whose aim should be to enhance the teaching capabilities of present faculty and also to build up a cadre of trainers especially equipped as teachers of community mental health practice. Such programs will need to be directed to the faculty of university-affiliated educational programs and to the preparation of much needed agency-based training personnel.

Whither Social Work in Mental Health?

The National Association of Social Workers (NASW) has stated a social work position which emphasizes a broad, encompassing philosophy of practice in community mental health. The scope of service envisions extension of community mental health to "significant social systems, other human service programs, and the community at large" (NASW, 1969). These objectives are indeed being achieved by the centers oriented to the comprehensive mental health service objective.

The converging forces behind social welfare and mental health suggest the need to move toward more effective collaborative engagement at state and local levels (Wittman, 1972). The social work educational establishment must look to its means for maintaining currency with practice in a growing and changing field with significant input for well-being of the individual, the family, the community. New methods for linkage of practice and education can be generated from settings in which interdisciplinary practice finds its best expressions. The future of social work practice rests firmly on its ability to apply the knowledge gained from the newer modalities of service delivery. The mental health center is one of these.

References

Bandler, Bernard. "Community Mental Health and the Educational Dilemmas of the Mental Health Professions," *Journal of Education for Social Work*, VIII, No. 3 (1972), 5–18.

Berg, Lawrence K., William J. Reid, and Stephen Z. Cohen. "Social Workers in Community Mental Health." Chicago, School of Social Service Administration, University of Chicago, 1972.

Brown, Bertram S., and James W. Stockdill. "The Politics of Mental Health," in Stuart E. Golann and Carl Eisdorfer, eds., *Handbook of Community Mental Health*, pp. 667–86. New York, Appleton-Century-Crofts.

Cassidy, Helen, ed., *Modes of Professional Education.* New Orleans, Tulane University School of Social Work, 1969.

Glasscote, Raymond M., *et al. The Community Mental Health Center: an Analysis of Existing Models.* Washington, D.C., Joint Information Service of American Psychiatric Association and National Association of Mental Health, 1964.

—— *The Community Mental Health Center: an Interim Appraisal.* Washington, D.C., Joint Information Service of American Psychiatric Association and National Association of Mental Health, 1969.

Greenblatt, Milton, Richard H. York, and Esther L. Brown. *From Custodial to Therapeutic Patient Care in Mental Hospitals.* New York, Russell Sage Foundation, 1955.

Grosser, Charles, William E. Henry, and James G. Kelley. *Nonprofessionals in the Human Services.* San Francisco, Jossey-Bass, 1969.

Hobbs, Nicholas. "Mental Health's Third Revolution," *American Journal of Orthopsychiatry,* XXXIV, No. 5 (1964), 822–33.

Joint Commission on Mental Illness and Health, *Action for Mental Health.* New York, Basic Books, 1961.

Jones, Betty Lacy. *Current Patterns in Field Instruction in Graduate Social Work Education.* New York, Council on Social Work Education, 1969.

Levenson, Alan I. "The Community Mental Health Centers Program," in Stuart E. Golann and Carl Eisdorfer, eds, *Handbook of Community Mental Health,* New York, Appleton-Century-Crofts, pp. 682–98. 1972.

National Association of Social Workers "Position Statement on Community Mental Health." New York, The Association, 1969, Xeroxed.

National Institute of Mental Health. *The Comprehensive Community Mental Health Center.* Washington, D.C., U.S. Government Printing Office, 1964. Public Health Service Publication No. 1137.

Ozarin, Lucy D., Saul Feldman, and Fred E. Spaner. "Experience with Community Mental Health Centers," *American Journal of Psychiatry,* CXXVII, No. 7 (1971), 88–92.

Panzetta, Anthony F. *Community Mental Health Myth and Reality.* Philadelphia, Lea and Febiger, 1971.

Smith, M. Brewster, and Nicholas Hobbs. *The Community in the Community Mental Health Center.* Washington, D.C. American Psychological Association, 1966.

Smith, Neilson F. "Interdisciplinary Training for Community Mental Health Service." 1972; mimeographed.

Southern Regional Education Board. *After Graduation: Experiences of College Graduates in Locating and Working in Social Welfare Positions.* Atlanta, Ga., 1970.

Williams, Richard H. *Perspectives in the Field of Mental Health.* Rockville, Md., National Institute of Mental Health, 1972.

Wittman, Milton. "The Social Welfare System: Its Relation to Community Mental Health," in Stuart E. Golann and Carl Eisdorfer, eds. *Handbook of Community Mental Health,* pp. 127–35. New York, Appleton-Century-Crofts, 1972.

WILLIAM GELLMAN

Vocational Rehabilitation and Social Work

THE CONCEPTUAL and institutional bases of social welfare programming in the United States are in a state of flux. The exponential nature of American societal transformations is altering the goals and methods of the social welfare delivery system. The social services are enveloped in a maelstrom of change which leads to surprising intersections in the helping disciplines and reactions that will modify their roles and responsibilities. The evolvement of the United States into a postindustrial economy is accelerating the process. New demands for social service resulting from the interaction of hitherto unserved groups with emerging social pressures is generating social problems which appear to be beyond the scope of present social services. Sussman (1972) foresees marked changes in the systemic configuration of social services and in the interrelationships between helping professions such as vocational rehabilitation and social work. Richman (1971) believes the current organization of social services lacks a substantial theoretical base. The consensus is that the social service system requires reexamination and reformulation of its rationale and service methodology.

President Nixon's message "Delivery of Social Services" (1972) iterates a similar theme in calling for a more effective and more integrated system for the delivery of services to individuals and groups. The message states:

These many [social service] programs were established one-by-one over a considerable number of years. Each of the target problems was examined in isolation, and a program to alleviate each problem was devised separately—without regard to programs which had been, or would be, developed for allied problems. The result is . . . a bureaucratic jungle. . . . The unintended administrative snarl frustrates needed efforts to treat the whole person.

The Presidential message poses the question of operational unification of apparently disparate social service programs such as vocational rehabilitation and social work. A similar problem exists on the theoretical level. The separation of theory and practice both within and between the helping professions is indicative of a need for an integrative conceptual system as a theoretical underpinning for practice. The demand for an organized framework of knowledge for social service suggests a pretransitional state antecedent to the development of a unifying theory similar to periods in the natural sciences preceding the appearance of the periodic table in chemistry and the theory of relativity in physics. A similar trend toward integration is occurring in the vocational rehabilitation–social work subsystem. Both helping professions seek to develop a substructure which relates similarities and differences in practice to a theoretical framework rather than empirical constraints. The absence of a rationale for coordinating delivery systems in the two social services reflects the present level of professionalism within these fields and the influence of extrinsic factors which make it difficult to formulate a general theory. Among these are the *ad hoc* organizations of services imposed by the urgency of immediate problems; a theoretical orientation of service-oriented disciplines; focus upon delimited problem areas; and pseudoprofessional barriers to interdisciplinary cooperation.

Examination of the relationship between vocational rehabilitation and social work, a relatively unexplored subject, is a first step toward the formulating of a generalized social service practice theory. Early articles and focus on methodology describe the interaction between the two disciplines as occurring at the operating level (Cooper, 1963; Hillyer, 1955; Moore, 1962). The descriptions suggest two parallel practice methodologies with occasional links to serve clients but without expectation of meeting theoretically or operationally. Mayo (1957) sees the programmatic relationship of the two helping professions as nonintegrative. A recent conference (National Rehabilitation Counseling Association, 1971) on role differentials in rehabilitation counseling and social work focused on existing relational patterns. It saw little evidence of a sustained relationship between the two disciplines. The conference emphasized the desirability of developing a theoretical and methodological substructure which can further joint action. McCauley's conference summary stresses the importance of continued exploration of the problem of relationship between the two disciplines and the need "to attain a sense of community . . . to contribute new modes of service, to seek innovative uses of economic materials and resources . . . and together, develop new goals with which both of our fields can identify without qualms" (McCauley, 1971).

The Development of Vocational Rehabilitation

While illness, injury, accident, and aging, the precursors of disablement, occur in all societies, the aftermaths vary from culture to culture. Sociocultural value systems tend to determine a society's attitudes toward the disabled and the social value of rehabilitating the handicapped. Decisions regarding whom to restore, the nature of the restorative process, and the time to begin rehabilitation are rooted in cultural patterns. Treatment is minimal if illness, injury, and accident are regarded as results of supernatural intervention or divine displeasure. If a society's view of illness is fatalistic, rehabilitation is left to faith. If man is seen as actively controlling events, and if the healing arts are assumed to be curative, rehabilitative measures are used. The treatment of lepers during the Middle Ages illustrates the significance of the concept of curability. "Regarded as incurable by the West, they [the lepers] were cast out. . . . In the East on the other hand, the disease was regarded as curable and therefore not particularly feared" (Haj, 1970).

Prior to the last quarter of the nineteenth century, most rehabilitative efforts to help the disabled were separated from philanthropic attempts to relieve the indigent. If the handicappeed were both worthy and destitute, charity and rehabilitation were joined. For example, St. Basil founded a hospice in Caesaria Cappadocia for the blind who were deemed worthy (Obermann, 1965). King Louis IX of France, who was later canonized by the Church, established a hospital in Paris to instruct 300 blind veterans of the Crusades (Haj, 1970). In such cases, the combination of rehabilitation and social work differed markedly from the limited services offered the socially unworthy who were destitute or afflicted with socially undesirable disabilities.

The second half of the nineteenth century was characterized by sustained advances in all fields: science, technology, the useful arts, medicine, and industry. The rapid growth of technological capacity led to the concept of progress and the belief that man and society were infinitely perfectible. The forward thrust of science and applied science resulted in increased capacity to control natural and social environments. The formation of voluntary welfare agencies at the close of the Victorian Age reflected the addition of humanitarian impulses to the conceptual mixture of control and progress. As improved medical care increased the possibilities of recovery and restoration for the ill and injured, the *Zeitgeist* led the Cleveland Rehabilitation Center to initiate the first formal rehabilitation program in 1899. Physical restoration, which the center used as the primary rehabilitation methodology, served as the model for early rehabilitation agencies. Rehabilitation emphasized the use of "all those medical measures which expedite recovery" and cemented a close working relationship with physicians (Kessler and Kessler, 1950). Rehabilitation, as the restoration of physical capacities, was part of the emerging medical technology. The medical orientation of the rehabilitation team restricted the participation of social work in dealing with social problems. The physical restoration model of rehabilitation was characterized by: (1) the physician as a leader of a hierarchical team; (2) focus on physical aspects of disability; (3) the use of a limited, tangible, specific treatment goal based upon physical capacity; (4) the assumption that psychosocial problems were outside the scope of rehabilitation; and (5) the view of social work as unrelated and disjunctive.

The inadequacy of this model became apparent when rehabilitation began to serve individuals in lower socioeconomic brackets. The model was inadequate for disabled persons facing poverty because of diminished work capacity or inability to secure suitable employment. The necessity of a vocational component led Pasteur to add a work goal to physical restoration in 1907 by establishing a vocational education school to train severely disabled persons for industry (Soden, 1949).

The transition from a purely medical approach to a combination of physical and vocational restoration culminated in 1918 with the United States federal program for disabled First World War veterans. The federal vocational rehabilitation program included the purchase of prosthetic appliances, vocational training, and assistance for veterans in training. Although vocational training was primary, the program faced difficulties because many veterans had social or familial problems which interfered with their vocational education. Efforts to deal with the nonvocational factors, including those within the scope of social work, imparted a quasi-social work character to the rehabilitation process (Obermann, 1967).

The administration of the vocational rehabilitation service provided a limited social service program at community training centers and used volunteers from veterans organizations to assist veterans with social work problems. The Veterans Bureau neither established comprehensive programs for dealing with social problems nor coordinated its activities with those of social service agencies. Psychological and social factors affecting the disabled client were treated as secondary and separted from vocational rehabilitation. The partial success of the veterans rehabilitation program coupled with an economic recession which limited employment possibilities for physically disabled persons led Congress in 1920 to pass an act providing vocational rehabilitation services for disabled civilians.

The act established a state-federal program in which states were given the responsibility for developing vocational rehabilitation programs for the physically handicapped with partial funding from the federal government. The state rehabilitation agencies equated skill training with employability and viewed the rehabilitative process as preliminary to vocational education. Funds were available for training and for services necessary to make training feasible. The overemphasis upon skill training excluded the psychosocial aspects of the rehabilitation process from consideration and left social work with a limited role.

The period from 1918 to 1943, the vocational education stage of vocational rehabilitation, was characterized by the addition of a vocational goal and the use of vocational training as the primary rehabilitation technique. The vocational educational model treated social and psychological difficulties as peripheral problems. The centrifugal approach to personal and social factors affecting physically disabled persons was both a cause and consequence of the limited understanding of social work concepts. The vocational education model restricted the possibilities for an effective working relationship with social work. It precluded formal cooperation between rehabilitation and social work and resulted in a relationship characterized by referral at a distance. The interaction was limited to referral supplemented by the sharing of information. There was little effort to coordinate client services or to take joint action to resolve general problems affecting both professions.

Rehabilitation's third stage of development began with the Second World War vocational rehabilitation program for veterans. More than six hundred thousand veterans were placed in rehabilitation training and almost eight million in other forms of training (Obermann, 1965). The introduction of vocational evaluation and counseling as prerequisites for entry into training programs added a psychosocial motif to rehabilitation. Veterans with personal and social difficulties received intensive counseling to improve their use of training services. Increased emphasis upon vocational evaluation exercised a catalytic influence upon the rehabilitation process and led to the formulation of notions such as work satisfaction and work adjustment. The job-placement goal was enlarged to include job satisfaction and to provide for a job change if a rehabilitated person found his job unsatisfactory.

The Veterans Administration program stimulated the growth of the civilian vocational rehabilitation programs which added new services, and the mentally handicapped as clients. Concepts of impairment, disability, and handicap were differentiated and used to define levels and types of disablement. The term "impairment" connoted a physical decrement; "disability" referred to the loss of functional capacity; "handicap" indicated a social bar or disadvantage resulting from societal prejudice toward a disability or impairment. Psychological and social factors were assumed to play important roles in determining the rehabilitative consequences of the disability, impairment, or handicap. The disabling impact of an impairment or a handicap could not be equated psychologically with the severity of a disability. Psychology joined medicine and education as a component in the rehabilitation process. Rehabilitation counseling added the technique of interpersonal relationship to the information-giving and guidance processes.

The methodology of vocational rehabilitation was expanded to include the concept of an array of services to assist clients. Services such as hospitalization, transportation, prosthetic devices, and maintenance during training were added to vocational education and skill training. Vocational rehabilitation worked with psychology, education, industry, and the employment services to increase the effectiveness of the rehabilitation process. Rehabilitation regarded social work as a means of helping individual clients deal with a limited range of problems and did not establish coordinated programs with social work. Although vocational rehabilitation established relationships with other helping professions, it retained a close tie with the vocational education system. The array of service was channeled into areas which fostered the disabled person's ability to undertake training and to secure competitive employment. Despite greater awareness of the effect of psychosocial factors upon rehabilitation outcomes, there was little attempt to integrate nonvocational components into the rehabilitation treatment process.

The Contemporary Concept of Rehabilitation

The Vocational Rehabilitation Act of 1954 marked the beginning of vocational rehabilitation's fourth developmental stage. The act intensified two trends evident in the preceding phase: expansion of the client group and the shift toward a psychosocial approach. The act "gave vocational rehabilitation the boost it needed to become a dynamic part of the fabric of services to people" (Whitten, 1971). The use of research-demonstration projects opened vocational rehabilitation to inputs from the helping professions and the behavioral sciences. The provisions of the act fostered the partnership of vocational rehabilitation with social and vocational community agencies. Subsequent amendments included provisions for the establishment and improvement of rehabilitation facilities and for services to the families of disabled persons receiving rehabilitation or facing postrehabilitation adjustment problems. The act added the socially disadvantaged, the deviant, and the dependent to the potential rehabilitation population.

As the program expanded, changes occurred in the conceptual and operational bases of vocational rehabilitation. The definition of rehabilitation need shifted from disability to handicap with its focus upon the social sphere and psychosocial factors hampering or diminishing ability to function. The psychological model replaced the vocational education model and generated a multidisciplinary approach which emphasized the use of teams and coordination of services and resources (Horwitz, 1970). The picture of the rehabilitant was changed from that of an atomistic man to one of a social man enmeshed in a web of familial and social institutions. Disablement was viewed as a continuing process affecting both rehabilitation and client adjustment after the termination of formal rehabilitation. Vocational adjustment supplanted job placement as the goal of vocational rehabilitation. The rehabilitation workshop emerged as the tool for vocational evaluation and work adjustment of the vocationally maladjusted client, whether disabled or disadvantaged (Nelson, 1971). The utilization of workshop techniques and other noninterviewing methods generated approaches to vocational rehabilitation practice which used concepts such as work role, work personality, vocational development, work adjustment, and work therapy (Neff, 1968). Recognition of the influence of sociocultural forces upon the rehabilitant brought social workers into the rehabilitation teams (Cooper, 1963). Subsequently, social work and rehabilitation agencies joined forces in cooperative projects serving deviants and the recipients of public assistance. Generally, social work assumed responsibility for the entry of clients into the rehabilitation program while rehabilitation coordinated postintake services, calling upon social work as necessary. Such projects did not eventuate in complete integration. The tendency was for the two professions to operate sequentially or along parallel tracks.

The Rehabilitation bill of 1972, which was vetoed by President Nixon, introduced a nonvocational goal for severely handicapped persons. While the implications of this proposed change are unclear at this time, the bill would have provided service to the severely handicapped with little or no employment potential. Improvement in physical, psychological, or social functioning would have become an acceptable rehabilitation goal for this group, with the vocational goal remaining primary for less severely handicapped clients. The probabilities are that the concept of vocational rehabilitation would have been extended to include unrenumerated productive and self-care activities which contribute to society and which have positive psychological or social consequences for a rehabilitant.

Lofquist (1968, p. 351) summarizes the current status of vocational rehabilitation in his definition of the field:

Rehabilitation deals with past, present and future behavior and with assisting the individual to find an optimal balance which will permit him to live as well as possible within the handicaps imposed by a disabling condition and in a manner consistent with his ability, aptitude, interests and personality factors; it involves active interprofessional participation in planning for and with individuals; and, whenever feasible, it points toward some measure of vocational adjustment as an ultimate goal. Most counselors would also agree that the rehabilitation effort would be facilitated by more attention to the development of ways of changing the attitudes of the public and employers (and perhaps of professional workers and their clients) toward the handicapped as a group and toward specific disability classes.

Lofquist sees rehabilitation as a multidisciplinary enterprise involving the theory and practice of psychology, medicine, and social work. Rehabilitation is maximally effective when these are integrated with educational and employment skills in a team effort which takes into account the desires, needs, and unique pattern of handicaps of the impaired and his family. The rehabilitation goal is vocational adjustment, attaining or maintaining the ability to function productively in a work situation.

This brief survey of the history of vocational rehabilitation focuses upon changes in goals, approaches, techniques, and operating concepts during its evolution as a helping profession. At each stage, vocational rehabilitation expanded the scope of programs. Job training replaced the initial goal of physical restoration and was supplanted by job placement, which in turn gave way to a mixture of work adjustment plus improvement in other life sectors. The service model shifted from physical therapy to vocational therapy with a psychosocial emphasis. The interdisciplinary teams took the place of physical therapists or vocational educators. Rehabilitation moved the locus of interviewing and history-taking to neighborhood offices. Workshops and industrial settings were used for field observation and treatment of clients as they engaged in ongoing activities. The rehabilitation workshop, using simulated situations, took over the functions of verbal therapy as the preferred method for modifying the rehabilitant's work behavior and preparing him for competitive employment. Situation and behavior modification techniques assumed greater importance. The beginnings of a theoretical framework for vocational rehabilitation practice occurred with the initial formulation of empirical variables, relating a sociovocational model of the rehabilitant to his major societal roles — work, family, social, and community. The use of a psychosocial, multi-disciplinary approach was accompanied by closer working relationships with social work. Rehabilitation, which during its early stages saw its problems as unique, began to realize the importance of sociocultural factors. Vocational training was no longer the method of choice but one of many techniques of assistance.

The relationship of vocational rehabilitation to social work passed through a number of phases as vocational rehabilitation matured and adopted a psychosocial approach. During the early periods dominated by physical restoration and vocation education there was little contact between the two disciplines. Rehabilitation saw social work as neither relevant nor involved. The social and economic dislocations caused by the world wars brought the two professions together to assist veterans who were unable to use their veterans' benefits constructively. The rapprochement was short-lived. With the appearance of a peace economy, vocational rehabilitation and social work moved their separate ways. As the psychosocial approach became more pronounced during the fourth stage, social workers joined rehabilitation teams in client service, with the rehabilitant linking the rehabilitation counselor and caseworker. Interaction was minimal at the administrative, planning, and research levels. When vocational rehabilitation extended its services to the disadvantaged, the two fields cooperated on joint projects. As both fields became aware of the higher incidence of disablement and impairment among low-income groups, the relationship grew. The need for cooperation was evidenced in reports such as the following:

Health insurance survey data on family income, age, and employment status
indicate that the lower income groups contain a disproportionate number of
older workers, persons known to have a high prevalence of chronic disorders,
activity limitations, and restricted activity associated with chronic disorders
(Lewis, 1964, p. 1005).

The overlap in clients and problems in low-income groups creates a
linkage between the two disciplines. In such joint programs with rehabilitation the social work roles are those of coworker, team member,
and specialist in psychosocial problems. The collaborative role is being
expanded. The integrative roles which are basic for a unified social
service delivery system have not evolved.

Recent Trends in Vocational Rehabilitation

Program expansion and professionalization, the dominant motifs of
vocational rehabilitation, will continue during the 1970s. Extension
of service to a broader band of clients calls for innovative programming capable of dealing with mutational problems in new settings.
Creation and evaluation of service programs in a changing society require the capacity to cope with immediate needs quickly and expedi-
tiously. Professionalization calls for the formulation of a theoretical
rationale, the setting of standards, and a conceptual system subject
to empirical verification—a slow process. The contrapuntal tension
between the basic and applied approaches is intensified by the cost-
benefit approach with its pressures for greater efficiency and more
immediate results.

In regard to the first motif of program expansion, the history of vocational rehabilitation is marked by the addition of programs and new
categories of clients, such as the mentally handicapped, the emotionally
ill, the disadvantaged, recipients of public assistance, former public
offenders, alcoholics, and drug addicts. The vetoed rehabilitation bill
of 1972, which would have added severely handicapped individuals
with limited vocational potential, would have continued the tendency
to serve all vocationally disadvantaged handicapped persons, including
the disemployed. The corollary to the expansion of clientele is voca-

tional rehabilitation's reaching out for unserved persons. One consequence is the movement of facilities for vocational rehabilitation services and programs from central city areas to neighborhood locations.
Itinerant service is being provided employed clients at their place of
employment. The resulting increase in accessibility and availability of
rehabilitation in nontraditional locations enlarged the number served
and made the composition of rehabilitation's clientele more representative of the universe of potential clients. Projects with industry exemplify
the use of on-the-job training in industrial or business organizations for
rehabilitative purposes. The training position serves as a steppingstone
for disabled persons moving toward competitive employment. The
program's success points to the possibility of utilizing industrial work
for therapeutic purposes after training industrial supervisors in rehabilitation techniques.

Professionalization of vocational rehabilitation, the second major
trend, reflected greater emphasis upon sociocultural forces incident
to the change in rehabilitation's clientele, from a predominantly middle-
class group to a diversified racial, religious, ethnic, and socioeconomic
clientele. The effect of subcultural values upon the rehabilitant's self-
perceptions and evaluations of external influences created service difficulties and raised questions concerning rehabilitation's empirical
approach. Rehabilitation undertook research to delineate the operational variables underlying the rehabilitation process and to redefine
vocational rehabilitation roles. Rehabilitation was considered a social
technology for facilitating the vocational training of rehabilitants. The
rehabilitator was seen as a change agent. The rehabilitant emerged
as a "consumer-participator." The vocational sector was viewed as
reciprocally related to, and influenced by, other life sectors. The vocational scene, which included the rehabilitant's familial, social, and
work groups, touched upon all other life sectors.

As a counterpoint to the changed perception of rehabilitation's dra-
matis personae, new concepts are emerging. A key theoretical variable
is the work role which links observable job performance with coping
capacity in the vocational area. The work role is a comprehensive pattern of behavior and attitudes connected with an occupation, job, or
task and socially identified as an entity in a work situation. All productive activities, whether remunerative or unpaid, are characterized

by conformance, demanding work roles which require a worker to conform to the work role and to behave appropriately for the type of work he is doing whether it be as lathe operator, housekeeper, caretaker, volunteer, or manager. The work role presumes the ability of the occupant to function productively if customary working conditions prevail. It assumes also that the individual can secure employment and adapt to work.

The prerequisites of the work role are related to three significant variables for vocational rehabilitation: the work personality, vocational preparation, and vocational adjustment. The "work personality" is defined as the manner in which an individual enacts a work role, the behavior patterns exhibited in a work situation. The observed "work behavior" is a manifestation of the work personality, an integrated, semiautonomous portion of the total personality Gestalt. The constellation of work behavior, attitudes, and values which the individual exhibits in work or achievement-demanding situations is a result of vocational development, the process by which an individual learns to work, to achieve, and to function in a work role. The process begins in early childhood with orientation to tasks and goals, and continues with the cultural shaping of responses to the demands of achievement in socially demarcated work situations. The semiautonomous work personality as modified by the experiences of working and achieving develops the attributes and competencies necessary to function properly in a work role. "Vocational adjustment," the end product, refers to the level and degree of adaptation to the world of work as defined by the compatibility of the work personality with one or more' socially accepted work roles. "Job adjustment," the more specific term, refers to the relationship between the work roles, characterizing a specific position and on-the-job behavior.

The utilization of empirically based variables such as the work role and the work personality in the rehabilitation process tends to substitute situational techniques for psychotherapeutic counseling as the primary vocational rehabilitation methodology. The trend to use realistic or contrived situations which permit the rehabilitant to enact a work role in a work setting is related to the treatment of culturally divergent disabled and disadvantaged clients. Realistic work situations comprise on-the-job training or work activities in typical business,

industrial, or governmental settings. For purposes of vocational rehabilitation, the realistic work situations should be sufficiently flexible
with respect to working conditions and type of supervision to permit
full- or part-time work. Supportive services are provided if necessary
to help rehabilitants cope with on-the-job problems such as prejudicial
attitudes of supervisors or coworkers or intrinsic or extrinsic barriers
to performance. A job coach meets periodically with the rehabilitant
and his supervisor to review the client's progress and to provide assistance as required.

Workshops are the principal vocational rehabilitation settings for
the use of contrived situational techniques to prepare clients for movement to a realistic work setting. The types of workshops serving disadvantaged persons through the provision of gainful employment are:
(1) rehabilitative, using a controlled modifiable work environment
and the rehabilitant's work experience to evaluate his work potential
and to facilitate his adjustment to a work role; and (2) sheltered, fur-
nishing work to vocationally disadvantaged persons unable to compete
in the labor market. The rehabilitative workshop uses realistic work
environments and working conditions as a setting for purposive work
directed toward creation of a product which has economic worth
in the competitive market and thus provides funds to pay the rehabilitants for their work. Work activities in the shop are graded by level
of difficulty, probability of success, type of task, character of supervision, work pressure, required work abilities, and monetary rewards.
Provision is made for varying components of the psychosocial work
environment which influence the nature and intensity of client stim-
ulation. The alterable factors in the typical rehabilitative workshop
are, in addition to the graded items, such factors as the work role, extent of work group participation, work group leadership conformance
demands, and autonomy. Rehabilitation counseling and other supportive services are avilable to the rehabilitant during his stay in the
workshop and while he searches for employment in the open labor
market.

Vocational rehabilitation reacted to the challenge of disadvantage-
ment by expanding the scope of rehabilitation and increasing program
effectiveness through research.

Industrialization, Postindustrialization and the Social Services

Social work and vocational rehabilitation evolved in the United States as meliorative responses to the transition from an agricultural to an industrial society. The growth of the helping professions paralleled the rise of industrialism. Their apogees coincide with the plateauing of industrialism. Despite a quarter of a century between the formal beginnings of social work and of vocational rehabilitation, the demands of industrialization imposed similar schemas on the disciplines. Both spurted ahead programatically whenever the pace of industrialization quickened or when they faced the social by-products of industrialism such as urbanization, protracted unemployment, industrial accidents, destitution, or occupational deskilling.

The heightened tempo and expansion of the social services during periods of industrial growth were accompanied by sharp transformations in their structure and functions. As industry formed regional and national aggregations, social service agencies followed a similar pattern. The rise of a professional managerial class in industry was paralleled by professionalization of vocational rehabilitation and social work and the replacement of volunteers by trained staff. As the tide of industrialism waxed, the social services saw poverty and disability as supraindividual, as social problems resulting from the dislocations of an industrial society.

Intense and widespread social problems appeared with the deceleration of industrial growth. The capacity and ability of the social service system were insufficient to meet the demands for services. Vocational rehabilitation and social work responded to the challenge of economic recessions by attempting to meet service requests and by promoting social reform. The directions taken by the social service field reflected the level of prosperity. Program expansion paralleled recessions. Professional growth correlated with economic peaks. The level of the economic cycle determined whether emphasis was placed upon professional growth or social reform. During periods of high employment, the helping professions focused upon improving service expertise; with low employment, programmatic reforms were stressed.

Recurrent periods of prosperity and depression expanded the scope of social service programs and increased the number and types of clients served by rehabilitation and social work. The cycle of service intensification and program enlargement continued until the second half of the 1960s. With the beginning of postindustrialism, the disadvantaged and disemployed sought full participation in the consumer-oriented service economy. New client-problem melds generated by the metamorphosis of industrialism to postindustrialism disrupted social service patterns and delivery systems. The disarticulation of the social service delivery systems coincided with the phasing out of industrialism. The relationship between the evolutionary patterns of industrialism and of the social services suggests that the sociocultural effects of postindustrialism will shape the future relationship of vocational rehabilitation and social work.

The emergence of the first postindustrial society in history marks a qualitative change in American socioeconomic patterns. A computer-based, service-oriented technology is supplanting the machine-based, production-focused industrial society. The *Wall Steet Journal* (October 12, 1972) reports that the transition from a manufacturing economy causes dislocation and unemployment. Bell (1967) sees the shift toward a postindustrial economic complex as accentuating social trends which will alter present sociocultural patterns. Among the more significant trends are:

MEGALOPOLITIZATION

The continued movement of population to major metropolitan areas is transforming the metropolis into the megalopolis. Demographers foresee three megalopolitan complexes in the United States, centering on New York, Chicago, and Los Angeles. The megalopolises will have a larger and more heterogeneous population than the metropolis. Interpersonal frustrations, social dislocations, and emotional problems will intensify as the growing concentration of population increases the pressures of adapting to a psychologically more crowded world. The megalopolis will be characterized by overcrowding and insufficient services. The redistribution of potential client populations within the megalopolis will render existing patterns of services and resources obsolete and increase the pressures for altering social service delivery systems. As cities merge, regional networks of agencies will be formed to serve larger territories.

INCREASED WEALTH

The wealth of the country will continue to grow. The median family income, $9,433 in 1971, will rise. The diffusion of goods and services will be greater. Payment of fees for social services will become more prevalent at all socioeconomic levels as augmented income increases the number of individuals able to meet the cost of service in whole or in part. Fee-paying clients will feel freer to reject services which they deem unsuitable. As the standard of living rises, more and more economically disaffected individuals will seek additional amenities. A larger proportion of rehabilitation's clientele will be former clients who are employed and seeking job replacement at a higher level. Although the percentage of the population (12.5 percent) considered poverty-stricken by current standards will decrease, the psychological gap between actuality and aspiration will widen for the poor and near poor. With the separation of income-maintenance and social service programs, rehabilitation will conduct upgrading programs for persons who are working below capacity whether they are employed clients or underemployed individuals at or above the poverty line. Rehabilitation and social work will devote more attention to the economically disadvantaged, persons who feel deprived economically.

POPULATION CHANGES

Youth and the aged will comprise a sizable segment of the 1980 population. Younger people, age fourteen to nineteen, will approximate some 25 percent, with older persons constituting a greater proportion of the total. Both groups require extensive, specialized services. Youth and young adults will come to grips with the precursors of adult problems: extension of the career development process over the totality of working life; the loss of social cohesion with greater occupational, social, and geographical mobility; and the need to replace obsolescent vocational or technical knowledge. Learning and relearning competencies, skills, and work roles, a continuing task at all ages, will be particularly difficult for the elderly who seek continuance of productive functioning as they adjust to new social roles.

MEDICAL PROGRESS

The progress of medicine will raise the actual and potential caseload of social service agencies as improved techniques for enhancing physical capacities and prolonging life increase the number of individuals who require specialized help to maintain themselves or to function effectively. The conquest of genetic deficiencies will decrease the number of congenitally handicapped persons. Rehabilitation and social service will assume increasingly significant roles in assisting the chronically ill to adapt to failing capacities. Social work will be concerned with fostering social reintegration, enlarging the capacity to cope, improving techniques for optimizing the use of residual abilities, and sharpening methods of compensating for reduced or lost abilities.

DIFFUSION OF KNOWLEDGE

The pattern of schooling will be modified as the school system is incorporated into a lifetime pattern of alternating school with work. Schooling will extend beyond the first three decades of life to become continuous with the work life. Current work-study programs involving part-time schooling and part-time work will be supplanted by a sequence of career-oriented, full-time schooling alternating with school-related full-time work. Career education will begin in primary school and continue throughout the working life with further schooling a prerequisite for job advancement. The integration of schooling into the vocational cycle will provide a new objective for social work and rehabilitation: improving a client's educability through preliminary preparation in the psychological, educational, and vocational fields. As the ability to learn and to achieve through learning is recognized as basic for vocational adjustment, supplementing and strengthening educational programs at all life stages will become focal in social service programming.

EMPLOYMENT PATTERNS

Kahn and Weiner (1967, p. 720) see a decline in the producing or manufacturing sector of the economy and greater importance for the service aspects. The rise of tertiary occupations which render service to specialized industries and to other occupations will speed megalopolitization. The authors point out that "since these [tertiary] occupations are heavily concentrated in the government, the professions, the non-profit groups and the like, this implies . . . a shift from the private business enterprise as the major source of innovation, attention and prominence in society." Employment will become more and more concentrated in government service and nonprofit institutions. The educational levels of job requirements will rise as service industries become professionalized and bureaucratized. The tendency to equate education with occupational competence will become more pronounced as advances in knowledge raise performance requirements in industry and government. Scholastic certificates will be used as evidence of occupational adequacy. Programs for school dropouts will place greater reliance upon specialized training for paraprofessional positions which are integrated into career sequences and permit vocational advancement. Occupational displacement and "deskilling" will occur more often and with greater rapidity, creating occupational obsolescence at irregular and unpredictable intervals during an individual's career. Changing social demands and technological improvements will result in a large percentage of the work force requiring reschooling to acquire new skills. Retraining the occupationally displaced and reorganizing their intellectual and occupational skills will become a continuing social need. The computer will eliminate a number of occupational levels as it takes over most functions of lower middle management, and necessitate a higher level of abstraction in the upper and middle echelons of industry, business, and government. The possibilities of promotion from lower to middle echelon will diminish. As occupational and professional ties are loosened, new dimensions of work satisfaction will be sought by employees to compensate for the diminution or loss of work identity.

SOCIAL ASPECTS

The quest for individual, community, and social values will become more pronounced during the second half of the 1970s as social atomism is accentuated by the growth of the megalopolis. In the absence of a socially anchored value system, questions of alienation and identity will become central. Social and psychological problems will intensify as earlier separation from the family takes place in more competitive social and vocational environments. Disruption of family patterns will render individuals more susceptible to social stresses and strains. The life-span pattern of alternating school and work will limit the energy available for other life areas. A recent study points out that work dissatisfaction will intensify social problems. The New York *Times* (Dec. 22, 1972) summary of the U.S. Department of Health, Education, and Welfare, "Work in America," reports that "work-related problems are contributing to a decline in physical and mental health, decreased family stability and community cohesiveness, and less 'balanced' political attitudes among workers."

A New Service Strategy

Moynihan (1967, p. 807) believes that the service strategy of the future will be an "income" strategy:

the concept of giving the poor the money with which to purchase what they need—be it proper housing or medical care—in the market is apt to be considered far more seriously in the future than in the immediate past . . . more and more services that have been thought to be located necessarily in the public sector will probably be contracted out to private enterprises—particuarly in areas where results are more important than processes.

The change in income strategy will replace the supraordinate-subordinate client-counselor relationship with a more equal relationship. All clients will pay fees for social service, using their own income or a community service fund. The transition from philanthropy, the provision of service, to a system of payment-for-results will give the client greater freedom in choosing or transferring from an agency. Government agencies will pay organizations for results rather than service. The orientation to achievement will lead to a systems approach which will deemphasize process and stress objectives. Specific goals and criteria to evaluate success of the process will be set for each client. The degree of success with clients will determine the amount of payment by individuals or agencies. Scott Briar (1972) reports that

The Department of Health, Education and Welfare has announced its intention to implement throughout the nation what is being called a "new, goal-oriented" social service system (GOSS). The system emphasizes, among other things,

separation of social services from financial assistance, a computerized information network, evaluation and accountability, and—as the label implies—specification of precise service goals for each client (p. 2).

The GOSS approach emphasizes two trends predominant in casework management: (1) the income strategy which separates financial
assistance from service; and (2) the benefit cost analysis framework.
The Allied Health bill which complements the GOSS emphasizes
savings and benefits inherent in joint service programming in a multipurpose facility. The strengths of the GOSS system appear to be: (1)
an increase in the amount and intensity of casework service available
to clients with the removal of financial components from the casework
domain; (2) possible improvement in service resulting from formalizing
and objectifying the evaluative process; (3) strengthening services by
focusing casework upon attainable objective and goals; and (4) enhancing casework efficiency by converting casework from a process-
oriented service to a goal-directed social technology. The possible
weaknesses of the GOSS approach appear to be: (1) In a pecuniary
economy, divorcing casework from financial assistance limits the ability
of the caseworker to aid the poor and near poor whose problems may
be created or exacerbated by insufficient funds; (2) Evaluation in terms
of benefit/cost analysis may overlook intangible gains and benefits
which cannot be converted into fiscal units; (3) The specification of
goals may tend to restrict casework services to those sectors which
generate measurable results. In the absence of a formal test of the GOSS
approach, the choice as to its use will be based upon value systems
emphasizing costs or casework gains.

Future Relationship of Vocational Rehabilitation and Social Work

Bell (1967) see   present-day trends as determining the future. The
pattern for the future relationship of vocational rehabilitation and
social work will be shaped in part by the socioeconomic characteristics
of the evolving postindustrial society, and in part by tendencies evident
in social work and vocational rehabilitation (Kahn and Briggs, 1972).

The goal of casework and rehabilitation counseling will be client enactment of societal roles. Occupational obsolescence and the increasing stress of constant job change and job retraining will define vocational rehabilitation's goal as improving the client's ability to function in a productive work role (defined as paid or unpaid activity which society and the role occupant deem to be purposive and contributory to the individual and to society). The more broadly defined concept of productive role provides for service to the severely handicapped with minimal vocational potential.

The social work role will be complementary, enchancing the ability of the client to function effectively in social and familial roles. Situational techniques using sociopsychological variables and environmental manipulation will be techniques of choice for improving role performance. The integrative and coordinative functions will assume greater significance as the social services move from preoccupation with reducing deficits toward expanding client opportunities for effective role performance.

Vocational rehabilitation and social work will focus on client goal attainment, stressing competencies necessary for improved functioning in work or social roles. The decentralization of social work and vocational rehabilitation will bring the counselor and social worker into the living and work communities. The family and work groups will become the foci of client service programs with treatment centering on the client's enactment of the appropriate societal roles in these settings. The vocational rehabilitation and social work functions will require multifaceted approaches reaching into all aspects of community life.

Client service will be predicated upon a holistic approach using a multiprofessional team. Specialized experts from a variety of disciplines serving on problem-centered teams will be available to assist the rehabilitator and caseworker. With the greater use of multiprofessional teams, problems of interdisciplinary communication will arise as the team draws upon a variety of data from varied life sectors. The team will need the capacity to monitor and integrate data and to ensure the interprofessional compatibility of the data. The functions of securing and providing information will be separate from counseling and casework.

It has been suggested that the human resources agency will constitute the organizational framework for vocational rehabilitation and social work functions. The trend toward the establishment of human resources agencies is fostered by fiscal and professional considerations. Fund limitations suggest the desirability of consolidating social services to decrease costs. Concurrently, the recognition that segmentalizing service may result in poorer service is leading toward integration at the practice level. Consequently, intake, evaluation, and initial service for vocational rehabilitation and social work will be provided in a multiservice, multipurpose neighborhood facility staffed by members of both professions. The vocational rehabilitation and social work postintake service models will stress coordination, integration, consolidation of service facilities, the unification of common functions, decentralization, and consumerism (Richardson, 1972; Twiname, 1972). Accountability and level of goal achievement will be key criteria for evaluating casework and counseling.

In the public welfare programs, the Community Service Administration of the Social Rehabilitation Service of the U.S. Department of Health, Education, and Welfare stated that its overall mission is "to maximize economic self-sufficiency and personal independence for individuals and families through a goal-oriented national social service system" (Bax, 1972). The formulation suggests a reciprocal relationship between vocational rehabilitation and social work at the planning, research, and administrative levels. The planning function will be directed toward maintaining or improving the social health of the family constellation and the role functioning of the individuals comprising the family. Social work will be concerned with social welfare legislation strengthening the social institutions which undergird the family. Economic and employment aspects will fall within the province of vocational rehabilitation. Social work will assume the responsibility for rebuilding the social environment and making it more hospitable for the disadvantaged and disabled. Both professions will join forces in creating institutional supports and avenues of opportunity for the socially dependent or handicapped, with vocational rehabilitation concentrating upon societal bridges facilitating reintegration of the disabled or disadvantaged into productive activities. The construction of a theoretical framework for practice, a necessary step in professionalization, will call upon both disciplines (Briar and Miller, 1971). The process will focus on the delineation of epistemic variables linking observational and theoretical data through research (Northrop, 1966). Role theory will play a major part in forging conceptual links between theory and practice. Research utilization and evaluative research, which are basic to program development, will focus on methods of determining program benefits and the type of population which can benefit from a given program (O'Toole, 1971). The similarity of the rehabilitation and social work models will facilitate joint efforts to incorporate research into practice and to study the process of the dissemination and use of research in the helping professions.

The probable organization of the social service system into a single human resource agency suggests that administrative direction will be in the hands of individuals chosen for their managerial ability. Knowledge of social work or vocational rehabilitation will not be a prerequisite for an administrative position. Socal service competence will be a requirement for middle-echelon positions which will be responsible for highly specialized social work or rehabilitation functions. The management of teams and the direction of the neighborhood multiservice facilities will be assigned to specialists in vocational rehabilitation or social work. The staff of the facilities will consist of "knowledge workers" and indigenous personnel who will serve as communicators. The knowledge workers will be individuals with a college degree who will perform intake, initial service, information, referral, and follow-up functions. Drucker (1969) believes that the separation of such functions will lead to "the emergence of a mass market in careers for educated knowledge workers, that is, for people with a college degree." The team approach and the use of work modules for intake and initial service will permit the knowledge workers to function interchangeably in those functions in both vocational rehabilitation and social work.

The projected relationship schema for vocational rehabilitation is one of unity at the intake and initial service levels with specialization at the second echelon, which handles severer problems and long-term clients. The multidisciplinary team will make possible integration without unification at the second echelon. Each discipline will differentiate and isolate work modules. Case planning will utilize these modules to construct a unified program for each client. Conceptually, the two disciplines will be joined through role theory, reliance on situational methodologies, the use of societal roles as client goals, and research in the utilization of social sciences in the helping professions. Social work will continue its holistic approach as the integrative core of the social service delivery system with emphasis upon familial and social aspects. Vocational rehabilitation will provide the psychological underpinning for role enactment through competencies and learning abilities which enable the individual to function productively.

References

Bax, James A. "Social Services: Today and Tomorrow," *Public Welfare*, XXX, No. 1 (1972), 27–30.

Bell, Daniel. "The Year 2000—the Trajectory of an Idea," *Daedalus*, XCVI (1967), 639–51.

Briar, Scott, and Henry Miller. *Problems and Issues in Social Casework*. New York, Columbia University Press, 1971.

Briar, Scott, "Money, Politics and Social Service," *Social Work*, XVII, No. 6 (1972), 2.

Cooper, Ruth. "Social Work in Rehabilitation," *Social Work*, VIII, No. 1 (1963), 92–98.

Drucker, Peter F. *The Age of Discontinuity*. Harper and Row, New York, 1969.

Haj, Fareed. *Disability in Antiquity*. New York, Philosophical Library, 1970.

Hillyer, Cecile. *New Horizons in Rehabilitation; the Evolving Concept of Rehabilitation*, "Social Work Practice in Medical Care and Rehabilitation Settings," Monograph 1. Washington, D.C., American Association of Social Workers, 1955.

Horwitz, John J. *Team Practice and the Specialist*. Springfield, Ill., Charles C. Thomas, 1970.

Kahn, Herman, and Bruce B. Briggs. *Things to Come: Thinking about the Seventies and Eighties*. New York, Macmillan, 1972.

Kahn, Herman, and Anthony J. Weiner. "The Next Thirty-three Years: a Framework for Speculation," *Daedalus*, XCVI, No. 3 (1967), 705–33.

Kessler, Henry H. *The Principles and Practices of Rehabilitation*. Philadelphia, Lea and Febiger, 1950.

Lewis, Doris K. "Prevalence of Disabilities in the Work Force," *Monthly Labor Review*, LXXXVII (1964) 1002–8.

Lofquist, Lloyd H. "Vocational Rehabilitation," in *International Encyclopedia of the Social Sciences*, XVI, 350–54. New York, Macmillan, 1968.

McCauley, W. Alfred. "Summary Statement on Role Differentials," in *Rehabilitation Counseling and Social Work Serving Disabled People*, Proceedings of the Conference of the National Rehabilitation Counseling Association and National Rehabilitation Association, 1971. Washington, D.C.

Mayo, Leonard. "Rehabilitation and Social Work," *New Outlook for the Blind*, LI (1957), 397–401.

Moore, Alice. "A Social Worker in a Rehabilitation Center: Personal Observations," *Rehabilitation Literature*, XXIII (1962), 330–37.

Moynihan, Daniel P. "The Relationship of Federal to Local Authorities," *Daedalus*, XCVI (1967), 901–8.

Neff, Walter. *Work and Human Behavior.* New York, Atherton Press, 1968.

Nelson, Nathan. *Workshops for the Handicapped in the United States: an Historical and Developmental Perspective.* Springfield, Ill., Charles Thomas, 1971.

New York *Times.* "HEW Finds Job Discontent is Hurting Nation," December 22, 1971.

Northrop, Filmer S. C. *The Logic of the Sciences and the Humanities.* Cleveland, World Publishing Co., 1966.

Obermann, Carl Esco. *A History of Vocational Rehabilitation in America.* Minneapolis, Denison, 1965.

O'Toole, Richard. *The Organization, Management and Tactics of Social Research.* Cambridge, Mass., Schenkman, 1971.

President of the United States. Message, "Delivery of Social Services," Washington, D.C., The White House, May 18, 1972.

Richardson, Elliot L. *Responsibility and Responsiveness.* Washington, D.C., U.S. Department of Health, Education, and Welfare, 1972.

Richman, Harold. "Role Definition and Professional Purpose," in *Role Differentials in Rehabilitation Counseling and Social Work Serving Disabled People.* Proceedings of the Conference of the National Rehabilitation Counseling Association and National Rehabilitation Association, 1971, Washington, D.C.

Soden, William. *Rehabilitation of the Handicapped: a Survey of Means and Method.* New York, Ronald Press, 1949.

Sussman, Marvin B. "A Policy Perspective on the United States Rehabilitation System," *Journal of Health and Social Behavior*, XIII, No. 2 (1972), 152–61.

Twiname, John D. "Federal Planning for Social Services," *Public Welfare*, XXX, No. 1 (1972) 25–26.

Whitten, E. B. "Disability and Physical Handicap: Vocational Rehabilitation," in *Encyclopedia of Social Work*, pp. 236–45. New York, National Association of Social Workers, 1971.

RICHARD SCOBIE
AND
ELAINE WERBY

Social Work in Public Housing

ALTHOUGH SOCIAL workers were prominent among the reformers who first lobbied for a more expansive federal housing policy, few became directly involved in the actual operation of public housing in the early days. It was not until much later that they began to participate widely in this public program. To understand the reason for this and the problems social workers still face working in public housing agencies one must first understand the context out of which the program emerged and some of the forces that helped to shape it.

Early Goals and Assumptions of
Public Housing in the United States

The public housing program in the United States was born in that crucible of social welfare policy formulation known as the great depression. The Housing Act of 1937, which established the federal role in this heretofore almost exclusively private activity, set in motion the basic financial mechanisms which were subsequently elaborated in the housing acts and amendments of the following years. Although many of the earliest supporters of the program emphasized the social objectives of better housing, the primary thrust of the legislation was to help the national economy, to stimulate the building materials and construction industries, and to provide jobs (Beyer, 1965; Meyerson, Terrett, and Wheaton, 1962; Schorr, 1963; Shermer, 1968). It was, in fact, only one of the many programs which constituted the New Deal effort to end the depression, and as such, public housing was viewed in most circles as a "property" program rather than a "social" program (Shermer, 1968, p. 6).

Writings of housing professionals in this period reflected an overriding concern with the technical problems of land acquisition, construction, and physical maintenance to the almost total exclusion of any comment on the social problems encountered in management. Even the pioneers who had been associated with preceding programs such as those constructed by the Works Progress Administration between 1935 and 1937 neglected to discuss the social implications of their work. This is not to imply that there was no enthusiasm about the "good works" nature of the by-product; there was, in fact, an almost crusading spirit associated with the slum-clearance aspect of many projects. Wiping out blight caught the fancy of many participants during those early years, but the assumptions they held about the power of "safe, decent, sanitary" accommodations (as the Housing Act stated it) to ameliorate most social problems unassisted were as unshakable as they were naive.

THE "HAPPY" YEARS

To some extent, during the early years of the program, the expectations of a relatively strife-free management task were rewarded. Prior to 1949, local housing authorities had virtually a free hand in the selection of tenants, and it was their practice to choose their residents very carefully. They tended to select a highly homogeneous and stable working-class tenant body drawn frequently from second- and third-generation European immigrants, a group of "temporary poor" who, suffering from the state of the national economy, were grateful for the chance to obtain sound housing at a lower rent than they could get in the open market. Families that were "different," female-headed, of a minority group, or with attitudes which offended tenant selection personnel were frequently screened out, ensuring a population which was largely likeminded with respect to one another and to the management. The developments themselves were usually constructed in stable working-class neighborhoods, further fixing their image and life style.

The Second World War came, and the national attention turned to the war effort, with public housing becoming a major mechanism for housing the workers in war industries and the families of persons in the armed forces. This provided local authorities with a new supply of "worthy" tenants; working or middle-class in life style, with intact families, and essentially homogeneous. With large numbers of eligible applicants, relatively few vacancies, and no legislation requiring them to accept "unworthy" or different persons, authorities were able to continue providing housing while avoiding involvement in social problems which were only to emerge later.

THE END OF THE "HAPPY" YEARS

The 1949 Housing Act ended the happy days of homogeneous tenant bodies and harmonious housing management. It did this by providing for massive slum clearance programs which were to displace diverse populations of very poor families by extending and broadening the federal mortgage insurance program, making it possible for working-class families who might otherwise have become public housing tenants to purchase their own homes; and by both expanding the public housing program and introducing provisions which would limit the program to very low-income families, thus assuring that displaced persons would get preference. Whereas in the late 1930s and early 1940s local authorities were enabled to select only the most obviously "deserving" tenants, since 1949 they have had to take "whoever was displaced by some other government agency's action, usually those who would not and could not be housed by anyone else." (Meyerson, 1962, p. 300). Most authorities tried to defend themselves by instituting more subtle screening procedures in order to retain their prerogatives, but gradually the impact of the 1949 act was felt.

This new mix of tenants changed the management function almost everywhere, especially in cities which embarked on massive urban renewal programs or other projects which required the relocation of large numbers of families. For the first time during this period many severely disorganized families were housed, and a sense of alarm spread through the ranks of the professional housers. As new developments built under the 1949 act were just housing their first occupants, a debate broke out nationally over what to do about "those" families who were presumed to be disrupting the social fabric.

While simultaneous occurrences in the social welfare field focused attention on a phenomenon called the "multiproblem family" (Buell, 1952), housing professionals argued among themselves over what could be done about "those" families, and the extent to which housing authorities were legally or morally responsible to do anything at all.

There were both "hard-liners" who held that public housing should accept only "normal" families which could demonstrate their ability to meet certain standards of behavior before admission (Seiler, 1956), and "soft-liners" who believed that housing authorities were responsible for the provision of social services and rehabilitative programs for their tenants when they needed them (Filker, 1956). What both hard-liners and soft-liners agreed upon was that the "problem family" was the cause of the bulk of management's problems; a diagnosis of questionable validity but one which was to be the basis of much of the activity of social workers for public housing.

This diagnosis, stressing the pathologies of individual families rather than economic, political, or organizational factors, was erroneous at least in the weight it was given, but it provided the cue for the entrance of professional social workers into public housing. If multiproblem families were the cause of most of management's woes, then, it was reasoned optimistically, social workers could deal with them effectively (*Journal of Housing*, 1959, p. 363).

Enter the Social Workers — in Disguise

The late 1950s and early 1960s were a time in which the over-all objectives of the public housing program were being reassessed in professional housing circles. It had been assumed in the beginning that the mere provision of sound housing would eliminate the social problems of the inhabitants. Now that it was becoming clear that this was not the case, many of the more progressive members of the housing community began pushing for a more expansive view of public housing's goals, one which stressed social goals above and beyond the simple provision of an apartment.

However, although expressions of this "social welfare" perspective found their way into official circulars, the manner in which the program continued to be funded provided few resources for local authorities wishing to respond to these newly stated social responsibilities. Instead, both legislators and housers held onto the proposition that the actual provision of services was still a "community responsibility." Thus while accepting, theoretically, the social goals of the program, they continued to delegate the operational responsibility and the expense of social services to "the community." As the response of "the community" was invariably erratic, some local authorities began to search for ways to stimulate health and welfare agencies to be more helpful and to increase the capacity of their own staffs to handle family problems. In summarizing his experiences in public housing in New York, David (1968, p. 96) concludes:

There is no argument—in theory—with the philosophy that public housing should not assume responsibilities that belong to the community. Despite the logic of this position, however, the de facto situation is such that community services have not been forthcoming in the required degree and in their absence public housing itself has been diminished. This is not a situation that can be answered through unsupported logic; pragmatic answers are required.

"Experimental" programs frequently involving social workers sprang up in several cities (*Journal of Housing*, 1959, p. 363). The housing authority in Syracuse created a new position on its staff, that of "coordinator of social services," whose job it was to consult with housing personnel and to organize social and recreational services in the developments (Weinandy, 1962).*

In Washington, D.C., the local welfare department was induced to locate its field offices in housing projects in order to make their caseworkers more easily accessible. Cincinnati emphasized community organization approaches to bring the services of a range of social agencies to bear on the needs of the projects. Gary, Indiana, stressed home economics training with the help of the education department. In Boston, several disciplines were brought together in a multiservice center in one development, staffed by a community organizer, a home econ-

---

*With the participation of Syracuse University this effort represented one of the first attempts of social scientists to measure the effectiveness of family casework with problem families. Interestingly, they concluded that the caseworker's role as advocate within the system was more important than her therapeutic function (Weinandy, 1964).

omist, a family caseworker, and an "area youth worker" with group work training (Boer, 1961).

As housing agencies began groping for answers to their new problems, there was simultaneous discontent in social welfare circles with the ineffectiveness of private social agencies in dealing with such society-wide problems as juvenile delinquency and poverty, and many social welfare policy-makers searched for new approaches that would make greater use of existing public institutions. The critics and planners focused on public education, public welfare, and public housing. With large concentrations of low-income families, public housing neighborhoods were seen as logical target areas for concerted social services and the housing authorities as natural bases from which to launch them. Thus, just as housing officials were beginning to feel overwhelmed with their problems and to seek assistance, social workers themselves began knocking on their doors.

With encouragement from both the social welfare community and the more progressive professional housing organizations, President Kennedy's Public Housing Commissioner, Marie McGuire, urged local authorities to add social service personnel to their rosters, and many of the larger authorities began doing so. In many cases these positions were filled with trained social workers, but rarely were they given titles that might imply that the housing authority was actually providing social services. Rather the prevailing policy continued to emphasize "community responsibility," and the social workers were disguised as "tenant relations aides," "management aides," and other bureaucratic euphemisms.

INSIDERS AND OUTSIDERS

These disguised social service positions were seldom well-integrated into the regular housing staff. Whether they were based within management or in separate administrative units, the social sorkers were usually regarded as outsiders by the regular staff and allowed little influence in actual decision-making.

In many respects the position of social workers in public housing from the beginning was similar to that occupied by their fellow professionals in many other host agency situations. While the broad goals of public housing, especially those stressing social objectives, were consistent with social work goals, social work skills were interpreted from the beginning as strictly ancillary to the central task, which was still seen as that of providing homes. Further, as the economic incentives and constraints involved in producing and managing housing have always overshadowed social concerns, social workers frequently found themselves at odds with management decisions and the men and women making them.

In addition, social workers rarely became a part of the "culture" of most housing authorities, that unstated but very real network of mutual expectations, roles, and institutionalized rationalizations around the "rightness" of operating procedures. This state of "separateness" was a product of several factors.

First, these social workers usually represented a different social and economic class from that of their coworkers. With middle-class backgrounds and a high level of formal education, they usually stood out conspicuously in dress, speech, and life styles among the rank-and-file management employees who, for the most part, shared the working-class and ethnic background of the earlier tenants. It was a classic case of Merton's "locals" and "cosmopolitans" (Merton, 1949, p. 189); "local" housers and "cosmopolitan" social workers working together but continually suspicious and irritated with one another because of the vast distances between backgrounds, style, aspirations, and world views.

Second, because they arrived with a distinct professional orientation with its own set of values, assumptions, and code of ethics the social workers were visibly independent of, and frequently in conflict with, the operating norms and goals of the housing agency. In this sense, social workers tended to glory in their separateness, to accentuate their different value system, often with more than a hint of moral superiority.

Third, their special relationship to certain tenants as "clients" placed them in a position of dual responsibility in which the interest of tenants and those of the housing authority were not always identical. The result was that these positions, and the persons holding them, existed as "grafts" *onto* but never *into* the organization as a whole.

EARLY ROLES

The roles played by these workers varied from housing authority to housing authority and with their location within the organization. They involved varying mixes of the traditional casework, group work, community organization, and administrative skills, but whether a social worker was called a tenant relations aide or a management aide, the primary role was usually that of family caseworker operating out of the management office. They received referrals from management, other social agencies, and the tenants themselves—and were dispatched, sometimes on an emergency basis, to assess the situation and take action, if indicated (this might range from short-term counseling, to referral to a social or health agency, to calling in the police or recommending an eviction). Described as "aggressive casework" by some, it involved the implied and sometimes the explicit authority of the public agency in the worker-client relationship, a feature which some commentators considered a positive "treatment tool" but with which few social workers were ever really comfortable.

In the largest authorities there were more specialized casework positions affiliated with the tenant selection process. These workers were employed to evaluate applicants for housing whose record or characteristics implied that they might be a potential problem to management. This entire practice has recently come into question both legally and in terms of its actual value or effectiveness.

Depending on the workers, the management setting in which they found themselves, and the flexibility of supervision, many management aides were active in organizing local interagency councils, service programs, and some tenant groups; the latter usually focused upon a specific concern, such as scouting, recreation, clean-up campaigns, and so forth. It was only later, in the late 1960s, that the notion of tenants organizing to have a voice in public housing management began to emerge.

The War on Poverty Era

The currents set in motion by the landmark Economic Opportunity Act in 1964 affected both the role of social workers within the public housing authorities and the public housing program itself. With the influx of new dollars designated, at least in theory, for persons of low income, public housing once again was a logical focus for action and program activity.

The size of some of the programs of the Office of Economic Opportunity (OEO) emphasized the need for planning and coordinating skills quite different from those of the case-oriented management aide, and the larger authorities again responded by hiring social workers with training and experience in these areas. However, once again, the role of the social worker was peripheral to the central management operation. The social worker occupied the role of program planner, broker for services, and advocate for the public housing cause. In the scramble for the critical OEO dollar, the social worker's charge from the agency was to protect its interests by ensuring the flow of funds and programs into public housing neighborhoods.

This was an especially exciting time for social workers in public housing. Not only was there the sudden opportunity to create new services and to experiment with new ideas, but the whole atmosphere was one of hope and optimism. Collaboration between public agencies, which had once been rare, suddenly, with the availability of new funds, became common, and public housing social workers for once found themselves where "the action" was.

In late 1967 and early 1968 the Department of Housing and Urban Development (HUD) issued two far-reaching circulars, each reflecting current social philosophy generated by the Economic Opportunity Act. Both circulars had implications for the role of social work and social workers in the public housing program. One launched the "modernization program" (HUD Circular 11-14-67); the second offered a restatement of the goals of public housing (HUD Circular 3-22-68).

"The Social Goals for Public Housing" circular was "intended to spell out the major social objectives of the low-rent housing program, and to stress the urgency of an intensive new effort to achieve them." In language somewhat reminiscent of early group work and community organization literature, the circular contained such suggestions for local housing authorities as: "Work with tenants in partnership to create a sense of community in the project, to promote citizenship, and to encourage tenants to put down roots and assume a responsible role in project affairs." The circular also called for aggressive leadership at the

Federal level to bring about a more effective program for tenant social services including:

The development of guidelines for the more effective delivery of social services, especially for better approaches to the hard-to-reach and multiproblem families . . . [and] closer cooperation with other Federal agencies and departments to develop more effective systems for coordination of services at the local level.

But, as always, "the urgency of the intensive new effort" was carefully balanced by financial feasibility criteria. In a carefully worded statement, Deputy Assistant Secretary Elder Gunther (HUD Circular, 4-24-68) said in referring to the Social Goals circular:

The implementation of these goals requires that Local Authority staffs include persons who, by attitude, training and experience understand how to work with low-income people and help them reach the extent of their capacities as persons, as earners, and as citizens. Present staff should be enabled to secure these new insights and assume the new responsibilities called for through special training. Where additional staff is indicated and is *financially feasible*, persons with specific professional training and experience should be added to the staff. (Italics added.)

If those at HUD were hesitant about spending money on social services, they were equally ambivalent about the role of professional social workers in the process. The Gunther statement continued:

Some of the work called for in the areas of tenant participation and improvement and expansion of community services can be well performed by persons who, although not professionally trained, have a deep concern for appreciation and acceptance of people. However, *where the size of the Local Authority warrants*, it is desirable to place staff personnel with the required special training and experience in the supervisory positions of the social service area. (Italics added).

It is interesting to note that nowhere in this or subsequent circulars is the term "social worker" used.

THE MODERNIZATION PROGRAM

The social goals circular buttressed an earlier circular (HUD Circular 11-14-67), which announced a modernization program "for upgrading those low-rent housing projects which for reasons of physical condition, location, and outmoded management policies adversely affect the quality of living of the tenants." To housers generally, the program was significant since it was a source of funds for sorely needed rehabilitation of physical structures.

A condition of eligibility for funding under the program was tenant involvement in the modernization plans of the local authority, including changes in management policies and practices and expanded services and facilities. While this condition produced some consternation among housers, local authorities were largely free to interpret and meet the condition in their own manner. Not only was tenant participation left undefined, but the federal agency earmarked the modernization funds *only* for physical upgrading, making no provision for increased staffing to promote tenant involvement. In spite of these inadequacies, the language of the modernization circular was to serve in many cities as catalyst for the formation of new, militant tenant organizations.

For the professional social worker in the public housing agency these national circulars provided official sanctions for the first time for much of his professional activity and for his professional value system. However, on the local level it could rarely be said that the host agency suddenly swung over, embracing a new philosophy and value system. Although the modernization concept did suggest defined social work tasks, the dominant value structure was left basically intact, and the social work functions continued to be seen by the rank and file as secondary to the task of providing housing.

LEGITIMACY — A MIXED BLESSING

Curiously enough, the bestowing of this institutional legitimacy created new problems for the social worker. Prior to the modernization program, the social worker had been involved and identified with the emerging, more aggressively independent tenant organizations, spawned frequently by OEO community action agencies. The militancy of many of these groups and the sympathy they had found among public housing social workers had often led the workers into an advocacy position vis-à-vis their own agencies. Since the host agency was often fearful of this new-style, organized tenant voice, much of the professional worker's activities had been carried out covertly. Stimulating institutional change through support of such tenant organizations had lent a sense of excitement and job satisfaction to the worker who viewed the *agency itself* as his client, or more accurately as his target for social change. To the tenants and their community advocates such a worker had been a "hero," and their admiration and respect had provided him with the support that was so frequently lacking within the agency itself. He had received similar accolades from his professional community, which saw his work as a pioneering effort.

Then as the public housing social worker began to move overtly into the task of tenant organization under the modernization program and with the tacit sanction of his agency, his actions began to be challenged and suspect both by tenants and by the professional social work community. The emerging tenant organizations frequently adopted the adversary model of the labor union, and within this approach, the social worker, despite his acknowledged value system and orientation, was viewed as just another part of management. Organizations assisted by him were viewed by many as company unions.

One effect, then, of the modernization program has been a new identification for the social worker in public housing. Prior to this program, the social worker had been, in Merton's terminology, a "cosmopolitan" in a bureaucratic structure dominated by "locals," using as his reference group the professional social work community and its value system. With modernization, the social worker became more closely identified with the agency itself. He became a "local," a houser, in the eyes of the community. Yet, within the bureaucracy, his identification continued to be somewhat muddled and confused. With official sanction to work with tenants, he tended to become part of the institution; yet, to the "locals" in the agency he was still an outsider, equipped with his own professional credentials, orientation, and allegiances.

In the day-to-day battle over the conflicting goals of the housing program—financial concerns versus social concerns—the locals still presumed (probably correctly) that the social worker would show his "true colors," forsake efficient management, and "side with the tenants." These perceptions of the social worker by both tenants and fellow workers not only circumscribed his role, but also frequently left the worker adrift without real support from either the bureaucracy or his professional community. Somehow when he had been clearly an "outsider," he had often enjoyed a more potent form of legitimacy than his new official sanction afforded him.

In view of this it is not surprising to find that in most cities forces outside the public housing agency were most active in promoting tenant organization and ensuring that the HUD regulations in this area were honored. Thus neighborhood houses, community action agencies, and OEO-funded legal assistance agencies played a major role in assisting tenants and shaping the direction of tenant organizations and their relationships to the public housing agency.

The roles played by the social worker in relation to tenant organization, then, tended to be prescribed for him by outside forces or events rather than emerging from a professional theoretical model. For those tenant organizations lacking their own resources, the housing social worker provided technical assistance and performed the administrative tasks necessary for the survival of organization life. When tenant organizations were able to secure funding to employ their own staff, the social worker served as liaison between the tenant group and the agency, interpreting policies and practices, arranging meetings, offering the tenant point of view in the agency's internal discussions. These activities are familiar to the traditional enabler role of the worker; however, as the only tasks sanctioned for him by the tenant organization, they tend to root the worker more firmly in the bureaucracy.

Tenant insights into housing authorities' internal power relationships have further circumscribed the role of the social worker in the area of tenant organization. In dealing and negotiating with management, tenants respond to the power structure of the agency, both the formal and the informal system. They have been quick to perceive that in most public housing agencies the social worker does not occupy a position of power, either formally or informally. Therefore, while the tenant organization may call upon the social worker for his skill and expertise in social service programming, he is frequently bypassed or omitted from negotiating sessions on management policies and procedures. In this way the tenant organization accepts and reinforces the low status usually placed upon the social worker by his agency. Conversely, in those rare instances where individual social workers do occupy high-status positions within the agency, tenant organizations do relate to them. However, most frequently these are not social work positions but rather such traditional administrative posts as manager or director of management.

NEW CAREERS AND PARAPROFESSIONALS

The modernization program, then, has presented a dilemma for the social worker in public housing, especially if his primary method and task is community organization. Neither has the role of the social worker engaged primarily in casework been immune from the impact of the modernization program. Consistent with the national search for new career opportunities for low-income persons, one of the stated goals of the program is increased employment opportunities for tenants. As tenant organizations cast their eyes upon possible employment opportunities within the housing authority structure, the staff position of management aide or tenant relations aide (or whatever title is employed to cover casework, counseling, and referral activities) was sighted as a potential goal. Arguing, with some justification, that tenants understand the problems of tenants better than anyone else, including and especially the professional social worker, tenants are demanding that such positions be filled by tenants.

The posture of the tenant organizations has been strengthened by the accepted employment practice of the OEO community action agencies and by HUD itself, as stated in the Gunther circular quoted earlier, and by the professional social work community which less than ten years earlier had been clamoring and lobbying for the employment of professional social workers by public housing authorities. Once again the professional social worker in the agency has had to defend the value of his professionalism and his status with his own peer group. While the social work profession has yet to come to grips with the issue, the social worker in the public housing program is being forced to articulate exactly what it is that the professional can and should be doing and what activities can appropriately be assigned to the nonprofessional or paraprofessional.

There appears to be agreement that at least supervisory positions, as indicated by HUD, should require professional training and experience. However, the number of positions at this level are for the most part available only with large housing authorities and even then are limited in number.

The potential battle for social work positions never really developed. It quickly dissipated into a theoretical discussion due to lack of funding for such positions. Paradoxically, the federal housing agency's "new effort to achieve the social goals of the low-rent housing program" came at a point in history when local housing authorities (particularly large authorities) were experiencing serious financial difficulties. The inflationary trend of the mid-1960s produced steadily rising costs in operations while rental income remained almost at a fixed level.

To ease the impending financial crisis and to forestall rent increases that would place public housing out of reach of the market for which it was intended, Congress took action in 1969, establishing a 25 percent rent/income ratio limitation and providing for operating subsidies to cover deficits between income and expenses (the Brooke amendment). Theoretically, these amendments to the Housing Act were a means of solvency for the public housing program. However, by the end of 1970 it was clear that even with the operating subsidies the financial problems of local housing authorities had not been solved and in many cases were even more acute. As a result, local housing authorities were being pressed on the one hand to reduce operating costs and, on the other, through the mandate of the modernization program and by tenant organizations, to expand social and community services.

Re-enter the Social Worker

New possibilities to achieve the goal of expanded social and community services, and with them new opportunities for social workers, came in June, 1971, through a memorandum of agreement entered into by HUD and HEW "for coordination and cooperation on a broad scale between the welfare and housing agencies on the state and local front." The agreement, among other things, called for cooperation between local housing authorities, state welfare departments, and other state and local governmental units in the development of local social service and rehabilitation programs in public housing. Such programs may include community organizations, group work, casework, legal services, education programs and child care, training in home economics, family planning, and so on, but not services that relate directly to housing management.

With 75 percent of the cost met with federal welfare funds under the various titles of 1962 and 1967 Social Security amendments, housing authorities may contract with the welfare agencies to provide the services, contributing 25 percent of the cost, or the authorities may enter into a purchase-of-services contract to provide the services themselves, receiving reimbursement for up to 75 percent of budgeted expenses. By the end of 1971 thirty local authorities had programs in operation, and many others were in process of developing them. Most programs include employment opportunities for tenants, most commonly in paraprofessional positions, such as day care teacher's aide, health aide, homemaker, and so on. Supervisory positions in local authorities tend to call for specific educational requirements, with professional requirements limited to few positions.

A review of the three largest contracts executed under the HUD-HEW agreement in 1971 (Atlanta, Philadelphia, Baltimore) reveals an approach reminiscent of the early social service programs in public housing and with the same potential for administrative and organizational problems. The services offered under these contracts consist primarily of individual and family casework and counseling services in child guidance, financial problems, mental health, and drug addiction; expanded child care services; referral services; and some group work services designed to involve tenants and their organizations in recreation programs, homemaking, day care, and child development centers. All the services offered meet the HUD-HEW criterion of not relating directly to housing management; nevertheless, they do relate, and therein lies the problem.

While it is too early to evaluate the success of any of the programs, experiential evidence suggests that there will be administrative and organization problems as well as role confusion. Where the welfare agency is supplying the services, the social worker can and will be viewed as the tenant/client advocate and will inevitably have to intervene and negotiate with management on his clients' behalf. As Janet Weinandy (1964) pointed out in discussing her work with problem families in a public housing project some years ago:

The social worker plays the role of intercessor between the client and the cold, cruel world of reality. This function has been frowned upon by the classicists in the profession, but it is now recognized as necessary and respectable for certain clients. Other names for this position are mediator and "fixer," and the role is analogous to that of the ward committeeman in politics, with the one difference that the social worker does not have to win votes, to stay in business (p. 455).

While the social worker may not have to win votes to stay in business, he will have to tread lightly in order to keep his job when he intercedes in that "cold, cruel world of reality" that is the domain of housing management. The potential for conflict between welfare agency and housing authority personnel is inherent when the worker plays the role Weinandy describes. Management will tend to insist that the social worker is there as a guest to help families with their problems, not to get involved in housing management. The worker will defend his intervention on the basis that the way the housing authority conducts or does not conduct its business directly affects his clients or his programs.

Nor can such conflict be avoided when the housing authority itself is the administering agent for the social service programs. In this model the social services program is once again "grafted onto" the management function, and the organizational and administrative problems described earlier can only be intensified with a greatly expanded social service staff. While the social work profession has accumulated experience in functioning within a host agency, these expanded social service programs in public housing will offer the profession a new challenge in working with a host agency whose professional expertise lies in real estate management and is not rooted in a humanistic value system. Elizabeth Wood summarized the enduring problems in this interprofessional relationship as early as 1960:

The language of some social workers concerned with the diagnosis of some families whose eligibility for public housing is in question is replete with phrases about deprived childhood, rejection by parents—I don't have to expand that list, do I? There is not a word in these diagnoses about the things that would concern a public housing manager: the housekeeping, rent paying, the way the children actually behave.

On the other hand, the definition of "problem" by housing managers is almost entirely within the context of a landlord and is concerned primarily with housekeeping, rent paying, moral standards, cooperation and compliance with regulations.

Thus the two professions are talking two different languages as to the job they presume to tackle jointly. The customary "goals" of the two professions are even farther apart (p. 4).

The potential for conflict further increases with the argument over the true nature of the problem facing the public housing program today. In discussing the financial crisis in the program, many housing "experts" in 1971–72 (Lilley, 1972; Starr, 1972), have once again diagnosed the problem as the presence of the large number of very poor and problem-ridden families who have found a home in public housing over the last decade. In spite of increasing evidence (Scobie, 1972) that the problems of public housing are systemic and rooted in broader economic and political structures rather than in the individual pathology of "problem families," the policy-makers continue to cling to the old explanations. Having accepted the old diagnosis of public housing's problems they have turned again to the old remedies, increased social services. Against this background social workers in these new, expanded social services programs may face unrealistic expectations. Whatever the stated goal of these programs, housing authorities (management) may perceive and expect that the social workers have arrived to solve the problem of the "problem families." Once again the mistaken diagnosis of public housing ills can lead to disenchantment with the profession when the social workers fail to provide the necessary solution. Further, if the social services programs fail to make a dramatic impact on such measurable management goals as improved rent collection, reduced vandalism, fewer crimes, less littering, it is doubtful that housing authorities will be willing to continue to invest their limited funds in providing 25 percent of the cost of these programs.

The Years Ahead

The future of social workers and of the social work profession in the public housing programs is inextricably linked to the program's financial future and the extent to which housers and legislators consider social workers capable of contributing something to the program. The federal housing agency has moved dramatically toward formal recognition and acceptance that housing authorities must have a sophisticated social management philosophy and must expand their shelter role. This new federal posture is expressed in operational terms in a June, 1972, HUD "Low-Rent Housing Community Services Program Guide" (HUD HMG 7471.1, 6-72). Outlining the functional role of a community services program within a housing authority, the Guide cites activities requiring professional social work skills and expertise; however, nowhere in this four-page circular are the words "social worker" or "social work."

The omission may have been deliberate, but it is hardly surprising. The social work profession is not highly regarded by the Nixon Administration. The profession has not been intimately involved with the public housing programs, either as advocates, defenders, or lobbyists, nor have many professional social workers chosen or fought for employment in public housing. With the HUD-HEW agreement focusing new attention on public housing as a vehicle for delivery of welfare services, perhaps the profession may find the program more compatible and attractive as an employment target.

However, even if the profession's image within the housing establishment were glowing, the problem of adequate financing for the public housing program remains. While the community services guide sets forth an exemplary and sensitive philosophy, the guide itself serves only as a list of administrative regulations, lacking the power of statutory requirements and the support of statutory financing.

Even with this new administrative philosophy, the federal agency has not abandoned its caution and concern with finances. After detailing the key services of a community service program and the methods to be employed in establishing it, the circular (HUD HMG 7471.1, 6-7-72), states:

Within budgetary constraints, priority consideration should be given to those services demonstrated to best enhance the Housing Authority's primary sheltering role and at the same time to be of optimum value in serving the economic, social and civic needs and aspirations of residents. (Italics in original)

Thus, little has changed.

Without new legislation to shore up the financial mechanism so that it is more responsive and reflective of current costs, the public housing program may simply die and with it those few opportunities for the professional social worker in traditional social work roles.

If the future is not bright for expanded traditional social work roles, what remains for those social workers who are still convinced that our large human service institutions must be primary targets for professional intervention? The only answer seems to be in the pursuit of career opportunities within the administrative structures of those institutions. For the public housing program this means that social workers would seek employment in management, as assistant managers, managers, directors of management, and in administration, as special assistants, deputy directors, executive directors. There they can offer their skills in human relationships, community organization, social planning, and social services in a manner which will be central rather than peripheral to the life and primary task of the agency.

For many social workers who feel bound to more orthodox or clearly defined roles this path may be difficult, but the potential for long-range effectiveness is great. With social workers occupying key roles throughout the administration of the housing authorities, the provision of specific social services might begin to be viewed not simply as a narrowly defined problem-solving service to management, but as necessary enhancement to any housing neighborhood. The profession could then begin to make a real contribution to the formulation and implementation of social policy in the housing field and to a public housing program better able to respond to its expanded mandate to provide "more than shelter."

References

Beyer, Glen H. *Housing: a Factual Analysis.* New York, Macmillan, 1965.

Boer, Albert. "The Community Service Center." Boston, United South End Settlements, 1961; mimeographed.

Buell, Bradley. *Community Planning for Human Services.* New York, Columbia University Press, 1952.

David, Preston. "Human Dimensions in Public Housing," Bernard J. Freiden and Robert Morris, eds. in *Urban Planning and Social Policies,* pp. 96–106. New York, Basic Books, 1968.

Filker, David. "Public Housing Management Must Accept Family Rehabilitation Responsibility," *Journal of Housing,* XIII (1956), 168–170.

Housing Yearbooks, National Association of Housing Officials, Washington, D.C., 1936, 1937, 1938.

Lilley, William, III, and Timothy B. Clarke. "Urban Report/Immense Costs, Scandals, Social Ills Plague Low-Income Housing Programs," *National Journal,* IV (1972), 1075–83.

Merton, Robert K. "Patterns of Influence: a Study of Interpersonal Influence and of Communications Behavior in a Local Community," in Paul Lazarsfeld and Frank N. Stanton, ed., *Communications Research,* pp. 189–202. New York, Harper and Row 1948–49.

Meyerson, Martin, Barbara Terrett, and William L. C. Wheaton. *Housing, People, and Cities.* New York, McGraw-Hill Book Co., 1962.

"The Problem Family—New Devices Are Being Tested for Prevention and Cure," *Journal of Housing,* XVI (1959), 363–66.

Schorr, Alvin L. *Slums and Social Insecurity.* Washington, D.C., Department of
. Health, Education, and Welfare, 1963.

Scobie, Richard S. "Family Interaction as a Factor in Problem Tenant Identification in Public Housing." Unpublished doctoral dissertation, Brandeis University, 1972.

Seiler, Bernard R. Letter to the Editor, *Journal of Housing,* XIII, No. 3 (1956), 80.

Shermer, George. *More than Shelter: Social Needs in Low and Moderate Income.* Report to the Commission on Urban Problems, Research Dept. #8. Washington, D.C., 1968.

Starr, Roger. "Which of the Poor Shall Live in Public Housing?" *The Public Interest,* No. 23 (1971), pp. 116–124.

U.S. Department of Housing and Urban Development, Office of the Assistant Secretary for Renewal and Housing Assistance. Circular 11-14-67; Circular 3-22-68; Housing Assistance Administration. Circular 4-24-68; Housing Transmittal Notice #12, HM 7465.12, 6-2-71; Transmittal Notice #1, HMG 7471.1, 6-7-72.

Weinandy, Janet R. *Families under Stress.* Syracuse, N.Y., Syracuse Youth Development Center, 1962.

———— "Casework with Tenants in a Public Housing Project," *Journal of Marriage and the Family,* XXVI (1964), 452–56.

Wood, Elizabeth. "The Social Worker's Job in Housing and Urban Renewal." Speech given before the National Social Welfare Council, 1960; mimeographed.

PART
TWO

New Directions

for Social Work Practice

SHIRLEY M. BUTTRICK

The Degreening of the 1970s:
Issues in Social Policy

THE DIRECTION of social welfare programs in this country for almost thirty years was established by the events and policies
of the 1930's. The era of the 1960s and the 1970s have ushered in new
conditions, new approaches, and new policies that promise to have
equally significant and lasting effects on the social services.

For the time being, the expansion in domestic social programs has
ground to a halt. A new conventional wisdom and a new social science
perspective spearheaded by the Cambridge Group* and the Brookings
Institution study of domestic programs, *Setting National Priorities: the
1973 Budget,* assert that continuing to expand programs bears little
relationship to improving them and that the existence of a program
may have little to do with efforts to solve the problem. The mood is
one of contraction and concern for fiscal relief with emphasis on consolidation and integration.

In spite of the immediate picture there is acceptance that the social

---

*The Cambridge Group refers to a group of thinkers such as Nathan Glazer,
Edward Banfield, Richard Herrnstein, and Daniel Moynihan. While there are others
who are not geographically located at Harvard, the association seems to be with
Cambridge, hence the designation. These writers while not necessarily agreeing
with each other do appear to assert that the unintended consequences of programs to
help the poor only make the situation they were designed to improve that much
worse.

welfare industry, broadly defined, is an expanding one. How social work and social workers will fare in that expansion is a moot question. Fundamental is the question as to whether current social work training provides the professional skills needed for the new trends and developments in the planning, administration, and delivery of the human services.

There are many who make the sanguine assumption that the expansion of the social welfare industry automatically means an expansion in the demand for social workers. (U.S. Department of Health, Education, and Welfare, 1965). This view assumes that one is dealing with a homogeneous labor supply and that the demand for that labor is equally undifferentiated. Actually, just as the demand for services will not be of equal magnitude (the need for health care outweighing others, for example), the demand for personnel also needs to be differentiated. In fact, it may be that an increase in the demand for a particular type of skill subsumed under the rubric of "social work" may well be antithetical to the demand for another labeled as such. To continue to view social workers as an undifferentiated supply of interchangeable parts merely muddies analysis.

An analogy here might be useful. In 1963 national attention was focused on a disagreement between the economic growth theorists represented by Walter Heller, then head of the Council of Economic Advisers, and Charles Killingsworth, labor market economist. The disagreement centered on ways of dealing with the then rising unemployment rate. Heller argued for increasing economic growth. Killingsworth, while agreeing that economic growth set the limits, contended that the obstacles were to be found in the shortage of needed skilled manpower in certain parts of the economy (1965, p. 146). In other parts of the economy, unemployment rates for those with minimal skills continued very high. Thus, there might be severe labor shortages at some levels along with large labor surpluses at others. In this situation, economic growth by itself would prove ineffective in offsetting the structural imbalance. The point simply is that an increase in the growth of the social welfare industry may well bring a demand for skills which are in short supply along with a surplus of existing skills.

Hopefully, a review of recent policy and programs will offer grounds for some educated guesses for predicting the demand for social welfare expertise. Another, not unrelated way in which to view the demand for, and supply of, social work manpower is through the concept of the service delivery system. The service delivery system provides a device for integrating otherwise disparate elements in the human services. It consists of an array of complicated attributes which tie together the services and the profession and bring meaning to the services rendered at the point of delivery.

The diverse and distinct activities comprising the delivery system provide an interesting perspective for differentiating the "homogeneous supply" concept. At the same time that the tasks and activities are differentiated, the connections between seemingly unrelated activities emerge very clearly. The idea that the specific elements of the delivery system are useful for determining relative need is intimately related to the idea that there can simultaneously occur both overeducation for some jobs and virtual neglect of others.

The point to be made here is that in the explication of the attributes or elements of a delivery system (and the expertise required for each element) exists a very real though unrealized potential for determining needed directions and priorities.

ATTRIBUTES OF A DELIVERY SYSTEM

When one looks at the delivery of a service, some of the elements which influence the outcome are the nature of the legislation, the regulations deriving from the legislation, the intergovernmental strategy, the organizational structure, and the interpersonal technology; in short, all those elements which make an impact upon the development and translation of a program into a human service.

How, for example, do human service experts advise an executive or legislator where, on what basis, and even which service dollar to spend? How does one estimate what it will cost to make services statewide in conformity with legal regulations (planned progression)? What organizational arrangements are required to operationalize a new program? What kinds of participation, accountability, and coordination will best achieve a stated objective? What kind of help do community groups need to secure funding? What, if any, personal or counseling interventions are implicated in the program goals? The answers to such questions serve to enumerate some of the elements of a delivery system, for the activities implicated range across the broad spectrum of service provision, service development, and social change.

By definition, a delivery system consists of such functional components as strategic planning, program planning, program administration, funding, and implementation procedures (Kahn, 1969). Such components make up the core of the planning, programming, and administration process. But much of the knowledge required for the "trade-off" issues related to the structural and functional aspects have not received sufficient attention. For example, to what extent should such functions as program policy and planning, program administration, and project operation be combined or separated? Should an agency performing program planning also operate projects for delivering services? Experience with community action programs has led some to prefer the Housing and Urban Development (HUD) format in which the prime grantee contracts with other agencies and providers for the delivery of services.

Another set of choices has to do with funding strategies. How, for example, should funds be allocated to ensure the protection of special target groups and yet permit enough flexibility to deal with local problems? Should allocations be based on population, measure of need, and so on? What should be the basis for the distribution of funds to state, counties, and cities?

Should federal formulas allocate funds to the states or should allocations be computed all the way to counties, with the funds passing through the state? How shall funding be used to establish recipient priorities? How does the setting of recipient priorities conflict with the concept of block grants?

What should be the priority afforded special groups (children and old people) if programs for them are integrated into a constituent service agency? Should special-purpose agencies then be established within a broad human resources agency?

If coordination is to take place, what kinds of provisions are needed as part of the delivery structure? What kinds of techniques are effective as incentives?

What groups should have active roles in making policy decisions, providing advice, and evaluating performance? How should such groups be chosen? While there now exist models of consumer participation which range along a continuum from advisory to policy-making, the relative weight assigned to consumer participation and the kind and extent of participation continue to pose sticky problems (Spiegel and Mittenthal, 1968).

What roles should the respective levels of government play in program administration? What structure serves best for different kinds of programs, given specific objectives? Recent legislation (mostly vetoed) indicates divergent notions as to what the intergovernmental role should be. The defeated welfare reform bill spoke to strengthening state governments; the defeated Child Development bill of 1972 endorsed a model heavily local which bypassed state control.

In one kind of intergovernmental model the federal government could provide funds and administrative authority directly to local, nonprofit, nongovernmental organizations. These local, nonprofit organizations representing cities or groups of political subdivisions would have the authority to administer programs at the local level. State and local government involvement would be advisory for review and comment on grant applications similar to that which existed under the Economic Opportunity Act.

A second alternative would designate new or existing government agencies at the city or political subdivision level to administer the federal programs. In this approach (similar to Model Cities), federal funds would flow to the local or multicounty agencies directly from the federal government, based on area-wide plans. The state's role would be restricted to organizing the network of local agencies within the state, reviewing and commenting on local grant applications. The chief difference between the two models is the nature of the local authority—governmental or nongovernmental.

Under a third alternative, the state government might assume overall administrative responsibility. Large cities and political subdivisions could be treated as mini-states and receive direct federal funding, and each state could designate local planning and administrative agencies. Federal funds would flow to the designated state agency, based on state plans, and then to the local designee. These are only a few of the possibilities.

Common to all is the need to determine the allocation of federal funds, the need to define the eligible recipients as well as the eligible providers, and the need to specify the type of financing mechanism. All models have to coordinate with other local programs, deal with the issue of final review authority, and with accountability for performance. To whom, for example, should the administering agency be accountable? To those who give the money? Or to those who receive the service? What is the optimum mix? Should the choice of alternative delivery structures be governed by the extent to which it holds program administrators accountable for performance? Clearly, any structure is workable provided that the program objectives are specified and an effective system exists to assess performance.

All these structures have both positive and negative features. Each has its own set of trade-offs between, for example, efficient administration and user involvement, between strengthening general purpose government and leaving major decision-making to small groups. Thus one model would increase federal access to the local operating level. In so doing it might reduce problems caused by uncooperative state and local government agencies but at the cost of promoting conflict with state and local establishments. It could further increase the burden of federal administration through the necessity of extensive federal grant management and monitoring mechanisms. Whether this is "good" or "bad" depends upon the objectives one is trying to maximize, which in turn depends upon a set of assumptions as to outcome (Marris and Rein, 1967). In general, there has been far too little appreciation by social welfare professionals of the trade-offs involved in implementing a program, and of the subsequent impact of those decisions on the service consumer.

This cursory review is intended simply to identify some of the elements of a service delivery system. The question is not so much whether social workers should be involved in those aspects of the delivery system (as well as with direct delivery) but rather what delineation of the skills and knowledge is required at different levels of that system in different functional fields of service.

Social Policy Trends

The documentation of accelerated changes in our society since the 1960s and the myriad programs responsive to these changes have been well-described. The rediscovery of poverty, the urban crisis, the ethnic stance, the black confrontations, helped produce the new concepts of the poverty warrior and the advocate working for institutional change (Brager and Purcell, 1965; Rein, 1970). The methodological response of social work to these developments was to strengthen community organization, seen as neighborhood work, and to focus more on organizational and bureaucratic theory. Advocacy was seen as most useful when it was successful in influencing or pressuring bureaucracies for more effective service delivery.

But "institutional change" concepts so popular in the 1960s imply different things: on one level, they imply that the principal difficulty is within the situational structure (Warren, 1971, p. 150). Viewed in that way, institutional change is neither within the purview nor the product of any one discipline. It lies within the political arena—the outcome of action by many social groups.

A much more restricted meaning of the term is that certain social agencies and certain patterns of service delivery are deficient or harmful, lack coordination or effectiveness, or are too remote from the felt needs and wishes of the clients. In the 1960s the response to a stated objective of institutional change was a plethora of neighborhood service centers, storefront delivery units, and crisis intervention techniques. As one result, the disparity between broad philosophic goals and "social services" as the means to those ends became pronounced. Clearly, as a response to the broader concept of institutional change, social services were not the cutting edge. The services' response to the narrower concept of institutional change has persisted and is part of the current emphasis on coordination and integration of services, systems analysis, techniques of program budgeting, data banks—in short, the emphasis on technology.

In any event, there has been increasing clarity about the difference between "system change" and "service change." Increasingly since the 1960s, in social work, attention has been directed toward the theoretical knowledge that can be applied from systems and organizational theory, the nature of power and influence, and the ramifications of, and resistance to, social change. The demand for particular skills and knowledge in the human services field has also been clarified. There have developed, in the course of the social engineering and social experimentation of the past decade, demands for particular expertise which promise to remain fairly constant. Many of the evaluative studies of the 1960s, for example, focused attention precisely on the lack of difference the new and much heralded social problems make. This may help account for the current skepticism about the effectiveness of programs along with the demand for programs of demonstrated value.

Trends just surfacing in the 1960s have become an accepted part of current social programs. The new careers movement provides one illustration. The deprofessionalization reflected in the shift from graduate to undergraduate training and the employment, for the delivery of personal social services, of those possessing lesser degrees than hitherto deemed desirable have now become part of operating procedures. Regulations since 1967 require that recipients of services be employed by the beneficiary program. As one result, the utilization of indigenous nonprofessionals has become a conspicuous and self-perpetuating part of the new professionalism. Certainly it is not difficult to envisage that "as reward systems are increasingly tied to actual measures of effectiveness and as such measures become meaningfully sophisticated another confrontation will be in the revelation that education has little necessary relevance to occupation" (Dumont, 1969, p. 12).

Available evidence points to future training in the direct service area (in the public sector) as being increasingly directed toward undergraduate, community college, and paraprofessional programs. If so, then the emphasis at the more advanced or professional level should be on the acquisition of more highly developed skills in consultation, supervision, and technical assistance to those who provide the less advanced direct service (clinical leadership).

Other innovations of the 1960s have also become institutionalized. Of such an order, regardless of "bureaucratic emasculation," is the concept of "maximum feasible participation." Programs of education, health, law enforcement, housing—anything that affects the lives of residents of a community—will for a long time to come be met with demands for citizen participation and community control. From here on, participants of a social welfare program will have something to say about its design and implementation, and that implies some sharing of power and revisions in traditional and basic distinctions between donor and donee (Lloyd and Daley, 1971; Moynihan, 1969).

If the shift in manpower for the social services is away from the old professional, away from graduate to undergraduate preparation, away from liberal to vocational training, the emphasis is also away from the federal level. The assertion now is that the federal government, while good at mailing checks, should leave such matters as the social services to the community. Currently this is defined to include state government or, more precisely, general-purpose government as represented through the office of the governor or the mayor.

DECENTRALIZATION, DECATEGORIZATION, AND RELATED TRENDS

The stress on the devolution of responsibility for all social programs, including social welfare programs, to local political units has major implications for service decisions. It is tied closely to the revenue-sharing approach and reflects a long-term trend toward forcing trade-off decisions to the local level and away from the categorical programs at the federal level. But there remains considerable confusion about the meaning of revenue sharing. Heller, testifying before the Senate Subcommittee on Intergovernmental Relations on February 23, 1973, stated that

general revenue sharing was conceived to fill a gap in the family of federal physical supports to state and local governments, to do something that categorical aids cannot and did not do; namely to provide direct general support to state and local governments in order to reduce disparities in their abilities to provide public services.

A second major function was to supply fiscal support in a way that strengthened the self-reliance and independence of state and local governments, and it was conceived as a net addition to the funds that the federal government would place at the disposal of the state and local governments. It was not intended to serve as a replacement for categorical assistance.

There are those who predict that the problems inherent in general revenue sharing will surface very quickly and that Congress will shortly begin to exercise control over the program. In fact, while the rising federal deficit is notorious, the traditional deficit of state and local government nationwide has been steadily declining. State and local governments, taken all together, seem to be moving toward a surplus chiefly because of the change in the birth rate. It may turn out that the federal government provided revenue sharing at the precise moment when the pressure on state and local treasuries began to slacken. Equally significant is the fact that in order to get revenue sharing approved by Congress, a distribution formula was adopted that scatters the money very widely. The social services money, for example, is distributed among the states in straight proportion to population, which removes it even further from any relation to need. Thus it may be another irony of our times that the effect of these revenue-sharing measures is to provide less money for those overtaxed cities where the social needs are the greatest.

There is also confusion about the differences between general revenue sharing and special revenue sharing (or conditional as contrasted with general-purpose grants). It should be recalled that categorical grants were, and are, intended to help people either directly through cash assistance or indirectly through the support of government programs. Eveline Burns in 1956 stated that the "more detailed and exact the defining standards, the more the control for the program is removed from the recipient governments" (p. 228). Yet the very purpose of the grant-in-aid device is to permit a high degree of state and local autonomy and initiative by removing or minimizing state and local limitations and differences. There is certainly validity to the criticism that the multiplicity of special-purpose grants adds to the complexities of administration, and that the level of federal funds has caused states to channel a disproportionate share of state revenues into the federally aided service program to the disadvantage of other state functions which receive no federal grant. Yet a major purpose of the federal grant is to distort state expenditures: federal money is made available because of the belief that certain services are underdeveloped and more money should be spent on them than the states or localities would.

The conditional or categorical grant implies national goals and responsibilities. The block grant (or general-purpose grant or general revenue sharing) gives each state a lump sum contribution toward its total expenditures and leaves considerable discretion as to the purposes for which it is to be employed. Again in 1956, Eveline Burns said that "it seems doubtful whether American federal taxpayers would be prepared to support substantial grants to individual states leaving the decisions as to their use entirely up to the states" (p. 230).

In short, the fear remains that the block grant might lead to still further neglect of those services whose value is not generally appreciated or whose clientele possess no strong political influence. The concern about that has led to special revenue-sharing measures in which money is targeted for a specific area (education, social services manpower) but the allocation of such money among the programs is left to the discretion of the state or local unit.

Special revenue sharing seems likely to survive, even if there are doubts about general revenue sharing. The question arises as to the structure for decision-making, the ways in which priorities for different programs will be determined at different levels of government. Negotiations now will have to be with different and traditionally less friendly (to social welfare) levels of government. What, then, shall the strategy be?

Related to special revenue sharing is the issue of service integration. The notion of service integration is tied to the basic assumption that the country has enough in the way of new programs and what is needed is reform of present institutions. In fact, the growth in the number of categorical programs since the 1960s has been astronomical, and that growth has made it virtually impossible for governors, mayors, county executives, to get a "fix" on the federal resources available to them. As is well-known, programs have emerged in response to the special pleading of identifiable interest groups, and there is now an impressive catalogue of special-purpose programs. In the process, jurisdictional jealousies, structural rigidities, and barriers to communication have been created. As each categorical interest has staked out its claim, it has sought to bring the full integrated array of services to bear on the problem for its constituency.

The sentiment, however, to rationalize the programs is strong. It derives from experience that suggests that those who require the services of any one program also need the benefit of others, and that tying together diverse categorical systems makes it easier for the consumer to get what he needs. It derives further from a belief that a service system dealing with the full range of an individual's or a family's need is more effective than one geared to provide single-purpose treatment (Buttrick, 1971, p. 136). This is the emphasis behind the proposed Allied Services Act and behind the push for some type of service legislation which is of the integrative, facilitative and coordinative type, at least on the federal level.

Tom Joe, in a study done for the Department of Health, Education, and Welfare (HEW), revealed that it was almost impossible for a mayor, for example, to coordinate HEW's subsidy programs (Lilley, Clark, and Iglehart, 1973, p. 294). Joe started with the problem of school dropouts in urban areas and postulated that a big city mayor wanted to marshal a city-wide dropout prevention program. Dealing with HEW programs alone was an attempt to enter an impenetrable jungle. In spite of this, he stated that a "simplistic put it on the stump and run" approach like revenue sharing was not the answer to the categorical maze. Revenue sharing, he felt, would simply transfer the fragmented programs now operating at the federal level to state and local governments. His conclusion was that the federal categorical structure needed to be repaired and not abandoned.

The now famous MEGA proposal* (HEW Reform and Simplification Plan), developed during Elliott Richardson's tenure as Secretary of HEW, proposed that a single service grant be funneled through governors, with a requirement that 90 percent of the money be targeted on the poor. Services could be provided to the nonpoor on an income

---

* The Mega proposal (Comprehensive HEW Simplification and Reform Plan) was prepared during Secretary Richardson's tenure at HEW. It represented a set of legislative initiatives designed to overhaul the HEW programs. The intent was to diminish the federal role and the categorical grant-in-aid structure and to give more discretion and funding to state and local governments.

scale. The governor would distribute the funds among local areas in proportion to their poverty population. Head Start was also included in this proposal which constituted yet another attack on the idea of paragovernmental structures; the idea behind many of the Office of Economic Opportunity programs of the 1960s.

Given the desire to decentralize services, institute special revenue sharing, and achieve service integration, it follows that the capacity of state and local governments and private agencies to provide and plan for these new arrangements must be considerably strengthened, and the trend in this direction is unmistakable. At the same time, however, the belief is also expressed that users of service should be able to exercise more choice, have more options, and that the monopoly control of services should be markedly diminished. There appears little appreciation of the conflicts inherent in these positions (Buttrick, 1970; Pascal, 1969; Ylvisaker, 1969).

Related to the above and currently receiving a good deal of attention is the "mixed delivery system," recognized more readily through purchase-of-service agreements. Here, the government is neither the provider nor the administrator, but rather a purchaser of services. What is to be purchased is defined by a contract relationship in which the services to be purchased and delivered are specified, preferably on the basis of results per dollar. The emerging belief is that the need for services could be met more effectively, responsibly, and economically if a new set of suppliers were encouraged to appear from whom services could be purchased either by governments directly or by the recipients. Thus there is marked emphasis on market incentives and the use of the private sector in providing social services, as reported in *Purchase of Social Services* (1971).

Significant, but receiving less attention, is the growing responsiveness of private firms to government contracts. The importance of these private firms and consultants in the formulation of social policy and the influences of decision-makers has barely been studied. Mike Causey writing in the Washington *Post*, states:

Private consultants have carved out a multi-billion dollar empire within government that threatens to take over policy making responsibility for major weapons systems, health and law enforcement programs from agencies that originally hired the firms for advice. . . . Many of the contractors who do an estimated $50 billion a year in business with the government are free from in-house federal conflict of interest rules.

In short, we have another arm of the Civil Service operating outside Civil Service with considerable influence and power; and we have a delivery system operating, along with the public, through purchase-of-service agreements. Both foreshadow major new developments and both heighten the issue of accountability.

THE "OPEN-END" AND SEPARATION OF SERVICES

As is by now well-known, the escalation of Title IV*a* social service spending made headline news in the summer of 1972. Some referred to it as "backdoor revenue sharing"; others, as an "open-ended raid on the federal Treasury" and a distortion of social policy. The passage of the Revenue Sharing Act (P.L. 92–512) effectively closed the end on the social services and with it an interesting chapter in the history of the social services component of the Social Security Act.

Three features of the social service authority help in understanding the developments. The first is the language of the social service provisions as modified by amendments during the 1960s. The language is broad enough to encompass almost everything. The services covered include any "service to a family or any member thereof, for the purpose of preserving, rehabilitating, reuniting, or strengthening the family and such other services as will assist members of a family to attain capability for the maximum self-support and personal independence."

In addition, such services could be provided not only to current welfare recipients, but to former and potential recipients as well. The law also allowed the states not only to provide such services themselves, but, since 1967, to purchase such services from other public and private agencies with federal support.

Another striking feature was the fact that for every dollar the state or localities offered the federal government had to supply another three. Most states were slow in recognizing the potential of the social service program, but some, through the ingeniousness of fiscal and other consultants, managed, as in California, to corner the social service budget. Other states were beginning to catch on to the technique of IV *a* funding and the possibilities of maximizing the federal dollar to obtain needed financial relief rather than necessarily supporting new services.

The social services caper of 1967-72 forced into the open what had already become a matter of national concern. It made it clear that monies had to be distributed equitably among states and that there had to be some way to see that real and needed public services were produced in the process. An important issue also implicated was whether social services, as opposed to income maintenance, for the lower-income segment of the population represented desirable public policy.

Also forced into the open was the fact that there existed no clear definition of what constitutes services and no formulations of goals in relation to measurable outcomes. As one consequence, the demand for defining the social services, the demand for goal-oriented services whose outcomes can be stated in measurable quantifiable ways has intensified. In one fashion or another, goal-oriented social services are accepted as a logical next step along with the development of management information systems, ways of defining and measuring output and input, and measures of cost-effectiveness.

Undergirding all of this was the to-be mandated separation of services from assistance payments. Recent legislation, in particular the 1972 amendments to the Social Security Act (P.L. 92-603) and the general Revenue Sharing Act (P.L. 92-512), introduce more confusion into an already confused separation issue. The statutory authority for separation is vague, the statutes themselves are contradictory. Separation now stems largely from administrative interpretation and implementing regulations.

Historically, as services were introduced into the assistance programs (1962 marking the victory of the services strategy), concern arose that services were really substitutes for adequate income-maintenance or harassment techniques designed to force people off welfare. But almost simultaneously, the 1962 service amendments were being extended to include federal financial participation for services to former and potential recipients. This actually encouraged separation by raising the possibility of developing a broadly based service system serving a broadly defined population.

Historically, the assumption of those who led the struggle to separate economic assistance from social services was that a clear problem of economic need existed responsive to the conditions of the market economy. Further, they assumed that these economic problems would be solved more rationally if they were part of the complex network of programs related to the economic stability of the nation. Aside from economic conditions, a broad and general need was seen for programs to promote psychosocial health. The conclusion was that there should be developed, either by public provision or purchase, a spectrum of social services geared to a total citizenry (Mencher, 1963).

Present-day separation was mandated against a philosophy that viewed the social services as tied primarily to the goal of the reduction of economic dependency (Rein, 1969, pp. 70-72). It was mandated against money payments and policies which were inadequate, increasingly restrictive, varied by state, and from a system (or nonsystem) of services designed primarily for the welfare poor.

Paradoxically, the political objective of getting people into the labor market (manpower strategy of 1967) tends to negate the structural objective of separation. It again defines the poor as people in need of rehabilitation, and hence standing in need of "services" by virtue of their deficient income. The fuzzy gray areas in present definitions of what constitutes "income" or "services" are dictated by, and functional for, accommodating this contradictory public policy.

Another aspect of the prevailing trend (recalling Warren's concern about technology camouflaging social change needs) is the installation of management systems that reflect superb "paper rationality" but little knowledge of the client and his problems at the direct delivery level (Stern, 1972). In short, if New York City's initial experience is typical, it means an increase in the number of people in the bureaucracy with whom the client must deal, an increase in the amount of paper flow in an already dense paper jungle, and mounting frustration of the client as he is shifted from one person to another with no one responsible, and no demonstrable improvement in people's lives.

In fact, the conditions existing at the time of "separation" should shortly lead to the rediscovery that the poor need services because they cannot navigate the system without them, and that income maintenance (inadequate public assistance by any name) cannot provide enough help, given the problems of the poor. In the meantime the groundwork has been laid for phasing out what many in an earlier era had hoped would be a free-standing public service agency. As Hoshino says:

Separation is neither a panacea for the problem of public welfare nor an unmitigated evil. What separation does is confront us with our unresolved conflicts about the nature and function of public welfare which, in turn, reflect our conflicting attitudes toward the poor and our ambivalence about dependency on public aid (1973, p. 4).

Yet from the time of hope, expressed as a belief in the availability of a network of public social services for all segments of the population, there has been a realization of how much was misunderstood and underestimated. Certainly underestimated was the pervasive problem of racism in terms of the cumulative effects of discrimination and selection throughout our systems of education, housing, and employment (Titmuss, 1968). Also underestimated were the difficulties that the poor and disadvantaged would have in manipulating an increasingly complex society. The existence of a hard-core minority poor, the issue of racism, and the lack of commitment for the public services all contribute to questioning the feasibility of "universalism" in provision. Today the question has really become how and whether there is another way to get programs to poor people without their becoming poor programs and how to discriminate in their favor without stigma. This is one of the great appeals of purchase of service and of all devices designed to maximize consumer choice and to "open" other systems.

Certainly one of the unforgettable lessons of the social programs of the 1960s was that programs designed just for the "welfare poor" were very vulnerable and could count on little mass support. Another lesson was that the "add-on" approach of the 1960s to program development would no longer suffice. Further, any notion that the federal government might actually run a social welfare industry (like health) has become thoroughly antiquated.

Implications

Whatever the perspective, the evidence is that the demand for knowledgeable people to shape the nature of the service delivery system will increase. The directive for the professional expansion of the social service professional with a repertoire of planning, policy, and pro-gramming skills seems undeniable, given the shifting nature of the social service domain and the changes recounted above (Stein, 1972).

The concern of many today that people who lack the substantive knowledge of social welfare programs are hired to administer such programs must be dealt with through the acquisition of the needed administrative proficiency and accountable management and through a strategy of interdisciplinary collaboration and education. For effective and desirable collaboration, there must be mutual advantage. What social work has to offer in such a trade is its access and the sanction for such access to its clients and institutions. It is a recognized profession with licensure and social sanction. It is further institutionalized within universities and it has a long tradition of administering social agencies and social programs.

One may still ask if, even with the acquisition of such specific skills, the demand for social workers in these areas will increase. The answer is mixed. There are other claimants to these activities. Social work does not now have the dominant position that it had when it institutionalized the personal services. That institutionalization provided not only for the professional monopoly of the personal social services, but also the opportunity (and the tradition) for social workers to move into adminis-tration and management. Today, however, institutions and organiza-tions interested in planning can and do turn to other disciplines for assistance. This fact introduces some important considerations as social work undertakes to strengthen its policy and planning components.

Yet these planning and policy components remain an integral part of the business of social welfare. And that business needs to be planned and managed in this as well as in more ideal societies. Social workers need to accept that there is nothing "bad" in becoming more technically proficient and nothing in the development of a methodology that pre-cludes commitment to fundamental social change. Change also needs its engineers. Inescapable (from a review of the trends) is the conclusion that in order to have future impact, social welfare professionals will need to learn state and local structures and develop proficiency in assisting states and localities in the technical and policy aspects of re-source allocation under revenue-sharing programs.

Another predictable thrust is in the development of new relationships with the business or private sector. Here is a virtually untapped market for the social services, and knowledge is needed about the nature of contracts, the details of performance contracting, and the purchase of services. The potential for profit in the human services is quite real, and if for no other reason, it can be anticipated that such arrangements will increase.

An expanded concept of welfare planning for the federal government is long overdue. Very simply, this means that the human welfare consequences of all programs and policies should be assessed, for policies in any one area have both intended and unintended consequences for another; for example, transportation programs have a welfare impact, and welfare policy is inextricably tied to tax policy (Cannon, 1973).

Finally, the time is ripe to reformulate, in collaboration with others, a domestic reform program which will embrace the development of a tax-and-transfer income redistribution system, a welfare reform system to include the working as well as the welfare poor, comprehensive health schemes, housing allowances, job-creation and training programs, and major educational programs to help areas with limited resources (Rivlin, 1973).

A major issue confronting the profession is the extent of the substantive and technical knowledge it can bring to this task in addition to its value commitment. Change also needs its engineers.

References

Brager, George A., and Francis P. Purcell. *Community Action against Poverty*, pp. 17–26. New Haven, Conn.: College and University Press, 1967.

Burns, Eveline. *Social Security and Public Policy*, pp. 227–39. New York, McGraw-Hill Book Co., Inc. 1956.

Buttrick, Shirley. "Innovative Ideas in Social Service Delivery," in *The Social Welfare Forum*, pp. 130–39. New York, Columbia University Press, 1971.

—— "On Choice and Services," *Social Service Review*, XLIV (1970), 427–33.

Cannon, William B. "Innovation in Education in a Time of Financial Adversity." Paper presented to the Council on Social Work Education, 1973.

Causey, Mike. *Washington* (D.C.) *Post*, September 18, 1972.

Dumont, Matthew. "The Changing Face of Professionalism," pp. 1–19. Bethesda, Md., National Institute of Mental Health, 1969; mimeographed.

Heller, Walter. Edited transcript of Remarks on President Nixon's Budget and Federalism, Before the Subcommittee on Intergovernmental Relations, pp. 1–

17. (Senator Muskie, Chairman), *United States Senate*, February 23, 1973, (mimeographed).

Hoshino, George. "Separation and Change." Paper presented at the National Conference on Social Welfare, 1973, mimeographed.

Kahn, Alfred. *Theory and Practice of Social Planning*, chaps. 5 and 11. New York, Russell Sage Foundation, 1969.

Killingsworth, Charles C. "Automation, Jobs and Manpower," in Louis Ferman Joyce L. Kornbluh, and Alan Haber, eds., *Poverty in America*, pp. 139–52. Ann Arbor, University of Michigan Press, 1965.

Lilley, William III, Timothy Clark, and John Iglehart. "New Federalism Report/ Tests of Revenue-Sharing Approach Identify Problems in Transferring Powers to Cities," *National Journal*, March 3, 1973, pp. 291–311.

Lloyd, Gary A. and John Michael Daley, Jr. "Community Control of Health and Welfare Programs," in *The Social Welfare Forum*, 1971, pp. 168–81. New York, Columbia University Press, 1971.

Marris, Peter and Martin Rein. *Dilemmas of Social Reform: Poverty and Community Action in the United States*, pp. 33–35. New York, Atherton Press, 1967.

Mencher, Samuel. "Perspectives on Recent Welfare Legislation Fore and Aft," *Social Work*, VIII, No. 3 (1963), 59–64.

Moynihan, Daniel P. *Maximum Feasible Misunderstanding*. New York, Free Press, 1969.

Pascal, Anthony. "New Departures in Social Services," *The Social Welfare Forum, 1969*, pp. 74–85. New York, Columbia University Press, 1969.

Purchase of Social Services (a study of the experience of three states in purchase of services by contract under the provisions of the 1967 amendments to the Social Security Act). Prepared by Booz, Allen, and Hamilton Management Consultants, Washington, D.C., 1971.

Rein, Martin. *Social Policy*, chap. 7. New York, Random House, 1970.

—— "Social Services and Economic Independence," in *The Planning and Delivery of Social Services*, Summation of a Conference Sponsored by the National League of Cities and the Center for Community Planning, HEW, pp. 73–78. Washington, D.C., National League of Cities, 1969.

Rivlin, Alice. "A Counter-Budget for Social Progress, *New York Times Magazine*, April 8, 1973.

Spiegel, Hans B. C., and Stephen D. Mittenthal. "The Many Faces of Citizen Participation: a Bibliographic Overview," pp. 3–20, in Hans B. C. Spiegel, ed., *Citizen Participation in Urban Development*. Washington, D.C., National Training Laboratory.

Stein, Herman D. "Conflict and Consensus in Social Work," *Assignment Children*, XIX (1972), 3–10.

Stern, Sol. "Down and Out in New York," *New York Times Magazine*, October 22, 1972, pp. 46–66.

Titmuss, Richard. *Commitment to Welfare*, pp. 124–36, New York, Pantheon Books, 1968.

U.S. Department of Health, Education, and Welfare, *Closing the Gap in Social Work Manpower*. Washington, D.C.: U.S. Government Printing Office, 1965.

Ylvisaker, Paul. "The Process of Social Service Planning," in *The Planning and De-livery of Social Services,* Summation of a Conference Sponsored by the National League of Cities and the Center for Community Planning, HEW, pp. 21–30. Washington, D.C., National League of Cities, 1969.

Warren, Roland. "The Model Cities Program," *The Social Welfare Forum, 1971,* pp. 140–67. New York, Columbia University Press, 1971.

GORDON ROSE

Issues in Professionalism: British
Social Work Triumphant

A KEY problem in understanding the progress of social work is its professional standing. It is impossible to discuss this without at least a brief dip into the difficult and disputed territory of the definition of professionalism. There is, in fact, a link between the problems of social work and the development of writing about the profession since one of the earliest contributions in this field is Abraham Flexner's "Is Social Work a Profession?" a speech delivered to the National Conference of Charities and Corrections (Flexner, 1915). Etzioni (1969) has implicitly answered the question by including social work in a book on the "Semi-professions"; but Greenwood's (1957) much quoted article, "Attributes of a Profession," seems to be more doubtful about this assumption.

Greenwood presents the basic list of characteristics of a profession which seems to have gradually evolved, despite variations, into something of a consensus. Greenwood's formulation of them is very loose, and a better summary is given by Leggatt (1970, p. 175):

(a) Practice is founded upon a base of theoretical, esoteric knowledge.
(b) The acquisition of knowledge requires a long period of education and socialization.
(c) Practitioners are motivated by an ideal of altruistic service rather than the pursuit of material and economic gain.

(d) Careful control is exercised over recruitment, training, certification and standards of practice.

(e) The colleague group is well organised and has disciplinary powers to enforce a code of ethical practice.

Everett Hughes's (1963) comment that the most important question is not whether particular occupations are or are not professions, but to what degree they exhibit the characteristics of professions, merely underlines the difficulty of giving any clear meaning to lists of this kind. Let us, for instance, take the case of plumbers. They undergo a long training which has both theoretical and practical aspects; they turn out in all weathers and show considerable devotion to an ideal of service (you may not be able to get a plumber in the middle of the night unless there is considerable danger involved, but you cannot get a doctor either; and the British police complain bitterly and repeatedly about the unavailability of social workers). There is considerable control upon the recruitment, training, and certification of plumbers, and a code of practice. There are national organizations (in England, certainly) of plumbers, but it is as doubtful if any code could be enforced as it is in relation to doctors except by striking a plumber off the list. (There is, of course, no list from which a university teacher could be struck, though nobody would doubt that they do well on points *a* and *b*.)

This kind of approach has lost ground in recent years largely because almost any examination of an actual profession, no matter how well accepted, tends to produce considerable areas of doubt as to the application of the criteria. There is obviously a good deal of difference between plumbers and doctors, but it is not immediately apparent from a recital of the provisos laid down above. One tends to become involved in assessments of what is meant by theoretical training, how far professionals are involved in producing new knowledge, what is meant by an ideal of altruistic service (every conscientious clerk has it), and the concept of the profession as a self-conscious, highly self-protective, social group which claims autonomy on the basis of expertise (and has convinced the community that this is so—a point much better made by Greenwood than by Leggatt).

Such criticisms have turned the attention of sociologists rather more to the consideration of professions as manifestations of social attitudes and changes in social structure. Professionalization is clearly a form of elitism, and one has to consider the characteristics of elites and what gives them prestige. Ben-David (1963) points out that a basic characteristic of modern societies is the central position of professions in the class system, and he goes on to argue that their support of liberal and welfare policies is as much in their own interest as industrial production is for the businessman. There may be some truth in this, but if so, these manipulations of society by professionals can only derive from their having achieved monopoly and high status. If it is monopoly, it is as Schumpeter (1951) suggests, a monopoly over a particular type of knowledge and practice to which society accords high status; thus the basis of the social accolade remains unexplained.

Leggatt (1970), whose article is mainly about teachers, lists a number of things which he argues militate against high status:

Principal Characteristics of Professional Teaching

Practitioner Group	Clients and Client Relations	Work Performance
1. Large size	1. Low-status clients	1. Based on low experience
2. Large proportion of female members	2. Clients confronted by large groups	2. Knowledge not created
3. Low social class	3. Compulsory relations	3. Holistic orientation
4. High rate of turnover	4. Protracted relations	4. Use of simple language
5. Loose organization	5. Emotionally charged relations	5. Performance hard to evaluate
6. Low autonomy	6. Multiple clientele	6. Isolation
7. Segmentation		

Leggatt's point is not so much that teaching is not a profession; indeed, he accepts that it is. What he is concerned to show are the reasons for what he claims to be the low status of the teaching profession.

Pehaps it would be useful to consider social work in relation to Leggatt's list. Under the heading of practitioner groups it is clear that social workers are a small group, but there is a high proportion of female members. (Leggatt quotes Great Britain's Sample Census of 1966 and the United States Census of 1960 to show that social welfare work has 52 percent females in Great Britain and 57 percent in the United States. The corresponding figures for teaching are 58 percent and 73 percent. If one were to take a narrower view of the social work profession, the proportions of females might be even higher in both countries.) Leggatt cites figures to show that a high proportion of English teachers in England and Wales are of lower-class origins; I doubt if similar figures exist for social workers. If one included probation workers and all the workers now in social service departments, the proportion might well also be high. We also know comparatively little about rates of turnover among social workers; although the appropriate figures have been collected for some years, they have never been published.

"Loose organization" Leggatt believes to be the consequence of a large number of partially disinterested women, which reduces the degree of loyalty to the organization; but this seems an extremely poor point since the teaching profession in England is extremely highly and effectively organized. "Low autonomy" refers to the fact that most teachers are public servants, as compared with higher-status professions whose members are more often self-employed. If he means the degree to which there is detailed supervision of work done, the teachers (and the social workers) are probably no worse off than hospital doctors below the rank of consultant. However, the suggestion more probably is that those who are self-employed have higher social status than those who are not, a debatable point. Also debatable is his reference to segmentation; that is, the considerable variety of levels and types of teachers and the splits in the national union organizations in both England and the United States. Why these should reduce the status of the profession is not clear, and one would have thought that the antics of the British and American medical associations are far more likely to bring disrepute on the medical profession than any of the teachers' organizations on their profession.

So far as clients are concerned, many of the clients of social workers are of very low social status, indeed are often rejected by society (but not the major categories of deprived children, the aged, and the handicapped). It is also not clear why Leggatt thinks that dealing with low-status clients is demeaning. Are criminal lawyers or personnel officers demeaned by this? The social worker, unlike the teacher, does not see his clients in large groups, nor is client participation compulsory. Leggatt argues that the long exposure of teachers to children and their families exposes their foibles and thus reduces the mystique of their craft; but this too is very doubtful, and it might as often induce admiration. Here also there seems to be no obvious reason why social status should be reduced—one does not particularly admire one's lawyer because one sees little of him. It is also difficult to see why the teacher's relationship with both adult and child, and the fact that this is emotionally charged, should necessarily reduce his status.

"Low expertise" seems to mean that the profession is dealing with behavior with which we all have familiarity, and with which we all to some extent have to deal. This has been a constant problem with social work, and much more so than with teaching where it applies especially to primary (elementary) education. The contributors to Etzioni's book seem to make a differentiation in status between the high school and the elementary school teacher, a differentiation which has much less force in England. A secondhand knowledge base is also a problem in social work, which does not even have the distinction of that section of the teaching profession which is in the universities producing research, which is widely accepted as of high academic status.

The "holistic orientation" refers to the response to the teacher by the pupil as a whole person, as evidence for which he cites pleasure in the return of former students. This goes against all the evidence on teaching which shows the teacher as seeing the child primarily as a responder and achiever rather than a "whole person," and Leggatt is quite wrong in putting the point. It is, however, very true of social work where this very strong feeling is one of the bases of the somewhat anti-academic tendencies of social workers. There is also a degree of contrast between teaching and social work in the use of language, particularly of jargon. This is uncommon in teaching but very common in social work, which cannot be accused of lacking its own private language. Leggatt also speaks of the divisive nature of classroom teaching which tends to lead to isolation of the individual teacher; but any professional relationship implies a privatized link between client and professional, and this does not help his case. Nor does his criticism that teaching is hard to evaluate; so is most professional work, and clarity of evaluation works both ways: one can display a mended broken leg, but it is difficult to hide a mistaken amputation.

It will be clear from the foregoing that Leggatt overstates his case. He does, however, illustrate very well the central problem of the sociology of occupations as it relates to professionalization; that is, prestige. A remarkably small amount of work has been done on the prestige of occupations and this largely to produce measures of class. The best works of this kind are by Glass (1954), Svalastoga (1959), and Blau and Duncan (1967). However, we know very little about the prestige of attributes of occupations of the kind cited by Leggatt, and he necessarily arbitrarily assigns high or low status to the various things he discusses. It follows that many of his judgments are highly debatable.

There is also a prior problem. Upon whose judgment are we to rely? It is probably true that in England most parents regard teachers as having high status because they deal in academic knowledge. This is not the primary source of status as recognised by most members of the working class themselves, but they appreciate it as showing high status in others. The traditional basis of the teacher's standing may have been eroded in the United States; this source of status remains very strong in England. But are the judgments of working-class parents a sufficient basis for assigning professional prestige to teaching or to social work? It seems highly unlikely; indeed, it is doubtful how far prestige emanates from the majority—consider "high culture," for instance, which is heavily rejected by the majority. Do we, therefore, rely upon the general social survey or upon the opinions of those who already possess some degree of prestige? Or are there professions which are of general high prestige (medicine seems the most likely candidate), and professions which are only of high prestige in prestigious quarters (the law, for instance, which is regarded as evil by many working-class people)?

If it is prestige which we are considering, we ought to look at the way in which professions emerge and the kind of hurdles they have to surmount in order to increase their status in the professional pecking order. Here we have some propositions put forward by Wilensky (1964) who offers these steps:

Full-time activity at the task

Establishment of university training

National professional association

Redefinition of the core task, so as to give the "dirty work" to subordinates

Conflict between the old-timers and the new men who seek to upgrade
the job

Competition between the new occupation and neighboring ones

Political agitation in order to gain legal protection

Code of ethics.

Wilensky presents these as a series of stages, but as Goode (1969)
has pointed out, examination of particular professions does not support
this, and they should be taken as areas in which progress might be
made. However, I agree with Goode that they "do not separate the
core, *generating* traits from the derivative ones. Many occupations and
activities have tried all or most of these steps without much recognition
as professions" (p. 276). Goode himself lists a number of attributes
which he reduces to two basic, generating categories: a body of abstract knowledge and the ideal of service.

Despite the fact that the service ideal is most frequently given a central place in the definition of a profession, it is extremely difficult to
give it a watertight definition which will pass the plumber test. It is
no use saying that it is the practitioner who decides upon the clients'
needs—so do plumbers. If the practitioner-client relationship is, in
fact, different for professionals, exactly how is it different? It is not
sufficient to argue that the profession demands real sacrifice from its
practitioners (I am following Goode's list); so do plumbing and, even
more, the police and the fire service. Are policemen and firemen professionals? Goode suggests that society believes that the profession
not only accepts these ideals "but follows them to some extent"; but
presumably it believes this of policemen and firemen too. Nor is it
good enough to argue that professions have strong sanctions about
the behavior of their members in relation to the service ideal; again,
so do police, firemen, and most skilled workers.

This is not to say that the service ideal is not characteristic of professions; obviously it is, but it is certainly not discretely so without
qualification. Perhaps this is to be found in the continuing relationship
which is enjoined by the nature of professional client contact, in which
the client is advised, instructed, or treated in some way which he thinks,
rightly or wrongly, cannot be done without reference to a wide basis
of high-status knowledge. This, however, is to return to the first head-

ing concerning knowledge. Perhaps the answer is that it is the type of knowledge base which discretely defines the professions rather than the ideal of service, although they would not be professions unless they also incorporated the service ideal.

It seems to me doubtful, however, whether one can define the progress of an occupation toward professionalization or within it by this sort of approach alone. The key factors in professionalization seem to be most closely related to questions of status; that is, how closely the profession is related to those things which society tends to regard as of great importance and ranks highly. On this basis we might suggest the following:

1. *Association with high-status knowledge*
   This usually means university-approved knowledge.
2. *Association with universities*
   This is a factor even though one is not closely associated with high-status knowledge. This is because the universities themselves rank high.
3. *Association with high social class*
   This does not necessarily mean that all practitioners are of high social class, but that there is a substantial relationship for the leaders of the profession. There is a chicken-and-egg problem here: whether the profession comes first and leads to high social class, or the reverse; but it is probably a hand-over-hand situation for those climbing the ladder.
4. *Association with activities which have high value to many people*
   This implies "people work," because this has higher status than work with things, but work with things is not excluded. Surgeons do not suffer in prestige because they use knives and saws and needle and thread; they use them on people, not on pieces of wood. Similarly, a number of professions which do not actually carry out people work directly, do things which are fundamental to people's safety and comfort. They build houses, roads, bridges, work which is more fundamental and more complex and expensive than the plumber's job.
5. *Association with beliefs in processes which have acquired a high degree of mystique*

This is often related to the knowledge base, but need not be so;
for example, belief in a deity.

6. *Association with power bases*
The universities themselves are, of course, a power base, but it
is usually necessary to be respected and assigned high status by
a major power base, usually the government, but sometimes by
another highly influential profession such as the church.

The above items are not, of course, sufficient to define a profession,
but they do give some strong pointers as to rungs of the ladder. The
high-status profession is to a considerable extent indefinable on the
basis of a categorical list because a particularly high valuation upon
one item may make another superfluous. These are simply some interesting characteristics which one may often observe. At least they pass
the plumber test, even if they may fail in other ways.

Social Work in Great Britain

SOCIAL AND ACADEMIC STATUS

This has been a long prologamena to an assessment of the status
of British social work, but it has brought us to some possible yard-
sticks. To start with, one of the most fascinating characteristics of
the development of social work in Britain was its association with high-
status people. Charity always did have an aura of saintliness and some
association with those of high status. The medieval abbess, in fullness
of time, was secularized into Octavia Hill, and the abbott became the
warden of the settlement. The settlement movement was, in fact, of
very great importance in England, as in the United States and a number
of other places, for it linked the university with the laborer. When
it became apparent that some form of training was necessary for the
emergent social worker, it was natural that it should be placed in the
universities. Elizabeth Macadam (1945, p. 22) quotes from Margaret
Sewell, the Warden of the Women's University Settlement in the 1890s,
who says:

It is significant of this new aspect that the universities took a leading part in the reorganization of so-called charity, and that the leading movements were largely recruited by men and women from the universities, and it followed almost of course that the need for some sort of specialized educational equipment was speedily recognised.

A joint committee of the Charity Organization Society and the National Union of Women Workers (later the National Council of Women) was set up in 1897 and was followed in 1901 by the London School of Sociology and Economics, with Professor Edward Gonner at its head. In 1904 Professor Gonner, later Sir Edward Gonner, on the suggestion of his friend Sir Charles Loch, of the Charity Organization Society, established the School of Social Science in Liverpool, which became fully incorporated in the University of Liverpool in 1917. (Note the high-status associations in that last sentence.) The University of Birmingham in 1908 was the first to register students intending to follow a social work career as internal students of the university and to accept full responsibility for their training, followed closely by the universities of Bristol, Leeds, and Manchester. In 1912 the London School of Sociology and Economics was absorbed by the London School of Economics and Political Science.

The First World War led to an increasing demand for social science trained students, the Ministry of Munitions offering grants for training welfare workers for munitions factories, and toward the end of the war there was a strong feeling that recruits should be trained for a preventive "war on poverty." (President Lyndon Johnson was not very original in his choice of phrase.) The result in 1917 was the founding of the Joint University Council for Social Studies to coordinate and develop the work of social studies departments in the universities, a task it is still doing.

It is noteworthy that the training provided was brought into line with the academic development of the social sciences. It was not thought, for instance, that what social workers really needed was a long apprenticeship associated with part-time attendance at an evening college; it was already too respectable and middle-class to be associated with artisan-type training. When skill training eventually arrived, as a result of the importation of child guidance from the United States in 1927, it was already packaged in a discipline, psychotherapy, rapidly attaining a degree of respectability, and it very soon gave rise to a professional course for psychiatric social workers at the London School of Economics.

These developments took more than middle-classness. Occupational therapy and physiotherapy, into which went many of the daughters of the upper middle class, never made the grade with the universities. No doubt this was partly due to the actual nature of the work, but doctors also use implements and medicines to cure people. The generality of the nature of the helping process in social work, its easy assimilation in the progress of the social sciences, and the absence of any established high-status profession dominating the field all contributed to the rapidity of this assumption of academic status; but the original links with the universities were undoubtedly crucial.

There was also the great respectability of its practitioners. The strong identification of charity with women became an asset in a period in which the intelligent middle-class woman with a private income, or a benevolent husband, was increasingly socially acceptable; and the intelligent nonsupported woman was beginning to find salaried posts. The conjunction of these events opened up a situation where there were enough people of high social standing to foster the university and government connection, and enough others to produce a flow of recruits.

And, of course, the nature of the job helped. It was clearly people work, but it was a nonroutine kind of people work, quite unlike nursing, which had only recently arisen from a long period of low reputation, and it was eminently respectable.

What social work did not have, however, were the last two points in the above list. The original social science development was very important since it created a link, subsequently expanded in the 1950s, with the academically respectable social sciences. The exploitation of the link with psychoanalysis did, however, introduce a mystique associated with skills, by no means as academically acceptable, but well bespattered with jargon and obfuscation. The interesting point about this, however, is the community reference. It may be true in the United States, but it was never true in England that the mystique cut any ice with the general public in the way that medicine did. It may have helped, and this is doubtful, to introduce skill training into the universities, and it certainly greatly helped to give social workers themselves comfort and status support, but as a community referent it did very little good. Indeed, the conditions have never existed in England where the psychoanalytic link could be exploited. The English social worker was always, and remains, squarely face to face with the main body of clients because his only real career structure is in the public authority, which cannot duck its difficult, lower-class clients. And one does not need to elaborate on the lack of association with high income.

ADMINISTRATIVE STRUCTURE AND TRAINING

These considerations, while they explain the remarkable speed with which social work acquired some of the accouterments of a profession, need to be related also to post Second World War developments.

On July 15, 1944, Lady Allen of Hurtwood wrote a letter to the *Times.* She said that in the plans for reconstruction one section of the community had been forgotten:

those children who, because of their family misfortune, find themselves under the guardianship of a Government Department or one of the many charitable organizations. The public are, for the most part, unaware that many thousands of these children are being brought up under repressive conditions that are generations out of date and are unworthy of our traditional care of children.

Lady Allen's initiative was rapidly backed by a tragic instance of the kind of problem she had outlined. In January, 1945, Dennis O'Neill, a boy boarded out by the local authority, died from neglect and ill-treatment. There was an immediate public reaction and a court of inquiry, which also emphasized the need for a new approach.

By the time the court of inquiry had reported, the Government had already set up in March, 1945, a departmental committee which came to be known as the Curtis Committee. In September, 1946, after publishing an interim report on training, the Curtis Committee recommended that the care of deprived children should be the statutory responsibility of a single local authority department, watched over by a single central department (the Home Office). The Children Act of 1948 at one stroke swept away the jumble of statutory authorities and substituted one single authority, giving it power also to register voluntary bodies.

There was, however, another consequence of Lady Allen's letter. For the first time, a department was set up in the local authority which came to consist mainly of social workers; by modern standards almost totally without professional training, but social workers nevertheless. Furthermore, they were social workers who had no direct link with the payment of means-tested assistance. The new departments took over from the public assistance departments of their local authorities all the homes and nurseries run by them, together with their staffs, and they thus inherited directly some of the functions of the poor law; but, starting with the Unemployment Assistance Act 1934, the functions of paying out money had been increasingly taken over by a central organization, a process much accelerated by the war and completed through the National Assistance Act, 1948.

There thus came into existence an organization dedicated to the objectives of supervision of children by trained child care officers, of placing out children, and of breaking up and reforming the large and soulless children's homes. The emphasis in the Curtis report was upon the last of these, but the Children's Department was to become an organization of social workers with its own chief officer, the Children's Officer, employed by local authorities and supervised by the Home Office, which had never been concerned at all with public assistance (a responsibility of the Ministry of Health), but had since 1914 a special section devoted to the interests of children.

By the end of the war, comparatively little progress had been made in professional training, as can be seen from Eileen Younghusband's (1949) two reports on the state of employment and training in the profession. These showed the progress of the basic two-year nongraduate social science course soon to be renamed "social administration" (Titmuss arrived at the London School of Economics in 1950); but beyond this was a mass of in-service training courses, sometimes with periods of academic training, the only exception being psychiatric social work. And over-all loomed a considerable problem which had been produced by the ease with which social work had acquired university status: the fact that this was a bottleneck in England, where the universities were traditionally highly selective. The way out of this was already obvious to Eileen Younghusband (1951, p. 173):

There are indeed only two possible solutions—assuming the present chaos not to be a "possible" solution. The one is to refuse to recognise grades of training in social work and to make available well-planned in-service training for those who do not qualify for admission to social science courses in the universities: the other is to provide one or two year courses at institutions associated with, but not part of, universities for those whose previous education and academic capacities do not fit them for a university course, though their personal qualities make them suitable for some forms of social work.

Miss Younghusband did not get her way until 1959, and the courses concerned were not, in fact, set up in educational institutions related to a university, but in the top layer of nonuniversity schools for further education. The general pressure toward the accolade of a degree has subsequently floated these up, and they have now become polytechnics in which many degree courses are taught, though they do not have university status. This may also be seen as a further instance of the continued standing of social work, but in terms of professionalization it was possibly a backward step. It fixed the training of the large majority of workers at a nonuniversity level, even though by this time there was a growing elaboration of university professional training courses of the "generic" type.

It is not the intention here to produce a detailed history of British social work but to consider only those features which are important in relation to its societal status. We leap, therefore, to the Seebohm report (1968). The report stems from two sources: a movement toward family casework and against specialization; and the general move toward the reorganization of local government and the National Health Service upon a basis which was also strongly biased toward unification.

The first of these movements started with pressure from two small but influential pressure groups: the Fisher Group headed by the wife of the Archbishop of Canterbury and the Council for the Welfare of Children. They strongly advocated the unification of departmentalized social work services on the basis that the whole family should be seen as a unit. The Home Office, in a report entitled *The Child, the Family and the Young Offender* (1965, p. 4), produced some proposals for discussion concerning the reform of the system for dealing with juvenile delinquents:

The proposals . . . for the reform of the law and practice relating to young offenders emphasise the need to improve the structure of the various services connected with support of the family and the prevention of delinquency. The Government believes that these services should be organised as a family service but the form and scope of such a service will need detailed consideration.

They proposed, therefore, to appoint a committee to consider this reorganization, and this was the genesis of Seebohm, whose purpose was "to review the organizations and responsibilities of the local personal social services in England and Wales, and to consider what changes are desirable to secure an effective family service."

The second factor cited, the move toward unification and reorganization both in local government and in the National Health Service, cannot be underestimated. Thus it is important to note that this reorganization was crucial for the setting up of a unified social work service in the local authority, since it removed its most influential competitor, the Public Health Department which contained most of the social workers outside the children's departments, and placed it clearly in a health setting with the other parts of the health service.

The Seebohm report recommended a larger unified department with a stronger claim on resources (the children's departments had been of very low status as against the two large local spending departments of education and health); a better career structure and thus possible recruitment and better people at the top; better training facilities; and the filling of some unsightly gaps in the provision of services.

It is interesting to note how many of these are really concerned with raising professional standing: more resources, a better career structure, better training facilities, and, one might add, a general increase in autonomy and a much stronger and more unified power base in the local authority. The point is not, of course, made by Seebohm; but it is rarely far below the surface in the report's 370 pages.

Much more interesting than the report's detailed recommendations is the ease with which the solution of unification was accepted, and the fact that it was so easily defended against the powerful health interests which for many years had retained their grip on a large part of the social work field, arguing, with justification, that much of the work for old people and the disabled was necessarily closely related to the health services. (It is interesting that the case for the social service departments was very largely made upon *family*, that is, children's services, and the largely single and isolated aged population was then subsequently drawn in.) The victory of a social service structure could not have been won without the general trend toward unification in the health services themselves, which would inevitably take them out of the hands of the local authorities. (Despite various suggestions in the major reports, there was never very much likelihood that the hospital system would be returned to the local authorities, who had in effect lost it during the Second World War, and this meant that unification involved a transfer of local authority services.) Nevertheless, one senses over and above this a strength in, and acceptance of, social work, which would need more research to explain, but which is buried deeply in the opposing trends toward large organizations on the one hand, and greater recognition of the autonomy of the individual personality on the other.

The net result, however, has been the creation of a large and powerful organization within the local authority, incorporating a considerable extension of the career structure particularly in the middle grades where senior and area officers now abound. Thus the basis for an extension of professional status has been considerably widened, though the full implications are yet to be worked out.

THE TRIUMPH OF BRITISH SOCIAL WORK

There is yet much to be unraveled in the rapidity with which British social work has advanced in the last twenty-five years. Nevertheless, one can discern some important factors which contributed to this.

1. A high-status start resulted in rapid incorporation in the universities. In the progress of social science, social work has not retained much status in the university world. It has produced little or nothing which would be accepted by the established social science disciplines (or, if it comes to that, by the medical disciplines) as good standard research. This is not surprising since it tends to reject "hard" research methods on the grounds that the social work process cannot be precisely described and analyzed by any research method which has re-

liability and validity. The incorporation of social work in departments of social administration has produced an uncertain marriage of those devoted to the objective analysis of social policy—who, rightly or wrongly, have standing in the research world and with the public authorities—and those who largely reject "objective" data of this kind in respect of their own operations, and are seen as producing practitioners for the public services, not ideas. The marriage has worked well on the basis of a division of responsibility between "basic" and "professional" courses; and it has solved the problem presented to the rapidly expanding social science faculties of how to incorporate in the departmental structure small, semi-independent groups of people running social work courses, who had next to no academic standing. It has, however, done little or nothing for the intellectual stature of social work—but then it does nothing for itself.

2. Social work has benefited from the growth of an autonomous, centralized structure which deals with income maintenance and makes means-tested decisions. This has had nothing to do with the social work profession itself but with a complex of objectives, values, and administrative problems. Nor was it inevitable that the strong reaction against the poor law would produce a division between income maintenance and the rest of its activities. The American solution of trying to combine the two was more logical though doomed, due to the American definition of politics not as the art of the possible, but of the hopeful. Perhaps the most important of these objectives was the totally mistaken expectation that means-tested benefits would wither away as comprehensive insurance-based benefits took over. The result of this was the belief that means testing was for clerks and had nothing to do with social work. Even when it became clear that means testing was not unlikely to wither, but was gathering strength, the authorities minimized its human aspects, relying upon the idea of the dispassionate operation of regulations with comparatively little discretion. Nobody loves a poverty means tester, and social work by this chain of circumstances escaped the stigma. At the same time, however, it failed many of its clients, and it is only slowly beginning to see itself as sufficiently identified with their interests in these respects to act as advocates. Not a small part has been played in this failure by the bias in training against quantitative research.

3. The institution of children's departments in the local authorities in 1948 had three important consequences. For the first time a wholly social work department with its own director was set up in a public authority. True, from the local authority's point of view they were of low status (many of them even had women as their directors!), but they were a clearly defined unit within the recognized organizational structure. Secondly, the setting up of these departments greatly increased government participation in a social work function. Up to this point the only real government participation had been with probation, which in England and Wales but not in Scotland had been and remains outside the local authority structure. As a result of setting up children's departments, the small number of government inspectors was rapidly expanded, regional offices appeared, and the civil service, administrative commitment was increased. A similar process took place in the Ministry of Health in respect to regional welfare officers (their equivalent to Home Office inspectors) after the publication of the Younghusband report in 1959, and the passing of the Mental Health Act in the same year.

Thirdly, the existence of a separate department in the local authority built up confidence that social work was a separate job and that it could be successfully done within a local authority setting. It became clear what the policy organizational and financial requirements were for a social work department, something which was very important to demonstrate to councilors who also saw themselves as social workers, and who learned to differentiate between what they did and the work of the full-time social worker.

4. Probably the most important result of the post Second World War developments in social work stems, however, from the social workers themselves. Those who operated the major power structures and those who worked in the field in conjoint disciplines met social work staffs at all levels and, despite their many prejudices, were largely impressed by their capacity to be helpful and practical. The people they met were not necessarily those with training, and this relates particularly to many of those who rose to controlling or inspectorial positions. It became apparent, despite the existence of many in social work roles who had a narrow view of their responsibilities, that there were in the field people of considerable quality who could operate within the power

structure, who very much impressed those who ran it, and who were patently helping people who needed help. All welfare states are basically run on compassion, not on economics, and the quality is present at all levels and among politicians and civil servants alike. Social work above all remains identified as the instrument of compassion, and its embodiment within the organizational structures of the state. What has been demonstrated is that this can be done.

The Professional Status of British Social Work

Is British social work a profession? As suggested above, it is probably more important to think of its general occupational status than to take a view which implies some kind of hurdles over which one has to leap before one can "make it" as a profession. A "semiprofession" presumably does not mean 0.5 profession but < 1 profession; but it certainly implies that being a professional is something fairly clearly definable, and this is doubtful. The best one can say is that some occupations have to varying degrees those characteristics which we think of as peculiarly professional.

On this approach it would seem abundantly clear that British social work has one basic component which runs through all professions: organization in small teams with a good deal of autonomy for each member. One finds this whether professionals are self-employed or employed by public bodies or by industry. If autonomy in judgment and working is a characteristic, then it is quite clear that British social work possesses it. Also clear is a basic ethic which operates in relationships with clients, and produces a familiar clash between organizational and occupational demands. There are also only two strong professional *cum* trade union organizations that pour out writings ranging from chat to serious discussions of basic problems, of self-conscious discussion and participation in conferences and similar gatherings, which is little different from other professions, since one does not expect any but a minority of practitioners to take much part. There is a university connection (though a nonuniversity qualification for the majority), and a strong power base firmly entrenched in the public authorities.

British social work is never going to be of very high status; it simply is not sufficiently central to high-status activities. Socal workers are never going to be among the most highly paid, although directors of social service departments and their deputies are now very highly paid. It is, however, impossible to deny that it has many professional characteristics, and that it is well-accepted as an important part of the public responsibility of the welfare state.

References

Ben-David J. "Professions in the Class System of Present-Day Societies," *Current Sociology*, XII, No. 3 (1963–64), 296–97.

Blau, Peter M., and Otis D. Duncan. *The American Occupational System*. New York, John Wiley and Sons, Inc., 1967.

Etzioni, Amitai, ed. *The Semi-Professions and Their Organizations: Teachers, Nurses, Social Workers*. New York, Free Press, 1969.

Flexner, Abraham. "Is Social Work a Profession?" in *Proceedings of the National Conference of Charities and Corrections*, pp. 576–90. Chicago, Hildmann Printing Co., 1915.

Glass, David, ed. *Social Mobility in Britain*. London, Humanities Press, 1954.

Goode, William J. "The Theoretical Limits of Professionalization," in Amitai Etzioni, ed., *The Semi-Professions and Their Organization*, pp. 216–33. New York, Free Press, 1969.

Greenwood, Ernest. "Attributes of a Profession," *Social Work*, II, No. 7 (1957), 45–55.

Hughes, Everett C. "Professions," *Daedalus*, XCII (1963), 655–68.

Legatt, T. "Teaching as a Profession," in J. A. Jackson, ed., *Professions and Professionalization*, pp. 155–56. Cambridge, England, Cambridge University Press, 1970.

Macadam, Elizabeth, *The Social Servant in the Making*. London, Allen and Unwin, 1945.

Schumpeter, Joseph A. *Imperialism and Social Classes*. Oxford, England, Oxford University Press, 1951.

Seebohm, Frederick. *Report of the Committee on Local Authority and Allied Personal Social Service*. H.M.S.O., Cmnd. 3703, 1968.

Svalastoga, Kaare. *Prestige, Class and Mobility*. Copenhagen, Gyldendal, 1959.

The Child, the Family and the Young Offender. London, Home Office, Cmnd. 2742, 1965.

Wilensky, Harold. "The Professionalization of Everyone?" *American Jornal of Sociology*, LXX (1964), 142–46.

Younghusband, Eileen. *Report on the Employment and Training of Social Workers*. Edinburgh, Constable, 1949.

—— *Social Work in Britain*. Edinburgh, Constable, 1951.

EUGEN PUSIĆ

The Administration of Welfare

THE SIGNS of the time spell change for both the field of administration and the field of welfare: administration is turning away from the traditional chain of command toward less rigid and possibly more complex relations among people at work; welfare is growing from a subsidiary and marginal helping activity into a wide network of programs using diverse methods, from depth psychology to macro-economics.

As both administration and welfare are changing so are the links between them. The old concepts and rules of social work administration will hardly be adequate for the modern administrator of the welfare systems of tomorrow.

What are the options for the new administration of the new welfare system?

Changing Trends in Administration

The following discussion of four types of cooperative systems and the three main varieties of administration are constructs to help our perception of reality rather than to mirror images of reality itself. They are simplifications in the sense of stressing one class of characteristics and disregarding mixed and transitional phenomena.

Administration is the activity of creating, implementing, maintaining, and innovating structure in human cooperative systems. Its main characteristics vary with the the type of cooperative system in which it functions. The characteristics of human cooperation depend on the activity itself as well as on the the type of technology employed. Cooperative systems move from less to more complex forms, so that in a certain sense it is possible not only to speak of stages in the development of cooperative systems, but also to distinguish four such stages.

FOUR TYPES OF COOPERATING SYSTEMS

The primary cooperating group. This group is convened *ad hoc* for a given task, a single action, and is coordinated by direct and personal contacts among its members. Examples range from a fruit-gathering group in a primitive tribe to an *ad hoc* interdepartmental task force in a modern government. While, however, the task force is the exception in modern government, which is based on a vast background of rules, institutions, and supporting services, in the primitive tribe primary cooperation might be the only form possible since the available material and human resources would permit nothing more complex.

The Leadership Group. This group depends upon the leader to assume the function of coordinating the activities of the members. In the leadership group there is already a simple structural element which distinguishes this from primary cooperation: the relation between leader and followers. This relation is relatively permanent; it lasts beyond the task at hand, irrespective of the activity in which the group is engaged. Examples range again from a tribal war band to a modern military unit under conditions of combat. While the tribe has no other means to wage war, the modern military unit is a part of a huge and complex organization; only in actual combat is it thrown back on personal leadership as the simplest and most convenient method to coordinate men under heavy stress.

The Bureaucratic Organization. Here the structure is composed of jobs or task elements obtained by dividing and subdividing a complex task into ever smaller and simpler elements; the people who perform the jobs are integrated by a superior-subordinate relationship based on the position of each job on a hierarchical arrangement (Weber, 1947). Almost all cooperation in industrial societies is organized in this structural type.

The Team Network. This highly complex structure is composed of

people as specialists (as sources of information) who are combined into
teams on the basis of equality among members. Teams are combined
into networks on the basis of their mutual interdependence in function.
Teams are today used increasingly within the framework of bureaucratic organizations for problem-solving purposes in those complex
activities which depend primarily on knowledge and skill, such as research, medical treatment, and architectural planning. They are found
increasingly in the fields of welfare. This is still an emerging form as
there does not yet exist any broad span of activities in society structured
as a team network.

The four types of cooperative systems can be called stages only in
the sense that in less developed, poor, agrarian societies there will be
hardly any cooperation structured as a hierarchic bureaucracy and even
less as a team network. The simpler types of cooperation, however, do
not disappear in more developed, urban, and industrial societies. All
types can be and are used according to the ends pursued and the means
available. Thus cooperation can be more structurally differentiated in
more developed societies.

TYPES OF ADMINISTRATION

Administration, an activity related to structure in cooperative systems, is itself likely to change according to the type of structure to
which it is attached. In primary cooperation there is no relationship
among the cooperating individuals beyond the task at hand and therefore no structure of any permanence. Administration cannot be meaningfully identified as a separate activity in this cooperative type. However, in the three more complex types (the leadership group, the
bureaucratic organization, and the team network) there can be found
a corresponding form of administration.

Administraion as the Extension of Leadership. In the leadership group
the creation, implementation, maintenance, and innovation of structure,
that is, administration, are in principle the function of the leader. He
holds the group together by charismatic appeal, by superior force, by
authority of skill and capability, by traditional habit, by rational calcula-
tion, or by whatever other means at his disposal. Whatever the situation, the reason for the followers to follow and to obey is always cen-

tered upon the personality of the leader, who defines the task and designates the means.

Beyond a certain size, however, the leadership group needs an extension of the leader's personality, the appointment of subleaders, of group members whose main function will be to assist the leader in his effort to maintain communication, to impose, as it were, his presence over an increasingly far-flung membership. As leadership groups continue to grow—and all empires of antiquity, for instance, are in their essential organization leadership groups—these locumtenential and auxiliary arrangements can become quite elaborate. Yet administration as the extension of leadership, however elaborate, is always distinguishable from other types by being predominantly personal. There are no functions or tasks in the abstract, but only functions deputized, tasks entrusted by a leader. There is no link from job to job, there are only links among people, from follower to leader. All duty and all loyalty are duties toward men, loyalties to leaders.

Administration as the Differentiation and Integration of a Task. Administration as a clearly separate activity in its own right is characteristic of the bureaucratic organization. The links which hold the system together are impersonal and obtained by dividing and subdividing a complex task, in the abstract, into more and more restricted components (Friedmann, 1962). The pyramidal pattern which results from this process is, at the same time, the device for integrating the diverse components, in action, into a meaningful whole. People are allocated the prefabricated task components as their individual but strictly functional jobs; they have to perform them as occupants of a given organizational position.

To make this system work, two activities are indispensable: a constant communication process between the decision-making top and the operating base; and a negatively defined group of activities that do not fit into the specialist job descriptions in the main pyramid and have to be filtered out into separate auxiliary or staff units. These two groups of activities are administration as it is best known to us, in hierarchic, bureaucratic organizations. The communications aspect of administration is the main duty of the hierarchy (Barnard, 1940), including all positions above the firing-line operatives. Auxiliary and staff units (for such tasks as personnel, finance, planning, buildings, maintenance, and filing) are, as a rule, attached to the main line of the hierarchy and have to be meshed with it.

Administration as the Handling of Information. The shortcomings of hierarchy are most visible in organizations with a high content of information and consequently have stimulated the team-network approach. Where successful operation depends on the fact that knowledge, skill, experience, and judgment must be dispersed throughout the organization and can no longer be concentrated at the top, the traditional line of command is ineffective. The administrators at the top can in no meaningful way direct the specialists at the bottom, and the latter, therefore, resent supervision; they come to feel that the distribution of benefits according to hierarchic rank is unfair. The whole process of reporting, directing, commanding, and listening to commands seems more and more, in the eyes of all concerned, a loss of time at the expense of the main activity the organization is supposed to perform.

It is feelings such as these that motivate the search for alternatives and the movement toward what we have called team networks (Bennis, 1969). This movement includes a change in type of administration. Though the new type is still far from complete, there are some indicators of its changing characteristics, and three aspects can be identified.

First, since the handling of information is the central activity in cooperative teamwork, no matter what its content, a variety of team networks will emerge based on interdependence of interests and/or needs. For example, what we have learned to call auxiliary and staff activities (personnel, finance, planning) will continue to exist as the responsibility of teams and groups of teams not directly attached, in the sense of subordinated, to any others. After all, the geometrically expanding research, development, and educational systems could be called "auxiliary" to the existing operating organizations with the same right. Thus the concept of "auxiliary" work is becoming obsolete.

Second, there is a shift in emphasis from the stabilizing, defensive posture of administration toward an innovative approach. Initially, administration concentrates on protecting the system in which it functions against disturbing influences from the environment. To that end both defensive and offensive strategies are used to prevent potentially dangerous impulses from emerging and to shield the system—or its "core technologies"—from their impact.

However, in the increasingly turbulent environments of today's society there are selective premiums on being able to innovate quickly and adequately (Emery and Trist, 1969). The ideal of administration is no longer stability but ultrastability, in the cybernetic sense, meaning some kind of ongoing identity through constant changes of almost all systemic parameters.

Third is the interest-adjudicating and conflict-handling function of administration, in which increasingly interested parties themselves are becoming involved through processes such as representation, bargaining, participation, and self-management. It is not unreasonable to assume, extrapolating present trends, that these diverse activities will in time become distinct functions and objectives of individual team organizations, and no longer be considered accessories of a bureaucratic monolith.

Our time will be rich in hybrids as dissatisfaction with classical bureaucracy is becoming more general, but an alternative solution is still far from complete. The field of welfare might provide an opportunity to make a virtue out of necessity.

Changing Trends in Social Welfare

In the development of social welfare concepts and services three broad tendencies can be distinguished on an international level, although there are wide spans of variation among countries and systems.

First, there is a widening circle of responsibility as the original concern with a marginal group expands towards an operational concept of general welfare (Titmuss, 1959). The riches of existence should be shared by each of us, and everyone should participate in bearing a part of the burden in order to achieve minimal security for all. In that generalized effort whoever is not a part of the solution is a part of the problem and the possible object of additional social welfare action. This action, however, is meaningful only against the background of normally achievable security; it is not a substitute for it.

A second and related tendency of particular relevance for the administrative problems of the social services is the expanding role of the state in welfare. While originally a concern of the church and private charity, social welfare has become a department of government. The political concepts and the ideological fixations of the Enlightenment in regard to the universal responsibility of the territorial sovereign for all that was happening in his territory was clearly affirmed (*Quod est in territorio etiam est de territorio*, in the words of Thomasius). The content of this responsibility included economic sufficiency, bodily security, and the amenities of life. There are striking similarities in the official attitudes of Eastern European socialism: the same assumption of a universal responsibility of the state, the same priority for the economic sector, the same attitude of active intervention in the life of the individual.

The idea that government is the best choice as carrier of welfare is by no means confined to Europe, nor is it rooted in ideological prejudice only. There is a solid basis in economic fact for this belief. The cost of welfare, even if only a first attempt toward a system of general welfare is made, tends to rocket out of proportion to the capabilities of any but the strongest mechanisms for accumulating the available surplus: that means the State. In this way financial necessity no less than political conviction brings government more and more into the field of welfare (Galbraith, 1967).

While the first tendency is related to conceptual approaches and the second concerns the locus of responsibility, the third deals with the concrete aspect of services. There is a growing variety of social welfare services available to potential clients and a progressively richer tool kit of methods to perform them. At the risk of gross oversimplification, we can speak of five groups of social services present in most developed, and even less developed, countries today: (1) economic assistance; (2) institutional care; (3) sociopsychological treatment; (4) provision of specialized information; and (5) social action. In each service there is a widening variety of content, diversity of method, circle of beneficiaries, theoretical sophistication, as well as educational prerequisites for the practitioner, remarkably different from the rudimentary forms of a hundred years ago.

These changing trends in social welfare throughout the world are essential background data for any discussion of administration in welfare.

Bureaucracy and Social Welfare

Government, and particularly public administration, is tied, possibly more than other systems, to a model of organization which is not necessarily the best for performing adequately in the field of welfare. The administrative machinery of government is built on the model of bureaucratic organization, a type of structure that is fairly general in industrial society. Its outstanding characteristics are, as noted, the impersonality of work relations, the division of labor, and the reliance upon supervision as a means of coordination and control.

Not one of these characteristics of bureaucratic organization is particularly congenial to social welfare. Much of social work is intensely personal in its relation to the client as well as in its link to other specialists, resisting any attempt at standardization and requiring careful individual distinctions from case to case. Even when highly complex, most social service activities cannot be broken down into simpler and easier components; the cases have a Gestalt that defies attempts to fragment them. For the same reason, the profession of welfare needs leaders but not overseers. It is not a coincidence that the term "supervision" has acquired a technical meaning in social work, denoting a process of educational exchange and professional interaction completely different from that of a first-line supervisor in industry (Kaslow, 1972).

This does not mean that there are absolutely no social services where bureaucratic organization should be adequate. Large-scale standardized programs of economic assistance and systems of social security fit better into the framework of bureaucracy than into any alternative model. But the majority of social services do not: in sociocultural treatment; in institutional care; in social action; and in most of the informational social services, impersonality, parcelization of the work process, and programmed supervision actually inhibit the achievement of the social service end.

Other important elements of social welfare activity clearly anti-thetical to bureaucratic organization and its structural norms can be identified:

1. Innovation in welfare requires central activities such as research, policy planning, and experimentation with new approaches to services. The elasticity, adaptiveness, imagination, and freedom from traditional patterns of thinking required for successful innovation are simply not possible in bureaucratic organizations constructed to follow faithfully the well-trodden paths.

2. The delivery of services requires responsiveness to the needs of the client and individualized attention to a growing variety of small-scale social situations. Since bureaucracy is designed to deal with the typical, not with the ideographically unique, its bias toward imperson-ality leads it to eliminate everything that is individually significant and unforeseen.

3. Social action requires initiative, charisma, and risk and has many characteristics of a social movement (Killian and Turner, 1957). Bu-reaucracy, with its conservatism, its overdeveloped internal complexity, and its inability to relate to any social micro-environment is the antith-esis of a social movement. Its unwillingness to take risks leads to in-action more often than to action, social or otherwise.

4. Bureaucracy gives birth to institutional interests directed toward the continuing existence, expansion, security, and stability of the struc-ture irrespective of its functional content (Michels, 1962). Institutional interests can motivate people to action just as powerfully as any per-sonal end; in their pursuit, members of the organization can be most ruthless and unscrupulous with good conscience because any personal gain that may accrue to them is only the indirect by-product of the greater glory of the institution to which all are so selflessly dedicated. It may also be noted that the obvious material interests of welfare per-sonnel push them into opposition to the interests of their clients, an opposition which is usually glossed over by ideologies of service.

By contrast, social welfare is a field where interests are numerous and the interest situations particularly delicate (Dahrendorf, 1965). There is a difference between potential and actual clients as well as between their respective interest positions; furthermore, various client groups are often competing for the same scarce resources. Thus the interest position of most welfare clients is more vulnerable than the position of any other group of users of public services.

All these factors make social services structured as bureaucracies questionable in regard to their ability to focus on the object of their services, the client group.

Administration in Social Welfare.

Is there any alternative to bureaucratic organization for the administration of social services? A search for alternatives that are practical (applicable within a reasonable time) must necessarily start with what exists and seek to remedy the negative aspects of the almost universal dominion of bureaucratic organization in the field of welfare. The comparative study of such attempts has uncovered a surprising number of new forms in various countries; this comparison alone should point to the possibility of applying these in nations other than their place of origin.

Is there, however, a systematic answer to the question of alternatives? Could a pattern be devised in which all these individual experiences and experiments would fit, that would provide us with criteria beyond pure trial and the correction of error? Since there is no such answer, it must be evolved piecemeal, a consideration which justifies the present approach.

The five classes of social welfare services (economic assistance, institutional care, sociopsychological treatment, specialized information, and social action) can be structured according to one of the four basic types of cooperating groups, and administered accordingly. However, there are a number of binding conditions that must be taken into account in each case when a social service is established and its administrative type selected: *(a)* the territorial reach of the service—local, regional, national, or international; *(b)* the time horizon of a service on the continuum, from short to long term; *(c)* the problem level considered for the service, from simple to gradually more complex problem situations; *(d)* the degree of specialization of the service or of professionals within the service, from all-purpose work groups with non-specialized members to progressively more detailed specialization.

Using the elements listed, a system of social services administration could be based on nine typical institutional forms, four oriented directly to the delivery of services to clients and five serving the system and its total functioning.*

ADMINISTRATIVE FORMS FOR SERVICE DELIVERY

The four administrative forms, which cover a vast array of services, include: first aid groups, treatment teams, treatment institutions, and social security networks.

First Aid Groups. These groups composed of volunteers or nonspecialized professionals, for the smallest territorial units, would be the most generally used all-purpose instruments for simple tasks such as providing information, triggering and directing small-scale social action, and mobilizing resources for special local situations which are not covered by the large-scale economic assistance services.

The administrative type of first-aid groups would be the leadership group or the even simpler, primary cooperative group (when no continuity in time is required). The advantages are simplicity and comparative economy that give the form widest applicability irrespective of the level of economic development of the environment. These groups, operating in great numbers, could take upon themselves the mass of simple welfare problems that today are either left untended or clog the channels and overtax the capacities of professional welfare services. In this way professional service institutions could turn to only those tasks that require their professional competence.

This type would include such already existing examples as: citizens' advice bureaus, providing information on social and other essential services through volunteers; neighborhood councils, consisting of elected volunteers within a community, for a broad range of social concerns with the power to initiate local referenda, to raise funds, and take some simple regulative decisions; community development groups, organized in various parts of the world according to the respective ideologies within the limits of available resources; and social welfare committees as parts of other volunteer bodies, such as trade unions,

* The titles are optional, used here primarily as shorthand designations.

hospitals, schools, and oriented toward welfare tasks for the clientele of the specific auspice.

Treatment Teams. For complex tasks of sociopsychological treatment that do not require institutional care, treatment teams, composed of highly trained specialists, can be effective. The wider the spectrum of specialties represented on the team, the wider the span of problems the team can handle, the longer the time span, and the greater the territorial diameter of its circle of action.

Treatment teams should be team organizations functioning on the basis of informational openness and positional equality of their members. They can serve as coordinating and consulting centers for first aid groups and, in turn, can depend upon the larger welfare institutions for support with expensive equipment and, possibly, some ancillary services.

The neighborhood service center is an illustration of this type, organized as an autonomous agency for the delivery of a variety of social welfare services such as economic assistance, information, and treatment. This can be viewed as a prototype of the future treatment team. It is different from the traditional welfare department in being, to a greater or lesser degree, independent of the governmental administrative system; however, it still retains a number of characteristics of bureaucratic organizations, particularly hierarchical relationships as well as its own auxiliary services, separate for each center.

There are, obviously, situations where a single individual can deliver a welfare service. These situations range from simple initiatives and interventions requiring no special training to highly trained and specialized services. An example of the latter is the private practice of social work. In the American context this form offers an important alternative since it removes the social stigma from the helping process, for welfare clients particularly (Piliavin, 1968). The system would have to develop a means of controlling possible abuses, perhaps through the policy-planning and coordinating teams. The treatment teams could serve as sources of consultation for the private practitioner.

Treatment Institutions. These organizations would continue to assume those aspects of sociopsychological treatment and rehabilitation that have the longest time requirement as well as a need for stability, comparative isolation, and an expensive material infrastructure (e.g. buildings, equipment). Their probable development would be from the present hierarchic organization to an association of specialized professional teams. One can expect that for a considerable time they will continue to have at least some of their own auxiliary support services, thus retaining a mixed character where teams will operate within a framework of bureaucracy, but with hierarchy being mitigated, as they evolve toward interdependence between the professional service teams and the auxiliary service teams.

Social Security Networks. These structures would administer the basic programs of economic assistance, including not only social insurance but all forms of benefits aimed at broad, general categories of people and situations defined by their characteristics in the abstract rather than case by case. They would continue to function as hierarchical organizations, tending toward automation of routine operations in their work process. Both their time horizon and their territorial reach would tend to be maximal, including a network of possible local branch offices. Special mechanisms of control by members and users should be perfected to counteract possible bureaucratic and technocratic tendencies in large social security systems. Their contacts with other operational parts of the service system should be systematic and constant as their benefits and interventions constitute the background against which special need situations are diagnosed and treated.

ADMINISTRATIVE FORMS FOR SYSTEM FUNCTIONING

The following five services function in terms of the total systems operation rather than in terms of direct services to clients.

Auxiliary Service Teams. These teams would handle personnel training, finance and bookkeeping, supplies procurement, maintenance of buildings and equipment, security, handling and retrieval of general information, and, possibly, other elements of internal administration. The central difference is that these services would no longer be internal to each operational organization but would function as autonomously organized agencies in specified relations, by contract or otherwise, to the operational services. Thus, just as most operational types in the social service system will be organized as teams, it becomes appropriate also to provide a similar structure for the essential auxiliary services,

thereby replacing the relationship of subordination by one of interdependence. This alternative has, in addition, the advantage of being
in most instances more economical and efficient.

Policy Planning Teams. These units are the main mechanism for
integrating a system of social services at whatever level of inclusiveness.
The name denotes the genus; many existing species (planning commis-
sions, community chests, and parliamentary committees) can be studied
comparatively, adapted, and developed. No other form than team organization could serve for an activity that has to involve high-level
professional specialists as well as the representatives of all major interest
groups concerned with welfare services: practitioners, consumers, and
clients. The boundary conditions depend on the size of the system to
be integrated, from local to world-wide. The integrating activities
include setting down the general rules for the system, planning its
over-all goals, determining priorities, as well as financial planning
for the system.

Research Teams. The fundamental tasks of analyzing and defining new
social problems, new methods, and new services for the solution of
problems, of evaluating existing problem situations, and of appraising
ongoing or projected services are assumed by research teams. Patterned
as team organizations, research teams can operate singly or in various
clusters suggested by considerations of national resources and/or
rare skills.

Two subtypes, for fundamental and applied or evaluative research,
will have to be distinguished and are likely to differ not only in their
goal orientations but also in the pertinent boundary conditions. Fundamental research teams are likely to have longer time horizons, a wider
clientele (not necessarily restricted by rational boundaries), the capability for approaching more complex problems, and a higher degree of
specialization in their personnel.

Research teams are also the most natural setting for higher forms of
training in the professions of welfare. Their links with the welfare
system are through contracts with individual operating service organizations or with the policy-planning teams.

Arbitration Teams. Existing forms of arbitration in several social
security systems, as well as specialized courts and quasi-judicial agencies in the field of labor and social insurance law, represent examples

that could be expanded for the adjustment and settlement of disputes throughout the system of social services. If the individual organization is autonomous and the links within the system are established through contract and other arrangements based on the adherence of all partners, a growing number of disputes concerning these compacts can be expected. In their handling the equal position of the contestants has to be respected, and disputes should not be allowed to stop essential services. Arbitration seems to fit best these two requirements: the parties are represented on the arbitration teams; and the arbitration methods are free from the cumbersome requirements of court procedure. The form is also adaptable enough, so that its boundary conditions—extension in place and time, problem level, degree of specialization—can be changed as the situation may require.

Coordinating Teams. These teams would be in charge of intrasystem as well as intersystem operating coordination. Team organizations, composed of delegates of institutions or networks in the social service field, would operate on a day-to-day trouble-shooting basis in all the myriad little frictions and problems that endanger the smooth flow of the service. The question of consumer- and public-interest representation on coordinating teams is open; possibly delegates of these groups should have simply the status of observers on the coordinating teams whose orientation is mainly technical. Here as well, boundary conditions depend on the size of the coordinating task.

These five teams function in relation to the social welfare system; but clearly the ultimate beneficiary of a well-operating system is the client.

The Dynamics of the Social Welfare System

A HYPOTHETICAL MODEL

The material basis of the system of social welfare services should be the planned distribution of the social product, available through governmental as well as nongovernmental channels, depending on the traditions and preferences of each country. These should be specified by policy-planning teams and administered by an autonomous and neutral banking system. The result of this arrangement would be the

availability of funds to organizations established by accepted procedures and fulfilling the generally required conditions of the broader
social system.

The formal initiative for establishing social welfare organizations
would belong only to the personnel providing the services and to the
potential consumers of the services. Both groups, suitably represented,
would express their intention to have the service established. Informally, the initiative should also come from research teams and/or
policy-planning teams which would not have a formal role in the creation of an organization but could stimulate the process by drawing
attention to a situation in order for the service-team members and the
consumers to begin service development.

The central task at this point would be the establishment of objective
criteria for both the need for the service and the conditions for its performance. When a formal offer is made by personnel and consumers
to establish a social welfare organization, applied research teams would
evaluate the needs and conditions; any negative finding would force
a reconsideration by workers and consumers, but would not be a veto.

At periodic intervals the results of a service and its continuing need
would be evaluated by applied research teams; the results would be
made public but need not imply immediate change in status of the
organizations involved. Negative findings could only influence policy-
planning teams to reconsider the allocation of resources for a given
purpose or to reformulate the conditions for the performance of a
service.

If potential consumers refuse a service, though there are professionals
who consider it necessary, policy-planning teams together with other
interested groups could initiate a change in the definition of the target
"consumer" group to allow for innovation and change in service delivery.

Protective services which are not voluntarily sought (psychiatric
care, drug addiction, child placement) should be performed only under
special controls, with evaluation at shorter intervals by policy-planning
teams together with interested community groups.

Conflicts of interests would have to be adjusted by consultation,
participation, and, where necessary, arbitration. The outlay in time
and resources implied in this process is the social consequence of a

complex society. Criteria of efficiency would no longer be applicable in the purely economic sense.

The achievement of new forms of cooperation and administration is not a purely technical pursuit. It involves interests, beliefs, and values, all things that move people deeply and irrationally. These deeper currents of motivation are bound to be affected by the changes in progress (Pusić, 1968).

Welfare becomes more and more related to the basic problem of security in society and in this way becomes a prerequisite for any innovating experimentation. New forms of administering the network of welfare services are therefore likely to have an even greater effect on deep-set feelings than administrative reforms generally. This means that any change is not simply a matter of convincing a few specialists of the justification of a case for change. It is likely to be a struggle of no mean intensity and long duration, an overcoming of resistances, a matter of commitment and of engagement. It is an effort required whenever there are, in Jung's words, "greater things that want to become real."

References

Barnard, Chester I. *The Function of the Executive.* Cambridge Mass., Harvard University Press, 1940.

Bennis, Warren G. "Post-bureaucratic Leadership," *Trans-action,* VI, No. 9 (1969), 44–51.

Dahrendorf, Ralf. *Class and Class Conflict in Industrial Society.* Stanford, Calif., Stanford University Press, 1965.

Emery, Frederick L., and Eric Trist. "The Causal Texture of Organizational Environments," in Frederick L. Emery, ed., *Systems Thinking,* pp. 421–576. Baltimore, Penguin Books, 1969.

Friedmann, Georges. *The Anatomy of Work.* New York, Free Press, 1962.

Galbraith, John K. *The New Industrial State.* Boston, Houghton Mifflin, 1967.

Kaslow, Florence W. *Issues in Human Services.* San Francisco, Jossey-Bass, 1972.

Killian, Lewis M., and Ralph H. Turner. *Collective Behavior.* Englewood Cliffs, N.J., Prentice-Hall, Inc., 1957.

Michels, Robert. *Political Parties.* New York, Free Press, 1962.

Piliavin, Irving. "Restructuring the Provision of Social Services," *Social Work,* XIII, No. 1 (1968), 34–41.

Pusić, Eugen. "The Political Community and the Future of Welfare," in J. S.

Morgan, ed., *Welfare and Wisdom,* pp. 61-96. Toronto, University of Toronto Press, 1968.

Titmuss, Richard M. *Essays on "The Welfare State."* New Haven, Conn., Yale University Press, 1959.

Weber, Max. *The Theory of Social and Economic Organization.* New York, Free Press, 1947.

LOUIS G. TORNATZKY

Experimental Social Innovation in Social Work

THE PRINCIPAL issue to be faced by social work as a profession in the coming decade is not whether it is relevant, or involved, or attempting social change. All these descriptions generally reflect the thrust of current social work practice. Rather, concern should be whether the relevance is real, the involvement is appropriate, or the change is positive. In short, the concern should be not over morals but methods. The modal comment used to end an article on social work practice is to say that "further research is needed." This has never been more true than now, yet the relationship between research and changes in field practice is moot. Social workers, like others working with real social issues, are largely using ill-defined methods, with unknown or negative outcomes, and often on unsuitable populations.

Consider the illustrious history of clinical social work and the related fields of clinical psychology and psychiatry. It has not been convincingly demonstrated that conversational interaction between client and worker has a predictable and consistent effect on the alleviation of symptoms, problems, or aberrant behavior patterns. The outcome research that does exist (Bandura, 1969; Bergin, 1966; Wallace, 1967) tends to support a view that verbal therapy may have *some* effect, but that in no way is the effect consistently positive or of appreciable magnitude. Yet, in spite of these data, which have been available for a number of years, many schools of social work continue to socialize their students into the role model of the clinical practitioner. Here the ac-

cumulation of negative data on the effectiveness of professional practices has had very limited impact on the modification of those practices.

The community organization orientation in social work practice
is subject to related criticisms. Here, however, the problem is a lack
of research, not an abundance of negative data. While representing
a broader-gauged approach with its interest in social change, organization building, community planning, and client participation, community organization has a limited empirical base. In an extensive review
of the empirical and descriptive literature on community organizational
practice Rothman concludes (1971, p. 102) that "there has been a striking paucity of research in community organization, a factor that has
inhibited the development of this area of professional practice in social
work."

Some hard questions about community organization practice need
to be asked and answered. What is the relationship between the establishment of an elaborate community planning apparatus and the
development of effective programs? To what degree does community
participation build "community" in a significant portion of the target
population? Do conflict and confrontation with existing agencies produce more and/or better public services? Can political solutions produce social innovations? Currently there is little data to answer these
questions definitively.

These comments underscore the need to find out how social interventions work, and how well they work. This impetus for the greater
reliance on data comes from other directions. As of this writing a strong
push for systematic program development and evaluation comes from
the chronic lack of funds for public services. While the expenditures
for these services have increased significantly in the last two decades,
the problems remain often unresolved or worse, and the problem of
a vanishing tax base continues. There are clearly emergent limitations
on the total amount of public expenditures that can be expected in
the next decade. Unless good solutions are found to new and recurrent
problems, the cost of bad solutions will always exceed available resources.

Aside from the limited availability of resources, we should become
skeptical about resources per se. There is a series of findings which
indicate that there is only a limited relationship between a good pro-

gram and an expensive one. The Coleman report (1966) found a limited relationship between educational achievement and indices of resource allocation such as class size and materials. In a recent study Fairweather, Sanders, and Tornatzky (1973) found a minimal relationship between the amount of financial and staff resources that mental hospitals have, and the degree to which they adopt innovative programs. Another author found only a limited relationship between the amount of public expenditures and the quality of public services (Sharkansky, 1967). While this general picture is not totally clear, a cynic might comment that increased expenditures for social services have probably produced higher salaries for social service professionals, a more elaborate administrative mechanism, nicer physical working conditions, and little direct benefit for the client. It does point out the need for a way of expending resources in a manner that will produce a more attractive cost-benefit relationship.

Along with the problem of getting more program for resources expended is the related problem of choosing among different approaches to solving different social-human problems. Much of the previous comments is related to decisions about single programs, or programs considered in the abstract. A related problem is when program continuation and/or termination decisions should be made. At the present time there is little systematic way to make a rational input to these policy decisions between program alternatives. The program developer has often little to go on other than his own hunches and/or professional opinion. Unfortunately, professional opinion often merely reflects an identification with a set of myths. The result is of course predictable in terms of duplication of bad programs, the creation of old programs with new names, and general confusion about what to do. The need is for an adjunct to the policy-making process which would clearly specify outcome information and costs as well as the probability of negative or null outcomes.

In addition to information about program outcome a means to communicate about program content is needed which will provide information about programs both good and bad and will serve to avoid duplication and waste motion. The problem of dissemination of program information is intimately related to the problem of finding a common language to describe either good or bad programs. In other words, programs on paper reflect more the language of the writer than the features of the program itself.

One can argue for a closer relationship between research and practice, but it would be foolhardy to ignore the problems of a closer liaison. As currently structured, the world of practice is divorced from the world of research, and vice versa. This is true whether one is considering theoretically oriented research or program evaluation research (as currently operationalized). Consider some of the disparities between the roles of practitioner and researcher. The practitioner's time frame is usually immediate in response to emergent crises; the researcher's time is longitudinal in response to reflective consideration of data. The practitioner is protective of a program; the researcher plays the role of skeptic and snoop. The practitioner's language reflects the real world and his clients; the researcher's language too often relies on statistics, arcane concepts, and academic protocol. The practitioner usually has some personal investment in, or identification with, his program; the program evaluation researcher must by definition be "objective." If considered systematically, the conflict between people who run programs and those who evaluate them is inevitable.

Unfortunately, most of the literature that discusses program evaluation research (Weiss, 1972; Zurcher and Bonjean, 1970) merely reiterates the above-mentioned problems rather than offering alternatives to the current model. However, the relationship between social research and social work practice can be considered as a special example of the larger problem of interinstitutional and intrainstitutional conflict and coordination. In his comprehensive review of the literature on the diffusion of innovation, Havelock (1969) incorporates the concept of "linkages" to account for how knowledge development interrelates with knowledge dissemination and knowledge use. A matrix of mutual communication and influence must exist between the disparate components of this system in order for research to have impact on practice. Similarly, in his general discussion of inter- and intraorganization coordination and linkages, Litwak (1961; Litwak and Hylton, 1962) mentions a number of variables which have direct relevance for the appropriateness of different linkage systems and organizational structures. These have special applicability to our current discussion.

Litwak argues that the nature of coordination or linkage necessary

between organizational units will largely be determined by the degree
of conflict, differences in structure and process, and degree of awareness of the need for coordination between the two units. Simple and
straightforward coordinating tasks can be accomplished by rationalistic
(bureaucratic) devices such as formal communications, memos, and
letters. In contrast, if a large degree of conflict and uncertainty exists,
coordination and linkage can only be achieved by informal process
and structure such as face-to-face interaction. For example, changes
in the parking assignments of workers in a factory might be made by
a note in the pay envelope; changes in working conditions and hours
would likely necessitate a considerable degree of face-to-face negotiation (linkage) between workers and management. If we consider the
inherent conflict, and differences in language, subculture, and process,
between the world of research and the world of practice, the difficulty
of achieving linkage should be apparent.

These comments are not meant to imply that a better program development and evaluation model will be sufficient to promote a greater
impact of research on practice. Unfortunately, the archives of funding
agencies are filled with the bones of well-run, well-evaluated, and
effective programs that never survived beyond their grant periods.
It is a moot point whether *any* new programs would be needed if those
past experimental programs that were successful had been implemented
on a widespread basis. Havelock's linkage notion (1969) also includes
the linkage between the product and the user. This is the link that
produces actual widespread social change. If it exists, the program
developer has succeeded; if it does not succeed, then time, money,
and good ideas have been wasted. The process of social change is in-
separable from the problem of getting research to make an impact on
practice.

The research model that needs to be implemented would have to
deal with a number of crucial issues:

1. It would need to work definitive information on whether social
interventions work or not, whether they work better than nothing
at all, and whether they work better than current practices.

2. It would need to expedite choices between alternative social interventions.

3. It would need to provide program descriptive information that is replicable and understandable.

4. It would need to attack the conflict between research and practice in such a way that a bridge of coordination could be constructed and maintained.

5. It would need to deal with the entire process of change, from innovation to adoption.

Experimental Social Innovation

What is proposed is a new professional role that social workers and others can come to adopt. This is the role of the experimental social innovator (ESI) as initially described by Fairweather (1967). Rather than traditionally separating practice and research, what this professional role will do is integrate these activities into a single comprehensive Gestalt. Referring back to our linkages between research and practice, we intend to eliminate the disparity of the two roles. This integration will be accomplished by having people become both practitioners *and* researchers, program developers *and* program evaluators, social change agents *and* students of the social change process. By being a part of the research process it will provide the decision-making device for determining whether programs work, and whether they work better. By combining the language of practice and research a more universal way of communicating about programs should eventuate. What, then, are the specifics of the ESI role. There are two general areas of action research: model building and implementation.

MODEL BUILDING

By model building it is meant that the experimental social innovator is to tackle the problem of ineffective social organization by the design of, and truly experimental longitudinal evaluation of, alternative social subsystems. This will be program development, but with some added activities. Not only will the practitioner-researcher be designing a program that he understands and feels, but one in which what is done is operationally defined so others could conceivably replicate the experiment. The hoped-for outcome of the program will not be "success," but specified and measurable outcome dependent variables. Input of clients to the program will be on the basis of their needs and desires, but also will be determined by such contingencies as the necessity for random assignment, the need to match client variables, sampling problems, and design requirements. If the total project includes multiple parallel or alternative subprograms, the project will be fielded in ways in which a legitimate scientific comparison between these programs can be made.

It should be clear that an argument is being made for a highly demanding type of program research: true experimentation. It is time for rejection of the sole use of correlational and survey techniques for evaluating social programs. Only the experimental model (Anderson, 1971; Campbell and Stanley, 1963) can allow for causal inference relative to program outcome. Only the experimental model necessitates the concrete operational definition of program content. Only the experimental model demands advance specification and definition of outcome criteria. In short, if research is to be done it might as well be good research.

All this is not merely academic chatter. The combination of a meaningful social program and a demanding experimental evaluation can be accomplished. An example would be instructive, and the community lodge model-building effort of Fairweather *et al.* (1969) is a good one.

The project was intended to take up the problem of recidivism of chronic hospitalized mental patients. From previous work of Fairweather (1964) it had been determined that the principal negative correlates of recidivism in this population were lack of employment and lack of social support, such as a family. Accordingly, a model subsystem was instituted in the community to which patients were discharged. This subsystem (the community lodge) incorporated group living, autonomous functioning, employment, and differentiated statuses for its members. Specifically, a communal dormitory was set up in which the former patients lived and worked together. The members had the power to manipulate formal and informal incentives, determine their membership, and establish their rules of living. A group-run janitorial business provided employment and status, and also served to reinforce the group structure and process. The staff role was largely one of furthering group autonomy until staff presence could be totally withdrawn. On a random basis volunteers were assigned either to the lodge, or to traditional aftercare facilities.

A sophisticated experimental design was employed, and outcome data was gathered for the experiment (lodge) and control (traditional aftercare) subsystems concerning employment, recidivism, behavioral ratings, and attitudinal items. Both subsystems were followed in this manner for a period of four years during which additional data were gathered regarding the internal processes of each system. Statistical comparisons between the two systems indicated an overwhelming advantage in terms of outcome criteria in favor of the lodge. Additional correlational analysis of internal process clarified and confirmed the rationale for designing a model subsystem that provided employment and social support. In other words, success for participants in the lodge system was related to the opportunity for group support and employment.

If we recast this plan into a series of discrete tasks and role demands we could get a clear idea of experimental social innovation model-building research. It should be reemphasized that *all* these tasks are to be accomplished by the ESI person or ESI team. Whether these tasks will be carried out by a single ESI person or a team is, of course, related to the size of the project. However, it should be pointed out that even in a team context all members of the team should be involved in all the subtasks of the generic ESI role. This weaving together of action-practitioner skills and research skills, will be apparent. The steps are as follows:

1. Defining a Problem. Here the ESI person relies on four sources of information. He relies on his own experiential knowledge, and observation in the naturalistic social context. He relies on the scientific literature. He relies on the expressed needs and complaints of those directly affected by the nonadapting social system. He relies on his own previous research. It should be emphasized that the definition of the problem relies just as much on the street knowledge of the client and practitioner as it does on formal information sources. The development of new social innovation must *always* be strongly influenced by ovservations of participants in the "real world."

2. Developing an Alternative. Here the most important parameters that

relate to the desired outcome or outcomes must be sorted out and designed into an operationally definable program or programs. In essence,
a service program is designed, but one which will keep its initial form
as nearly as possible for the duration of the research. By adhering to
the experimental modality it is essential that the operational details
of the program be specified. In other words, the program becomes
equivalent to the "treatment" as the treatment *must* be operationally
defined. Once again the importance of informal knowledge and input
must be emphasized. Yet the continuing input and influence of informal
sources should not be overemphasized. While one is indeed designing
a program, the fact that this program is also experimental research
cannot be denied. The initial design of the program *is* the operational
definition of the experimental manipulation. To maintain the integrity
of the experimental design the main defining features of the innovative
subsystem cannot be changed during the duration of the program.

3. *Designing the Formal Experiment.* Sampling units and procedures,
matching and randomizing, measurement and instrumentation, must
be dealt with. A control group must be designated and made comparable in all nonexperimental aspects. More often than not the control
subsystem is an existing social practice. For example, in the Fairweather
lodge study (Fairweather *et al.,* 1969) volunteer subjects were randomly
assigned either to the lodge (experimental treatment) or to the normal
hospital aftercare program (control group). In a context such as a secondary school setting, volunteer subjects might be randomly chosen
either to continue in their normal school program (control group) *or* to
participate in an alternative school social system (experimental group).
Thus, an innovation is not compared with *no* treatment, but with existing treatment of the problem under consideration. In this way the
objection of "denial of services" can be met.

4. *Action Phase.* The subsystems are put in operation as designed and
are continued for an extensive but predetermined length of time. Process and outcome data are collected. It should be reemphasized that
the ESI professional is engaged in both service and research activities
during the action phase. There is no complete separation of role except
in time and space. Thus, the ESI person or team is responsible both
for the individuals in the experimental program and for the continued
gathering of data.

5. Data Analysis. Data are analyzed to see if the innovative subsystem works. If it does, effective dissemination activities will be pursued. If not, but empirical clues are present to indicate how it might be changed, an additional model-building experiment might be in order.

IMPLEMENTATION RESEARCH

The problem of implementation returns us again to the initial problem of integrating research and practice. Much of the previous comments have been related to inputing science and technology to the artistry of the program developer. It is also desirable to input a research orientation into the adhocracy of the "change agent." In short, there is a need for implementation research. This research activity is an essential part of the ESI role. One of the difficulties in social innovation is to get institutions and individuals to adopt models which have demonstrated success in dealing with social problems. Social change did not result from the invention of the wheel, but from the widespread adoption of its use. Unfortunately, the tactics and strategies for getting institutions to change are often incomplete, or of undemonstrated validity. Not only does the ESI have an obligation to disseminate models that work, but he needs to define the parameters of institutional influence and adoption.

As indicated, the lodge research (Fairweather *et al.*, 1969) demonstrated a highly effective model program. The question became how to get those institutions most in need of such an innovation (state and federal psychiatric hospitals) to become aware of, and adopt, the model. It became readily apparent that there were little experimental data directly concerned with the problem at hand. The Fairweather, Sanders, and Tornatzky (1973) hospital change study has been an attempt to fill this gap.

From a tactical point of view, two phases of the experimental implementation project were needed. Phase I would focus on approaching and persuading the target hospitals in order to generate awareness of the lodge program, interest in its application, and verbal agreement to adopt it. Phase 2 would concentrate on an experimental effort in providing assistance to those institutions which wanted to adopt the program.

Phase I resulted in a complex experimental design aimed at a population of 255 mental hospitals. Four variables were built into the design: geographic locale (comparing urban versus rural hospitals); governmental affiliation (comparing state versus federal hospitals); formal organizational power structure (comparing entering the hospital at different levels in the organizational hierarchy); and alternative modes of persuasion (comparing written materials versus workshop versus demonstration projects as methods of persuading the hospitals). In addition to these manipulated variables, a host of internal process variables was measured during the experiment. This approaching and persuading phase of the research took nearly two years to accomplish, during which a team of researchers crisscrossed the country by telephone, letter, workshop, and demonstration counsultation. These efforts resulted in a smaller sample of twenty-five hospitals which were persuaded to adopt the lodge program. Two adoption-assistance conditions were established. For half of these hospitals the research team set up face-to-face action consultation visits; for the other half of the hospitals, a do-it-yourself manual was prepared which outlined in a stepwise fashion the specific tasks of lodge implementation. All of the twenty-five hospitals were followed up for at least one year, or until either a lodge was established or implementation activities died for lack of interest.

Without going into the specific findings of the study (see Fairweather, Sanders and Tornatzky, 1973) we should emphasize that what was being attempted was an effort to implement social change in the form of an institutional adoption of an innovation and study the change process at the same time. The research team had limited belief in the "knowledge" concerning change in such an organizational context, and their skepticism was at least partially borne out. Many of these variables which were theoretically important were not empirically so, and vice versa. What should be appreciated is the likelihood that every implementation effort has a somewhat different set of change buttons to push. The strategy to follow, and the specific tactics to use, should be distilled from the literature, personal experience, and a strong dose of hard data derived directly from change efforts.

Such ESI implementation research can be considered as a set of discrete tasks, some of which have direct research implications. Consider the following:

Defining the Target(s). Who, or what, needs to be moved to obtain widespread adoption of the change? What characteristics of the target institutions have potential implications for the change effort? In the hospital change study it was felt that state hospitals versus Veterans Administration hospitals and urban versus rural hospitals were considerations with implications for change, and these variables were directly examined in the experimental design. In an experiment designed to implement an educational innovation, different degrees of change, or processes of change, might be observed comparing public versus parochial schools, or wealthy versus poor schools. If there is doubt regarding the effect of such variables they should be built into the research design. It is interesting to point out that most of these steps would come under the research rubric of "defining the sample." Yet, divorced from the research process this step of thinking through the target of a change effort would likely result in more effective change agentry. Here, perhaps, a research concern could lead directly to more efficient practice. Getting operational definitions is merely good tactics.

Defining the Parameters of Approaching and Persuading. Who, and how many people, should be contacted? How should they be contacted? What modes of communication should be used? In what social context should persuasion efforts be made? What specific behavioral commitments need to be obtained and when? All these questions and others more directly related to the idiosyncratic features of the specific innovation need to be considered, and either controlled for, measured, or manipulated in the experimental implementation design. This is not to deny that many change tactics are difficult to define operationally. What is being argued is that many of them can be, and one can learn a great deal about the relative efficacy of change tactics by subjecting them to the rigor of experimental evaluation.

Defining the Parameters of Adoption. Given a willingness to adopt whatever potential support activities need to be engaged in, the specific nature of the innovation will have a significant impact on the degree of these activities. For example, a decision by a medical practitioner to adopt a new drug need only be followed by sale and distribution support activities. In contrast, the decision to adopt a lodge innovation necessitated months of group effort, consultative support, role change, and so on. The potential support activities need to be catalogued, and those most clearly relevant should be examined in the context of an implementation research.

Recycling of Implementation Research Data. Clearly, the data obtained in implementation research should be used to foster further social change. For example, an initial implementation research might compare methods *A*, *B*, and *C* in fostering the acceptance of an innovation. The research might discover that method *C* works, that *A* and *B* are useless, but that a combination of *B* and *D* might work. A second implementation effort might directly compare *C* and *B+D*, thus both gaining further tactical information and continuing the change activities.

From these descriptions of principal ESI activities—model-building and implementation research—it should be clear that what is proposed is a complex professional role. The intent is to develop a strategy of social change that is bounded by data and rationality. It should also be clear that this role includes, and extends, many aspects of traditional social work roles. The question that must be raised is: what are the training requirements for such a role, and how might traditional social work curriculum be modified to incorporate such a role?

The ESI Professional and Social Work Training

Social work training would seem to be an ideal locus for development of an ESI role. Of all the social science related areas it has the clearest service orientation. Its curriculum is explicitly multidisciplinary. Its students and faculty are typically chosen from among those who have had previous experience in service settings. As a profession it is established, yet sufficiently flexible to allow for a new direction. Yet there are some difficulties.

PROBLEM FOCUS RATHER THAN PROCESS FOCUS

While social work is ostensibly addressing itself to social problems, it is more likely perpetuating schools of social and therapeutic intervention. Both within, and between, schools of social work are large and powerful fiefdoms competing against one another both for resources and for a constituency. The behaviorists, the clinicians, the community organizers, the income strategists, all at best coexist, and at worst do not interact. From the description of ESI activity it should be apparent that what is needed to develop is a commitment to problem solution. Social work training needs to be more eclectic in its general approach and more skeptical about the universal efficacy of any one intervention approach. This eclecticism should not be the "seat-of-the-pants" variety but a data-based one. Rather than a commitment to particular interventions, there should be a commitment to a process which will enable a rational choice between intervention strategies and tactics. The criterion should be what works, and not what is congruent with the prevailing ethos of the field.

EMPHASIS ON PROGRAMMATIC RESEARCH

The emphasis on effectiveness and program utility can only be bought about if there is a concomitant commitment to programmatic research of the type that we have described. Model-building and/or implementation research should be at the core of social work training. The ESI-oriented social work professional should have the opportunity during his graduate training to engage in model-building and/or implementation research of a longitudinal nature. This commitment to programmatic research is no minor one. By "programmatic research" is meant a single-minded attack on a social problem that would proceed ideally from initial model-building, through implementation research, and eventually result in widespread adoption. Needless to say, the time frame is not months, but years.

At the least, the research skills base of social work needs to be expanded. This might necessitate an extension of training beyond the master's degree in social work. It is apparent that most social work professionals are only vaguely familiar with parametric and nonparametric statistics, multivariate correlational techniques, experimental design, quasi-experimental design, and so forth. Aside from mere familiarity with these skills, their programmatic importance needs to be understood. There is only limited appreciation of these skills as "tools" in a career of program development, problem solution, and change agentry. The utility of the scientific method needs to be reemphasized and its use on trivial problems reduced.

MULTIDISCIPLINARY PERSONS

While social work training and curricula incorporate material from many disciplines, the total impact is likely to be fragmented rather than coherent. Sociology, economics, and psychology, for example, should not be taught as separate disciplines, but as interrelated alternatives. Once again, problem orientation can serve as an integrating feature. The intent would be to make disciplinary inputs add to understanding and solution of the problem rather than the problem fitting the discipline.

ORGANIZATIONAL SUPPORT AND ACADEMIC NORMS

The training program that we have been describing is clearly in contradiction to many prevailing academic norms. It involves significant reciprocal alterations in faculty as well as student roles. To succeed it must have some changes in the organizational reward system and structure of the university, and of the profession.

For example, since the research focus of faculty and students will be on longitudinal programmatic efforts, frequent publications will be impossible. The publication ethic will need to be altered. Similarly, since the training and research program will be directly action-oriented, a significant, continuing effort will be needed to develop and maintain liaison with the community. Academic separation will be impossible to maintain. In addition, a more explicit problem focus might necessitate a structural reorganization of some schools. Currently, schools of social work are divided into huddles of community organization specialists, clinicians, behaviorists. A more functional organization would be along the lines of problem definitions and task forces.

TOWARD DEPROFESSIONALIZATION

In addition, the social work profession will have to tolerate a greater degree of ambiguity about its role and tasks. While it may seem paradoxical to discuss deprofessionalization in an article aimed at changes in a professional role, there is evidence to the contrary. The social history of the professions in this country indicates that hidebound conservatism closely follows the achievement of a certain level of prestige. In recent years that has been a growing concern in social work about the trappings of professional status, licensing, maintaining the boundaries of the guild. To maximize the potential impact of the profession, perhaps a greater tolerance for ambiguity needs to be nurtured. Clearly, with only a commitment to applying ESI methodology to social problems, the specifics of "what social workers do" can only evolve in the context of the changing society, and in the light of emerging data.

What, then, have we trained? An action researcher. A problem-oriented researcher. A multidisciplinary person. A program evaluation specialists, clinicians, and behaviorists. A more functional organization stitutions. All of these are compatible with the generic ESI role that has been developed here and all could significantly add to the thrust of social work as it currently exists.

References

Anderson, Barry F. *The Psychology Experiment.* 2d ed.; Belmont, Canada. Brooks/Cole Publishing Co., 1971.

Bandura, Albert. *Principles of Behavior Modification.* New York, Holt, Rinehart, and Winston, 1969.

Bergin, Allen E. "Some Implications of Psychotherapy Research for Therapeutic Practice," *Journal of Abnormal Psychology,* LXXI (1966), 235–46.

Campbell, Donald T., and Julian C. Stanley. *Experimental and Quasi-experimental Design for Research.* Chicago, Rand McNally and Co., 1963.

Coleman, James S. *Equality of Educational Opportunity.* Washington, D.C., U.S. Government Printing Office, 1966.

Fairweather, George W. *Methods for Experimental Social Innovation,* New York, John Wiley and Sons, Inc., 1967.

——, ed. *Social Psychology in Treating Mental Illness.* New York, John Wiley and Sons, Inc., 1964.

Fairweather, George W., David H. Sanders, and Lewis G. Tornatzky, *Creating Change in Mental Health Organization.* Oxford, England, Pergamon Press, 1973

Fairweather, George W., et al. *Community Life for the Mentally Ill.* Chicago, Aldine Publishing Co., 1969.

Havelock, Ronald G. *Planning for Innovation through Dissemination and Utilization of Knowledge.* Ann Arbor, Mich., Center for Research on Utilization of Scientific Knowledge, Institute for Social Research, University of Michigan, 1969.

Litwak, Eugene. "Models of Bureaucracy That Permit Conflict," *American Journal of Sociology,* LXVII (1961), 177–84.

Litwak, Eugene, and Lydia F. Hylton. "Interorganizational Analysis: a Hypothesis on Co-ordinating Agencies," *Administrative Science Quarterly,* VI (1962), 395–420.

Rothman, Jack. "Community Organization Practice," in Henry Maas, ed., *Research in the Social Services: a Five-Year Review,* pp. 70–107. New York, National Association of Social Workers, 1971.

Sharkansky, Ira. "Government Expenditures and Public Services in the American States," *American Political Science Review,* LXI, No. 4 (1967), 1066–77.

Wallace, David. "The Chemung County Evaluation of Casework Service to Dedependent Multiproblem Families," *Social Science Review,* XLI, No. 4 (1967), 379–89.

Weiss, Carol H. *Evaluating Action Programs: Readings in Social Action and Education.* Boston, Allyn and Bacon, Inc., 1972.

Zurcher, Louis A., Jr., and Charles M. Bonjean. *Planned Social Intervention.* Scranton, Pa., Chandler Publishing Co., 1970.

THEODORE LEVINE

Skill in Practice as a Problem in Public Welfare

THE NEW culture heroes of social work, as well as of other helping professions, have become the activists (Grosser, 1965), the advocates (Wineman and Wineman, 1969), the policy, planning, and social action people (Thursz, 1966). Our longing for relevance and our fantasies about the role of professions in the creation of public social policy pose simultaneous threats to our future capacity to provide qualitative, urgently needed human services and to make an impact on public social policy. Policy without sound program can be at best wasteful and at worst a fraud. It is my further contention that among the most serious issues facing professional social work is the negation of skill in practice (Rein, 1970). The need for skills in the planning, administration, and provision of direct services to people, and skill in the practice of social policy, loom as critical issues facing professional social work and the field of public welfare.

The Context: Organizational and Professional

The Community Services Administration is that unit within the Social and Rehabilitation Service of the U.S. Department of Health, Education, and Welfare (HEW) which is charged with the administration of those social services provided for in Titles I (aged), IV (families and children), X (blind), XIV (disabled), and XVI (a combination of aged, blind, and disabled) of the Social Security Act, as amended in 1967.

While the case material drawn upon occurred during the period of September, 1970, to November, 1972, and the social service regulations in effect during that time are undergoing change, the need for skill in practice applies to any new social service regulations or legislation as well as to other human service programs.

The list of services provided by the children's regulations (Title IV) and the adult regulations (Titles I, X, XIV and XVI) of the 1967 amendments were extensive. Child care services, foster care services, services to meet particular needs of families and children (including assistance with educational problems, consumer education, homemaking, and housing problems), health-related services, legal services, and day care were among those services listed in Title IV. The adult regulations included protective services, services to enable persons to remain in, or to return to, their homes or communities, services to meet health needs, self-support services for the handicapped, homemaker services, services to individuals and groups to improve opportunities for social and community participation, among others.

The lack of sound services, in spite of available federal policy and funding, was alarming. The so-called "state plan" for social services was not a plan at all. Although much was made of it, it was more of a grant-in-aid agreement than a plan. The document frequently "committed" the state to the wide range of services which federal policy permitted. It was not unusual for a state to copy verbatim portions of the federal requirement. Federal or state staff, for the purpose of stimulating, monitoring, or evaluating either the social service program or the utilization of those federal dollars claimed for it, was minimal. The states, with few exceptions, developed sketchy, uneven service "systems."

The discrete service most extensively developed with the use of social service dollars was day care. The dollars provided day care for large numbers of children in day care centers. Exactly how many, or whether the numbers served or the quality of program was commensurate with the dollar volume, was unknown. The quality of staff, cost per child, services rendered, indicated wide variation within the same city. Other services which the state plan "committed" the state to for adults and children were completely lacking. Some states (more than will ever own up to it) claimed 75 percent federal reimbursement for so-called "service workers," who in reality were income-maintenance workers. These workers were basically overloaded with the eligibility function, although some provided services. While 75 percent was claimed, federal regulations provided for a 50 percent reimbursement rate for income-maintenance workers. In some states the purchase-of service mechanism was extensively utilized. Information concerning precisely what was being purchased, or for whom, was difficult to ascertain. States, rather than making judgments on which services they would provide directly and which they would purchase, engaged in what was referred to as a "hatch 'em-and-match 'em" approach. If the 25 percent state share could be directly provided or "donated," the state would enter an agreement and draw down the 75 percent federal dollars.

Money, while an important part of the problem, was by no means the sole answer. The "games" which federal and state people played with each other ranged, on the one hand, from complete and utter lack of accountability for millions of dollars to the most intricate reliance on the minutia of federal and state regulations on the other. When money was available, even though limited, lack of skill in practice at all levels frequently resulted in waste or minimal service at the delivery point. The person eligible for a day care service, a homemaker service, a counseling or protective service is entitled to the best which can be offered. The chaotic nature of public welfare at the state and federal level, of course, has its ramifications at the point where a client meets a worker.

The public welfare system has been obsessed by issues surrounding the money payment, has neglected social services, has not implemented service opportunities, and has not demonstrated its capacity to deliver. There are gaps between social policy and legislation and a systematic inability to deliver sound, good-quality human services. To be sure, there are spots and oases of sound practice.

It was within this context that the separation of social services from the money payment took on the most serious ramifications. It was clear that until a regulation requiring a separate administrative and delivery system for the social services, apart from the money-payment system, was developed, the chaos would remain. This, from a practical viewpoint, was more critical than those many sound arguments of a theoretical nature. It also became clear, however, that separation alone would in no way guarantee the delivery of sound services.

Finally, it must be noted that the federal establishment's response to human service has been the creation of a categorical jungle. The provision of social services resides in volumes of federal legislation and scores of federal bureaus and agencies including Housing and Urban Development (HUD), Department of Labor, Social and Rehabilitation Service, Health Services and Mental Health Administration, Office of Child Development, Office of Economic Opportunity, Veterans Administration, Department of Agriculture, and HEW. In addition, each agency has its own maze: Social and Rehabilitation Service has within it the Youth Development and Delinquency Prevention Administration, Administration on Aging, Rehabilitation Services Administration, Medical Services Administration, and Community Services Administration. Furthermore, each program has its own legislative base, criteria of eligibility, rules of federal financial participation.

The product of this maze of categorical legislation and eligibility is waste, inefficiency, vast areas of unmet need, and countless man hours spent in search of the elusive gods of service integration and coordination. I have experienced no successful mechanism, under our system, for an orderly assessment of the nation's human service resources in relation to its needs. This failure is covered up by talks of goals, priorities, management techniques (e.g., PERT) and the newest proposal, the Allied Services bill. All of these mechanisms are a response to symptoms rather than to causes.

A root cause of the symptomatic response lies in our legislative process, the "system," if you will. Any legislator may propose, and the Congress may dispose. The relationship of one program to another, the merit of an approach based on facts, the proportion of our resources to be spent, are the products of trade-offs, vested interests, election year politics, the relationship of a given Administration to key states. Once one leaves the politics of the Congress, the politics of the federal bureaucracy, the states and the cities takes over. States and localities, while victimized by the federal chaos, have considerable capacity to add to it.

In the absence of a clear assessment and articulation of national goals and legislative provision of the resources necessary to achieve the goals, there seems to be an almost mystical reliance on organizational format and management technique. The organizational or systems analyst has been imbued with the same omnipotence that an earlier day ascribed to the psychoanalyst. While competent management analysts and competent psychoanalysts have major contributions to make toward the solution of organizational and individual problems, these are both tools which can be productively utilized only after the mission, goals, and resources have been committed.

While the variety of policy debates centering on all human service systems rage, children are entering classrooms, patients are entering clinics and hospitals, fourteen or fifteen million Americans are entering public welfare agencies. To ascribe all the inadequacies of these service systems to the policy level is not valid. I am convinced that the specific application of social work skill and knowledge, at the delivery point as well as at the policy level, can make a major difference to those seeking service.

EXAMPLES OF INADEQUATE PRACTICE

The following vignettes demonstrate the deleterious effects of lack of knowledge and skill in practice upon program and clients. The lacks include skill in interviewing and listening, planning and implementing a service program, working with a group, knowledge of the elements of a particular service, and knowledge of, and ability to express one's professional difference. The material includes examples from the delivery point, administrative, and policy-making levels. While recognizing the overlapping naure of the knowledge and skills mentioned, for the sake of clarity I will preface the illustration with an indication of the skill missing and the level at which it occurred.

1. *Lack of skill in interviewing and listening at the service delivery point*

Shortly after assuming my position as Chief, Community Services, Social and Rehabilitation Services, Region III, HEW, I arranged a visit to a county welfare office in a rural area. The visit included an opportunity to talk with some workers, supervisors, and paraprofessionals. One young, male caseworker on the job six months and recently separated from his money-payment function, said, "I'm new. I know what eligibility is, but I have no knowledge of what a social service is or how to offer it. Now that I have nothing to do with the money payment, I don't know how to begin talking with my clients."

I also went with a worker from that agency to see a client, a young, white, unwed mother, living in a shack with her baby in rural isolation. The social worker was a mature woman, born in the county and resourceful in terms of arranging and providing for tangibles. During our brief visit this sincere, giving woman either did not hear, could not hear, or chose not to hear several clear though faint references to the client's aspirations for herself and her baby, her concern about her isolation, her concern about her family's view of her and the baby.

The above occurred in a state agency which rightfully prides itself on its well-administered, finely separated program. Separation in and of itself is not a solution.

2. *Lack of skill in working with a group at the administrative, consultative level*

An experienced federal official with a major role in designing service delivery systems, who thinks clearly and creatively and writes well, was invited to provide consultation to a state agency staff. After twenty minutes with them it became apparent that he was uncomfortable in working with a group of people and threatened by some of the state staff who were negative and critical. His counterattack resulted in a heightened degree of anxiety on the part of the group which further blocked opportunities for mutual learning and assistance. The state agency staff made it quite clear they would not request consultation from this individual again.

3. *Lack of skill in planning and implementing a service program at the administrative level*

One state agency entered into over $2 million worth of purchase-of-service agreements with local housing authorities. The key pace-setting contract with one housing authority was broad, diffuse, and full of global references to global needs. It demonstrated a complete lack of planning and specificity as to target groups, kinds of services to be offered, staffing patterns, expected outcomes. The social workers at the state and local housing authority level prided themselves on their capacity and creativity in attracting federal dollars. The net result of this "creativity" bordered on disaster.

A second state agency, with federal encouragement and financial assistance, hoped to develop 100 additional day care slots. Two small buildings, each to serve fifty children, were to be built in the Model Cities area. Construction problems abounded, and the building could not get started. The children and families were not being served, the available service funds were not being utilized. State and Model Cities staff, including paraprofessionals and parents, were spending countless hours "fighting" over the facility. In consultation with the groups, the regional office proposed beginning the service by hiring staff, purchasing necessary equipment and supplies, involving the parents in determination of the most suitable homes and alternative sites for interim use until the buildings were completed. When the buildings were ready, an established program with children, parents, and staff would consequently also be ready to move in. Key staff in the Model Cities and state agency expressed appreciation, saw us off at the airport, and did nothing. No children or families were served until the last finishing touches were put on the buildings, one year after the target date.

4. *Lack of knowledge of the elements and issues in a particular service at the administrative level*

A third state agency, with the use of Title IV*a* funds, contracted for the provision of services to unwed, pregnant adolescents. The program, already in operation, enjoyed somewhat of a reputation for the comprehensiveness of its services and its use of paraprofessionals. My discussions with other state agency employees who have had to refer clients, and with staff and board members of that agency, indicated very poor administration; a range of service possibilities minimally utilized because of inexperienced staff; and a lack of ability to entertain issues of sexuality, contraception, educational alternatives, abortion, work with fathers and families. Although the agency did arrange for delivery, *post-partum* checkups and infant day care, the program was minimal and unimaginative. With Title IV*a* funds, this minimal program was greatly expanded and lauded.

A supervisor in a state agency called our regional office with a typical "Will Title IV*a* pay for . . . ?" type of question. He had just received a "very exciting" proposal in regard to the group care of children from a local community group. After indicating the constraints and possibilities inherent in IV*a*, I asked, "Can you tell me a bit more about the program?" In response to my questions about the facility, staffing patterns, ages and referral sources of children, costs in regard to clothing and food, arrangements for medical and dental care, schools, and work with families, it soon became apparent to us both that much more than "Will Title IV*a* pay for all or part of it?" was at stake. The administrator said, "Thanks a lot. In addition to the funding, there's a hell of a lot I better learn about group care."

    5. Lack of a sense of professional self and inability to express one's professional difference at the administrative level

As a "fed" I met many people at all levels who did not know how to listen or how to respond to the feelings beneath the words and gestures of another person. To work in the federal or state bureaucracy is to witness daily many people, including social workers, who do not know how to handle a whole range of role and authority issues. The phenomenon of able people quaking in their boots when faced with bureaucratic rank is sad to see. The ability to state responsibly and helpfully one's professional difference is all too often lacking.

I am reminded of the urgent phone call from the Office of the Secretary of HEW which interrupted a staff meeting to request certain information from each of our states. The chairman of the meeting, who was Acting Regional Commissioner for the day, immediately began to divide the assignment among the various departments. I asked, "Do we know the purpose of the information and who is requesting it?" Rumors always abound in the bureaucracy, several regulatory and legislative issues were in the hopper. It would help in seeking the information to have a sense of context; furthermore, the chief state administrators of the public welfare programs were entitled to know the reason for such a request. The bright administrative assistant who had brought the message to the meeting said, "I think it comes from the Under Secretary's office, but your questions are good ones. If you are continuing with the meeting, I'll check it out and get back to you." About an hour later the young man returned, and with a smile on his face said, "No one knows." He went on to describe how, starting with the person from whom he received the call, they worked their way up the ladder. After having spoken to half a dozen people, all of whom had a part in relaying the message down and none of whom knew why, they gave up. "We decided the only way to find out would be to call the Under Secretary, and we couldn't do that."

6. *Lack of practice experience and self-awareness at the policy making level*

An understanding of the tension and pressure at the delivery point (that place and moment where client and worker meet for the purpose of receiving and rendering a service) is essential in the writing of regulations. While there are other essential elements, for the social worker, within the constraints of the legal base, the implications of the regulations for the delivery point must be a guiding principle. This presumes, however, that those writing the regulations have by virtue of their own experience, or access to the current experience of others, knowledge of the situation at the delivery point. Before a federal regulation is issued, it has been through considerable negotiation. Program people may have one perception of the possibilities contained in the law, fiscal people still another, general counsel a third; in addition, there are frequently "turf" issues among the bureaus which a new regulation generates. Negotiation invariably involves trade-offs; the politics of the bureaucracy comes to bear on the final version. Without knowledge and experience of the problems at the delivery point, major service prerogatives can be traded off. Frequently, those who write, review, or negotiate regulations are light years away from the pressures at the delivery point.

A provision of the service regulations was concerned with the group determination of eligibility. The regulation and subsequent policy issuances held that in public housing, or formally designated poverty areas, all residents could be eligible for services under certain conditions, on the assumption that a high percentage of people living in those areas were probably eligible for service as current, former, or potential recipients of public assistance, the three eligible categories. Furthermore, there was considerable precedent in a variety of federal programs (health, mental health, Office of Economic Opportunity, HUD) where the concepts of target areas and social indicators as criteria for eligibility were well-ensconced in existing regulations.

However, fiscal people and others had visions of large numbers of ineligible people taking advantage of this and wanted the provision eliminated. The issue, in my view, was worth a major battle, for within it were important immediate as well as long-range ramifications for service delivery. Our prime negotiators capitulated, however, indicative of a central failure in the system. These key individuals, by virtue of their lack of experience in the morass of eligibility determination, and their lack of self-awareness (ability to divorce their need for recognition, approval, and getting the regulations out, from client and program need) only mustered an inadequate attempt to retain group eligibility. They collapsed before the attack of the conservatives. Perhaps those forces would have prevailed in any event. Yet the lack of vigorous defense indicated to me a lack of awareness of professional role and obligation from which to draw support and sustenance. In addition, a lack of knowledge of practice was demonstrated by many participants throughout the many discussions of the role of private agencies and how they should function in relation to the purchase of service, the design of a program and its financial requirements, the necessity for cash in a service unit, agency auspice and its effect on the nature of the service rendered.

The Profession and Service Delivery in Public Welfare

The provision of social services is the historically and institutionally sanctioned function of the profession of social work. It is an obvious statement that the field has undergone many changes: the methods of provision and the theoretical and practical formulation surrounding provision have changed; the definition and modalities of service have altered; the number of settings in which services are provided has greatly increased; the knowledge base in social science has expanded; the public sector has assumed responsibility for the provision of social services. Most recently, the emergence of black awareness and the concept of consumer participation are having a major impact. Yet the basic charge remains: to respond, reflect, and offer leadership in regard to the prime area of our obligation, the provision of social services. This is not to deny professional social work's prophetic function in favor of its priestly function or to claim total allegiance to "St. Sigmund" rather than "St. Karl" (Chambers, 1963). Rather it emphasizes that the provision of service is at our core and our roots, a fact of great import since the primary public instrumentality for the provision of social services, the public welfare system, is in deep, deep trouble.

The line worker in public welfare is frequently overwhelmed and has not been properly trained to offer a service. While administrators, academicians, and members of the professional community debate the issues of graduate and undergraduate training, thousands of public welfare workers are ill-equipped to perform either the income-maintenance function or the service function. While the debate rages over separation of services from income maintenance, and the administrative level at which it must be complete, when all is said and done, at least at this point in our history, we are separating an inadequate money-payment system from a nonfunctioning social service system. A separated social service system staffed by people who have not been equipped with the necessary resources to render services will yield little. Unless form and substance are placed in the separated shell, the separation surgery may result in the demise of public social services.

A baseline claim for a professional must be the possession of knowledge and expertise although the degree of knowledge and expertise residing in any one member of the profession will vary. The collective knowledge of the profession, however, must be clearly identified, be able to be implemented, and result in a product which is clearly more effective than that of the nonprofessional, or a member of another profession. It is my contention that the social work profession knows more about the delivery of specific human services, including homemaker services, day care, counseling, leisure-time services, child care services (including foster care and adoption), protective services, group services for the aged and youth, than law, medicine, public administration, public relations, business administration, and so on. As a profession we know more about the utilization of community resources, supervision, staff development and training than any profession active on the human service scene in America today.

When I say we know more, this is not to be mistaken for we know "all" or that others know nothing, or that we have nothing to learn from others about specific aspects of service. The profession has an obligation to transmit its expertise in offering a human service at the delivery point. Millions of public welfare clients who need help are being seen by staff of public welfare agencies. If service delivery is at the core of our professional claim, this demands that any graduate of a school of social work must have a working knowledge of the range of social services and beginning competence in the delivery of one or more social services. While this approach may not have the appeal of a variety of other graduate school offerings, skill in practice is essential. While the university may be one important locus of such activity, it will have to look to experienced practitioners from the field to serve as instructors.

An understanding of the human condition, of growth, pain, of potential and limitation, a compassionate understanding of people and their attempts to negotiate a variety of interpersonal and social systems, the understanding of a professional helping relationship, and the ability to translate these into the effective delivery of a human service, are in my view nonnegotiable, core elements of professional education for social work. The ability to verbalize, to feel, to advocate, to conceptualize this understanding is insufficient. The professional must be able to act it, to do it, to demonstrate it.

Professional schools and the professional association must become intimately related to the public welfare agency. Trained social workers can help see to it that policy and available funds result in sound human services. Institutes and other formal arrangements between our professional associations, universities, and state departments of public welfare, including specific curricula for currently employed service workers, are among many vehicles which can be utilized.

If, however, service delivery is at the core of our professional claim, and the nature of service is intimately related to a variety of policy issues, how will the profession make an impact on those policy issues? While broad-gauged positions are important, while commitment to a value system is essential, in and of themselves they are not sufficient.

The Practice of Social Policy

The first step in assessing our role in policy formulation is to take a hard look into the mirror of reality. Social work professionals do not create social policy. Professional rhetoric does not create change. The most effective instruments for change in social policy must come from forces outside the profession. We may help, but let us never delude ourselves that the social work profession will bring about basic change. We are neither omnipotent nor impotent. What can we do? Porter Lee (1937), in a paper entitled "Social Work as Cause and Function," described the essential task of translating causes we espouse into functions which are institutionally lodged. To espouse the cause of children or minority groups without the resulting expression of this cause in a program aimed at achieving the goals of the cause, falls short of the mark. Statesmanship devoid of workmanship is ineffective (Pray, 1949). Once again the effectiveness of a profession is measured by its ability to do it!

As we gaze into this social policy mirror, we have to ask ourselves: What can we do? Whom do we do it with? Whom can we provide leadership to? Whom need we take leadership from? I want to state some thoughts on the practice of social policy. Please note the phrase "practice of social policy." My intent is once again to distinguish a professional capacity to act and to produce, based on knowledge, from intent. While the practice of social policy requires a value base and a theory, it also requires specific knowledge and skill.

There are at least two critical levels where one can make an imprint on policy—the legislative and the bureaucratic or executive. There is a parallel situation between the state and federal level. Every government program is rooted in law. As any private agency executive knows, knowledge of, and relationship with, one's board is critical. The board in this case is the U.S. Congress or the state legislature. If the profession wants to make an impact on social legislation, it must have a thorough knowledge of the workings of the legislature and its committees (Cohen, 1966). Vital information which does not get into the right hands at the proper time is ineffectual. There is no magic in the legislative process; it is complicated, but it can be learned. The men and women who run the legislature (United States or state) must be dealt with if social policy is to be affected. Dealing with Congressional staff is frequently of greater importance than direct contact with the legislator himself. The profession cannot rule out finanical contributions and other forms of recognition as tools of influence. These must be well-targeted and goal-oriented. This will undoubtedly create value and role tensions among social workers. In this highly politicized nation, however, the profession must confront itself on these issues (Brager, 1968).

Some similar points must be made with reference to the bureaucracy. There are little-known "special assistants" to the departmental secretary, undersecretaries, commissioners, and middle-management people who wield great influence in departmental policy formulation. Legislative initiatives also come from the bureaucracy. Social workers have colleagues throughout the bureaucracy who can be sources of considerable help and influence.

The writing of a federal regulation or a program regulation guide is another key point at which policy is made. At times, hours of debate and pages of memoranda are written on provisions in a law which are not specific and have to be made so in a regulation. The law states that those who are "likely to become" a recipient of public assistance are eligible. Thus the definition of "likely to become" in the regulations becomes critical. Definitions of services and eligible populations are subject, of course, to fiscal restrictions, Congressional intent, and legal review. Nonetheless, those who write regulations can begin from a constrictive or an expansive base. They may have a sound understanding of service delivery issues or a meager one. Skill in the analysis and preparation of relevant data is important. The ability to translate the myriad of individual problems residing in agencies into the social indicators they are is most important (Schwartz, 1969). A working knowledge of potential allies and oppenents becomes critical.

Professional education for the complete practitioner must include sufficient content (conceptual and practical) to produce a working knowledge of the legislative and executive branches of government and their impact on social policy and services.

The practice of social policy requires an understanding that policy in this sector, as in all others, is never one-dimensional. The utilization of nonprofessionals and indigenous workers is as much a function of employment strategy and the health of the economy as it is a social service strategy. The ability to understand the potential implications, in a variety of areas, of a given proposal is essential. When at a high-level meeting data are requested on the "programmatic implications in New York and California" of a particular proposal, one must realize that "programmatic implications" can mean political ramifications.

While the profession needs leadership and expertise in the area of social policy, all social workers and all curricula must attempt to develop beginning competence in the practice of social policy.

As this is being written we are witnessing what appears to be a systematic attempt to dismantle the programs and philosophy of the Great Society by the Nixon Administration. Reduction in human service funding, curtailment of funds for training in the human services, elimination of entire programs and agencies seem to be the order of the day. The social service titles referred to earlier are in the process of being cut to ribbons. The painful fact, however, is that much of that being eliminated in HEW and elsewhere has not been effective. The truth is that throwing dollars at problems will not necessarily solve them. The answer to these harsh realities, however, is not the sharp curtailment of spending for human services. It is rather, in my view, a reformulation of the use of the dollars, including more sharply defined national and local goals, definitive plans for meeting the stated goals, and greatly increased fiscal and program quality accountability at all levels. Revenue sharing, as currently proposed, for all its slogans, will not achieve these ends.

The nation will one day right its course. The pressing problems of urban decay and poverty will have to be met. During these difficult days we must hold to what we know, practice what we espouse, and join with others in the continuing struggle for just social policy. We must continually strive to ensure that every dollar which policy provides results in competent, person-centered practice.

The struggles for adequate policy and sound delivery are inextricably related. No worker, regardless of his position in the agency or the function of the agency, can avoid this truth. No school of social work or group of practitioners can afford the self-indulgent turf issues between "practice" and "policy."

There has, in my view, been a pattern of masochistic self-depreciation evident in much of social work's literature and utterances. Sound day care, sound adoptions, first-rate homemaker services, services to unwed parents, protective services for the aged, help for groups of people to achieve their rights, while neither new, radical, nor revolutionary, are urgently needed by millions of Americans. Social workers skilled in the practice of offering a service and in the practice of social policy can make a difference. A key target of our activity, whether we are formally in the public welfare network or outside it, must be the public welfare system and the millions of Americans entitled to its service.

While we press on for new formulations, approaches, and knowledge, we must affirm our knowledge of the social services and see to it that they are provided in a manner which enhances individual, group, and community dignity. We must participate in the battle for sound social policy through specific efforts which demonstrate our knowledge and skill in practice and yield results. This is the need, this is our obligation.

References

Brager, George. "Advocacy and Political Behavior," *Social Work*, XIII, No. 2 (1968), 5–15.

Chambers, Clarke A. "Social Service and Social Reform: a Historical Essay," *Social Service Review*, XXXVII, No. 1 (1963), 76–90.

Cohen, Wilbur J. "What Every Social Worker Should Know about Political Action," *Social Work*, XI, No. 3 (1966), 3–11.

Grosser, Charles F. "Community Development Programs Serving the Urban Poor," *Social Work*, X, No. 3 (1965), 15–21.

Lee, Porter R. *Social Work as Cause and Function, and Other Papers.* New York: Columbia University Press, 1937.

Pray, Kenneth L. M. *Social Work in a Revolutionary Age.* Philadelphia, University of Pennsylvania Press, 1949.

Rein, Martin. "Social Work in Search of a Radical Profession," *Social Work*, XV, No. 2 (1970), 13–28.

Schwartz, William. "Private Troubles and Public Issues: One Job or Two?" in *The Social Welfare Forum, 1969*, pp. 22–43. New York, Columbia University Press, 1969.

Thursz, Daniel. "Social Action as a Professional Responsibility," *Social Work*, XI, No. 3 (1966), 12–21.

Wineman, David and Adrienne James. "The Advocacy Challenge to Schools of Social Work," *Social Work*, XIV, No. 2 (1969), 23–32.

SIMON SLAVIN
AND
FELICE DAVIDSON PERLMUTTER

Perspectives for Education and Training

THE FUNCTION that a profession performs for society, the system of educational preparation for its performance, and the organization of the profession itself can only be examined within the context of the social system in which it is embedded (Parsons, 1964). Consequently, the barefoot doctor in China, the *felsher* in the Soviet Union, the medicine man in Africa, or the midwife in Great Britain can be understood only in relation to his own professional medical system as well as in the broader historical-social-political-economic context of his respective society (Fry, 1969).

Similarly, a discussion of education and training for social work must be placed in its historical context. Thus Gordon Rose's discussion of social work in Great Britain in this work demonstrates the divergences in the ideological climate, the political and organizational structure for social service delivery, as well as the differentiated system for manpower training in contrast to ours.

It is therefore necessary to preface the presentation of a conceptual model for education and training for social work practice with a discussion of the social environment.

The Social Environment

The decade of the 1960s may in the long run be viewed as a crossroad in the development of both a philosophy and a program in social welfare. While it may be difficult to measure the effectiveness of specific projects per se, the legacy of the 1960s may in fact be the unanticipated consequence of a total system's change (Levitan, 1969). Therefore, we suggest that in spite of the reverse pendulum swing in national policy of the 1970s it is essential to view the development of social work in social welfare from a broader perspective, along a continuum; consequently, it is important to consider the trends in both decades, the 1960s and the 1970s.

The persistence of poverty in a society of affluence and its attendant social dislocations, including systematic discrimination against non-whites, systematic structural unemployment, and the failure to provide adequate housing, led to broad-based social unrest in the 1960s as blacks joined with whites and the poor with the nonpoor to press for a solution to these fundamental problems. A response to this malaise occurred in various central sectors of society and was no longer shunted aside to be dealt with by those institutions traditionally concerned with social problems (churches, voluntary welfare organizations, and civil rights groups). The dramatic response of the government and the university to the malaise demonstrates the ideological shift, as the political and academic establishments representing the total society became participants in what can be broadly termed "the welfare process."

THE GOVERNMENT

This discussion of government initiatives highlights those directly related to manpower development and training, all having long-run implications for the future of social work in our society. They can be briefly identified as follows: the affirmative action mandate, the career ladders program, the emphasis on accountability and quality control, revenue sharing, the separation of services from income maintenance, as well as community control and consumer participation.

Several implications are clear as a result of this listing. First, social work must expand to include all levels of manpower concerned with the delivery of social services since "social workers, viewed as an occupational category, exhibit an extraordinary amount of diversity" (Scott, 1969, p. 83). Second, roles must be clearly differentiated so that advanced training guarantees advanced performance.

Could we plan for different levels of training, ranging from those trained at the university level to the aide or auxiliary at the field level so that at a desirable time the necessary proportion of personnel will be employed at all levels? Some countries may put the emphasis on an initial development of high-level workers; others may see the need more strongly at the local level. Could a nucleus of workers be employed at all levels within a framework of future objectives so that necessary cadres of service will be expanded as and whenever the need arises (Gindy, 1970, p. 41)?

Third, the addition of new bodies of knowledge to the current repertoire, such as an expertise in cost-benefit analysis and an increased research capability, is essential for the administrative roles at the expanding diverse and decentralized points in the system, within the public sector and without. These three points have been explicitly cited in this volume by Keith-Lucas, Kahn, Gelman, and Scobie in their discussions of changing roles in their fields of competence.

It is not enough to cite the implications for educational programs; it is also essential to be cognizant of the conflicts created by these factors. First is the conflict created by the new manpower strategy which is designed to meet an employment objective in the economic sector while meeting a service delivery objective in the welfare sector. These two objectives are not necessarily compatible and often lead to a second conflict: the mere provision of manpower to provide service does not guarantee quality of performance. This relates to the central thesis of Levine's chapter: that quality of service has been lost in the public establishment where other objectives take precedence. A further conflict results from the revenue-sharing mechanism wherein a political objective can displace a professional one, thus *de facto* pulling the new career programs out of the welfare arena.

In planning for social work education it is essential that the implications of the new initiatives and their conflict-laden aspects be explicitly handled.

THE UNIVERSITY

The social environment of the university, affected by the malaise of the 1960s, included a thrust for change as students became disillusioned with traditional academic arrangements (Reich, 1971) as well as with the emphasis on science and technology (Roszak, 1969). In addition, the spiraling cost of education stimulated a variety of new structural mechanisms, all relevant to social work education.

The consolidation of time for obtaining degrees was introduced by various professional schools. City College in New York City reduced its medical degree preparation from eight to six years, and the relationship to minority and poverty needs was clearly explicated by the college president:

We also hope to encourage and motivate larger numbers of minority students to enter medical careers so as to provide inner-city areas with more physicians and other health professionals (New York *Times*, 11/28/72).

Some schools of education combined the bachelor's and the master's degrees into four-year programs, and some schools of social work offered an MSW based on a five-year continuum of education.

On the undergraduate level, students were pressing for studies related to social welfare and urban problems. In addition to the introduction of the bachelor's degree in social work, field work became an added dimension to urban studies, sociology, and political science. The development of community colleges and the associate in arts certification was a further educational innovation, of importance especially for mental health technicians in welfare programs. Further university changes included, among others, the provision of external degrees, the open university, and the acceptance of relevant work experience for academic credit.

The emergence of various programs in social welfare created a competitive thrust in the domain where social work once reigned supreme. For example, in the human services programs at Pennsylvania State University social work was not even included. Consequently, one can argue that social welfare as a societal function has attained broader acceptance than heretofore but that social work as a profession has yet to demonstrate its unique competence.

Issues in the Differentiated Use of Social Work Manpower

Social work as a profession has for some time been concerned with the differential use of social work manpower. As early as 1959 Wolfe dealt with this issue in a National Association of Social Workers (NASW) publication, *Use of Personnel Without Professional Training in Social Service Departments;* throughout the 1960s the literature has been replete with discussion of this topic (Epstein, 1962; Farrar and Hemmy, 1963; Heyman, 1961; Weed and Denham, 1961; Wolfe, 1961).

However, in addition to the rhetoric regarding its value there exists a literature which attempts to provide an analytic basis for task and role differentiation. Blum (1966) makes a crucial point when he argues that the definition must reflect the client's interests as opposed to "a professional definition of the role." Thus it bodes well that from the outset the social work literature reflects an awareness of the dilemma of professionalism and control, a myopic bias frequently encountered in literature concerned with the professions (Rosengren and Lefton, 1970).

The complexity of this endeavor cannot be overstated; not only is the precise definition of tasks and roles a difficult one, but the additional need to define qualifications, skills, and personal attributes appropriate to their performance is complex indeed—a task of high priority for the profession (Alexander, 1972).

The components of this process have been identified:

A functional classification design derives from the program objectives of the social welfare system itself. Analysis of the objectives leads to a delineation of the tasks to be performed in fulfilling the program objectives and to a clustering of these tasks in terms of scope and range of responsibility, complexity and difficulty of performance, particular knowledge and skill required, degrees of decision-making responsibility, and extent of autonomy in practice (Wolfe, 1972, p. 21).

The task becomes one of defining the relationship between the components: scope and range of tasks, complexity and difficulty of performance, knowledge and skill, responsibility and autonomy.

Richan's model for determining roles of professional and nonprofessional workers has been frequently cited in the literature since it was one of the first attempts to discuss this issue (Richan, 1961). Moreover, it merits attention because of its clear and simple definition of conditions and responses as he specifies two crucial variables, client vulnerability and worker autonomy:

When both client vulnerability and worker autonomy are high, the greatest professional knowledge, skill and discipline are needed. When clients are highly vulnerable but set procedures and external controls are appropriate, the specialist—with technical training around specifics—can be used. When an operation essentially like that of the professional, yet with less vulnerable clientele, is called for, the person with a "preprofessional" kind of education is indicated. Finally, when external guidelines and controls are available and clients are least vulnerable, use can be made of lay persons with only brief in-service training around specifics (Richan, 1961, p. 27).

Schwartz and Sample (1972) in an experimental project concerned with the organization of work groups in a department of public assistance used three sets of criteria:

(1) presence or absence of a major social problem, (2) presence or absence of client motivation and client capacity for using service, and (3) the client's degree of social vulnerability or the extent to which he constituted an immediate threat to the public (p. 18).

The authors point out that they have expanded the "vulnerability" concept from Richan's psychological definition which focused on impact of service to include, in addition, an emphasis on the impact of the environment on the client as well as the potential threat of the client to others.

Discussions of programs which have differentiated their use of manpower can be cited. One basic guideline underpins them all: the responsibility for teaching, training, supervising, screening, and management rests with the professional (the MSW), whereas the less highly trained staff perform "the newer social and educational therapies (companionship therapy, activity group therapy, tutoring, group counseling, and retraining)" (Sobey, 1970, p. 106). Richan (1972), Carlsen (1969), and Denham and Schatz (1969) focus on the tangible services which the non-MSW can effectively provide. Barker and Briggs (1968; 1969), in discussing a series of studies which involved professional and nonprofessional staff, found that the trend is toward using the BSW as "doer" and the MSW as "director" of social work task forces of the future. While the "outer boundaries" have as yet not been reached regarding the extent of activities which can be performed by a nonprofessional, team leadership, training, and supervisory roles are appropriate for the MSW (Rivesman, 1971).

One consequence of this task differentiation is the emergence of a team approach to service delivery, "that is, a team including staff with varying levels of education . . ." (Anderson and Carlsen, 1971); this coincides with the trends identified by Pusić's discussion, in this volume, of administration in social welfare. While Briggs (1973) presents a different conceptual formulation for manpower differentiation and training based on an array of twelve social work roles, the administrative implications are similar: the use of a team model for social work practice which maximizes the contributions of all levels of manpower.

This brief review of the literature attempts to draw attention to a central area of concern for social work; it is not designed to be more than suggestive of the work already done and needing to be done. Although the formulations were made in relation to direct service delivery, the discussion is also applicable to the roles in research, policy, and administration presented in this volume as well as the educational model which follows.

A Model for Education and Training

DEFINITIONS

A redefinition of professional and preprofessional roles is fundamental to this discussion of an educational model for social work. Whereas the field has in the past defined professionalism as beginning at the master's level, preprofessionalism at the bachelor's level, and paraprofessionalism at the high-school level or less, a new differentiation is herein offered.

Professional social work is defined to include those who are trained for professional roles with degrees in social work at the bachelor's, master's, and doctoral levels. This specialized professional training at the university level, furthermore, provides a framework of professional ethics and social responsibility (Parsons, 1964). It should be noted that the acceptance of the bachelor's degree as the first professional degree is not unusual and occurs in education and engineering, among others.

Preprofessional social work is defined to include those who work in the field in less autonomous, more specified roles and who may have other than professional training. This includes those with bachelor of arts degrees, associate in arts certification (AA), as well as paraprofessionals. The value of this dichotomy is that it emphasizes the essential difference between professionals and nonprofessionals as one of "kind" rather than "amount" of training. NASW in 1973 worked out a similar classification for differential social work practice. The relevant characteristics of these professional and preprofessional roles are highlighted in Table 1.

Table 1. Professional and Preprofessional Roles in Social Work

	Professional	*Preprofessional*
Role performance	Autonomous	Nonautonomous
Tasks	Diffuse	Specific
Knowledge	Conceptual, generalizable	Case-task defined
Education	Professional curriculum	University or other
Orientation	External-interdisciplinary	Internal-organizational

UNDERLYING ASSUMPTIONS

This model is based on five assumptions which must be made explicit. First, this model aims to provide a rational system for manpower preparation in which all levels and modalities of practice are articulated and linked one to the other.

Should not training levels be so structured as component parts of a whole system to permit a unified system of training, and so provide opportunities for professional development as well as for promotion in the social welfare administrative hierarchy? Should not such a system of structured training accommodate the training of the volunteer and auxiliary as well as the intermediary and other senior-level positions (Gindy, 1970, p. 41)?

The systemic interrelationship of the parts cannot be overemphasized. While many programs offer a rhetoric concerning continuity and linkages, in fact the entities are discrete units. This model aims to operationalize this assumption by facilitating the progression through the various levels.

A second assumption is that education and training are interrelated components for professional preparation: professional education is viewed as providing a philosophical, conceptual, and analytic base for professional practice with knowledge that is generalizable but which will serve the specific case when needed. By contrast, training is focused on the unique and specific tasks which need to be performed to meet an organization's objectives. While the term "training" is frequently used generically, the distinction made here is of striking importance. (Though the boundaries between education and training are relatively clear, there are often elements of each in the other.)

The third assumption is that professional preparation cannot progress in a vacuum; education, training, and placement must be viewed as vital aspects of one process. This premise is based on the experience in social work education, where there is frequently a fundamental disparity between educational objectives and field needs, a problem created by both partners. For example, public welfare departments have generally failed to define the objectives of the programs in terms of reentry points into the system, and workers were put back into the same organizational slots after completing their professional education (Thompson and Riley, 1966); furthermore, the direct practice and/or clinical model of training was not appropriate for the supervisory and administrative positions obtained upon graduation (Schwartz and Sample, 1972).

A fourth assumption, which follows from the third, is that planning must become an ongoing function of educational institutions, based on continuous communication and feedback between schools and the field of practice. This is not a throwback to an earlier era when schools of social work were agency training units; rather it is an attempt to develop a rational and informed basis for institutional behavior based on an open-system model of continuous exchange between the relevant parts of that system. This is essential for the healthy performance of any professional school, be it law, medicine, engineering, or social work. Whereas to date the feedback has usually been crisis-oriented, on an *ad hoc* basis, a continuing mechanism for planning is herein assumed. A fifth and final assumption is that this, as any educational model, is not fixed and final, but flexible and formulative, to be continuously revised in relation to new findings from the field.

The model attempts to evolve a clearly articulated and linked educational system for professional and nonprofessional roles by presenting an analytic framework upon which curriculum design is based. It does not attempt to designate specific course content.

THE EDUCATIONAL MODEL

This model is concerned with the two personnel groupings discussed above, preprofessional and professional.

The Paraprofessional. The first preprofessional level is primarily a practice experience. Community residents, hardly distinguishable from clients in their social characteristics, but highly motivated for service, began to play an important part in manpower development efforts of the 1960s. The similarity of cultural factors and life-style qualities made it possible to reduce social distance, create conditions of easy access and relationship, enhance communication, and make positive use of the vast knowledge that accrues to life experience, including recipient-of-service experience, in the process of providing services in a wide range of programs.

Selection of personnel at this level is based more on what people *are*, on their personal qualities, than on what they *know* of the intricacies of the helping process. Position in the community, participation in the institutional life of the area, and a feeling for people in need provide indications of potential capacity for staff roles in social programs. Readiness to learn and to accept organizational goals and educational and administrative controls figure significantly as criteria for selection.

The use of paraprofessional personnel calls for thoughtful programs of training within the agencies that employ them, and by agency personnel. Learning here is clearly prescriptive, restricted by organizational goals, procedures, and guidelines, all within the specific framework of organizational policies. Training content mirrors agency expectations and activities, and delineates performance requirements. Its focus is job-related and agency-oriented. The limits of worker discretion and initiation, as well as the realms of choice in problem-solving behavior, are significant aspects of such training. Location of accountability mechanisms and sources of professional help and supervision similarly figure importantly in program content.

While in-service training prepares personnel for effective staff functioning, encouragement to enroll in educational programs and facilitation of such activity are significant challenges to agency administrators. Several mechanisms lie at hand to further this latter objective. Some agencies provide a sequence of courses for employees that enlarge their areas of professional awareness and that constitute an internal certification system for upgrading to positions of greater responsibilities. Other agencies have arranged for courses to be given by educational institutions that carry beginning professional content, often with university credit which can be subsequently certified for credit toward the degree. Still another illustration is the move toward on-site courses by universities that serve as early inducement to engage in full-time study for eventual professional certification.

The Associate in Arts Certification. The second preprofessional level requires programs which must be carefully planned in order to be conducive to effective job performance as well as to provide a broader orientation to social work and its educational and vocational possibilities (Brawley, 1971). Education for personnel at this level must have its own integrity in order to utilize the unique competence of the preprofessional, to give job satisfaction, as well as to clarify the contribution in relation to the total welfare picture.

In a tight employment market paraprofessionals can be utilized not because of a shortage of professionals but because some agencies are unable or unwilling to meet professional salary standards. This is a very serious danger (Sobey, 1971, p. 7).

If the roles are clearly defined and the tasks clearly differentiated it will be more difficult to substitute levels inappropriately. However, the educational background is essential in providing mobility, either horizontally or vertically.

Criteria for admission into these certificate programs are still primarily the candidate's experience and interest in the human services role, now coupled with a desire for education. Candidates need not go through normal academic admissions channels. While program content is practice-oriented it is also designed to serve as an introduction or link to academic work. Thus the student can complete the program as an end in itself in order to obtain horizontal job mobility or choose to move into an academic or professional undergraduate program for vertical mobility. The following discussion provides a case illustration of an educational program for this preprofessional level.*

Prior to 1968, many child care agencies were employing untrained, poorly screened, and often psychologically unfit persons to give direct service to children. In-service training, provided by the agency, was often too little and too late, so that children suffered from the trial-and-error methods of workers in the process of acquiring new skills. In addition, the high cost of staff turnover was a major budgetary concern. Child care workers, who had the most critical role in the development of the children, had no role as members of the decision-making agency team. For a worker who had achieved a high level of competence and responsibility in one agency there was no reliable method by which he could transfer to a comparable level in another agency and no possible way he could transfer "credits" he had earned in in-service training to higher education.

Using a model for generic preservice training of child care workers, financed by the National Institute of Mental Health and made operational by an interdisciplinary faculty in the Department of Child Psychiatry at the University of Pittsburgh, Temple University began selecting and training potential child care workers in a two-year, preservice certificate program (Figure 1). Goals of the selection process were to assess the applicant's potential for the field as well as to communicate the requirements of the training program and of child care as a career choice. Areas of consideration included style, attitude, personal characteristics, and readiness (motivation, maturity). Danger signals, which become contraindications for selection, included hostility, moralistic judgments, punitiveness, and rigidity, among others.

Applicants represented wide ranges of difference in age, social and economic status, ethnic and cultural origin, educational preparation, practical judgment, and experience with children. Classes were formed with maximum heterogeneity in order that people could learn to value differences.

Many mature "certificates" have returned to the university, adding

---

* This case illustration was prepared by Fran Vandivier, Director, Child Care Training Program, School of Social Administration, Temple University, Philadelphia.

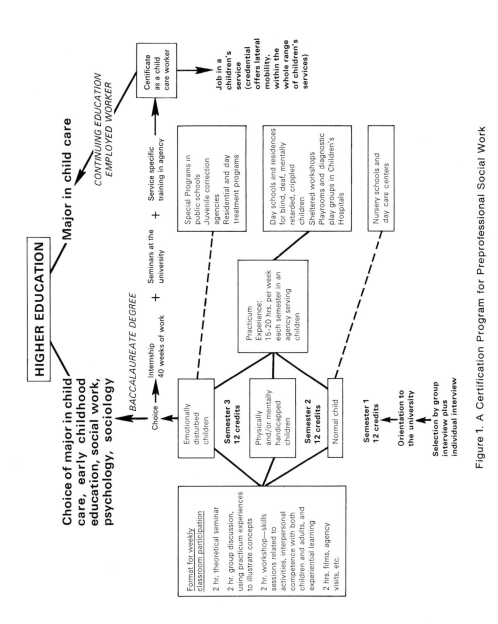

Figure 1. A Certification Program for Preprofessional Social Work

liberal arts courses to their "Introduction to the Profession" (the three-semester certificate training) to work toward a baccalaureate degree, mainly out of concern for their own developmental process. Younger, less mature trainees were often encouraged to seek a four-year educational experience before they took jobs, to compensate for their lack of practical experience or relevant life experience.

The Bachelor of Arts Degree. The third preprofessional level also provides manpower for the less complex tasks of the field. These students receive an academic background which consists mainly of theoretical and abstract content, coupled with their interest and motivation to work in the field. Thus their personal qualifications are different from those of the preprofessionals, whose cultural base and personal identity are in themselves the essential qualifications. While the BA program may offer some field experience, it is a relatively superficial exposure rather than an in-depth educational experience generally, related to specific course objectives rather than to the total educational experience.

Preparation for social work performance is through in-service training and supervision in the place of work, while linkage to the educational system is through continuing education provided by the university's professional school. Linkage can also be made to the MSW professional program as a result of experience in the field.

The Bachelor of Social Work. The first professional degree must have as its basic objective preparation for the entry level of professional practice. The objectives formulated by the Council on Social Work Education are as follows:

Program objectives shall reflect the values of the profession of social work. Preparation for beginning social work practice must be a stated educational objective of an undergraduate social work program. The program shall further specify its objectives in relation to: the mission of the educational institution of which it is a part, the human needs in the region identified by the parent institution as its service area; and its student body (CSWE Doc. #73-210-1, January, 1973).

This beginning level of professional education must prepare the practitioner for the autonomy necessary in areas of direct service discussed in the section on task and role differentiation. (The profession is beginning to recognize this reality; membership in NASW has been available to bachelor's degree social workers since 1970.)

The criteria for admission are more complex than in the earlier level, combining both the standard academic university criteria and the qualitative, personal attributes of the applicant. This is a crucial point in the system's linkage, for here lies the opportunity to encourage non-professionals with suitable background to enter the professional stream, thus recognizing nonacademic work and training background.

As specified by the Council on Social Work Education, the program should include: (1) a liberal arts base consisting of "knowledge in the humanities, social, behavioral and biological sciences"; (2) social work content, including "practice, social welfare, policy and services, and human behavior and social environment"; and (3) "educationally directed field work" (Doc. #73-210-1). The undergraduate social work program at Temple University offers a case illustration. Approximately one third of all course work deals with professional content; the balance is divided on a two-to-one ratio between general education and professionally related courses.

Students begin a three-year professional sequence of courses in the sophomore year. The concentration on professional content increases in each successive year, with the final year essentially devoted to class and field courses in social work. Preceding and surrounding this professional concentration are courses in natural sciences, humanities, and introductory-level social and behavioral sciences which provide a broad base in general education. The third segment of this tripartite program includes professionally related content, including social research and more advanced social theory courses drawn from psychology, social psychology, political science, sociology, and economics.

Practical field experience is attached to the social work courses in the sophomore and senior years. The former is intended to introduce students to the reality of an organized service delivery system and to test interest, commitment, and capacity for professional work. There is a year-long senior seminar together with a two-day-a-week field work experience in a single social agency, where the intimate and intricate relationships between theory and practice provide the substance of student learning.

There are two ways in which this BSW program is linked to earlier levels of training. More and more students who have completed a two-year AA program have transferred to the university for full baccalaureate certification. Some come directly from the community college, others after an interregnum for work in the human services. Care needs to be given to individual assessment of content mastery so that debilitating repetition of earlier studies can be avoided. Students from preprofessional programs are helped to succeed in the BSW program through various mechanisms. Initial courses taken by these students are given by program personnel and conform to the objectives of the initial professional offerings of the undergraduate sequence. A variety of support services is provided, including counseling, intensive advising, individual and group tutoring in basic skills, study skill sessions, remedial classes, and financial aid. Other courses provided by the university as required by the BSW degree follow or are taken in tandem. In time, these students merge into the regular student body both in the undergraduate department and in the university. Thus movement from preprofessional to professional status goes on apace. Many students continue to work in their agencies, undergoing transition to student and to professional more gradually. In time, many of these students will enroll in graduate programs, including those offering MSW degrees.

It is important to recognize that graduates of these programs will be full-fledged professionals, knowledgeable and trained in direct practice, capable of performing autonomously, requiring the usual supervision. This level will in many ways be comparable to the former level of the MSW entrance position.

The Master's Degree in Social Work. This must now be viewed as the second professional degree for advanced practice in the field; it can be built on the BSW as well as on the undifferentiated BA, as at present. Entrance into the MSW must assume knowledge of social work and social welfare, including history, philosophy, social policy, and practice issues, as well as experience in direct service delivery. Flexibility in the design of the MSW program is critical in terms of this integrated and interrelated model since the needs of the BSW will differ from those of the BA. Thus the linkages between the BSW and MSW programs must be carefully constructed in order to maximize past education as the basis for advanced work. All too often MSW programs give lip service to this linkage but in fact are not prepared to offer more intensive and/or specialized content areas. An important contribution has been made by the Council on Social Work Education, which has authorized that graduates of an approved BSW program can receive as much as a year of advanced standing in an accredited master's degree program. While each school will determine its own pattern, alternatives could include advanced standing in the MSW program and substitution of courses for greater specialization.

The program's objectives must clearly include new and advanced roles as it helps develop new expertise. These new roles and competencies, enumerated in all the chapters on functional fields throughout this volume, include administration, research and evaluation, policy and planning, supervision, staff development, and consultation. While some schools may include advanced training for direct practice at the master's level, we are not discussing that pattern since it has traditionally been part of the master's program.

The criteria for entrance into the program are twofold: the stringent academic criteria of graduate professional education and demonstrated competence in the practice role.

One distinctive difference in the MSW level, and one which forms the rationale for this volume, is the assumption that advanced practitioners should be experts in the functional field in which they plan to work. Consequently, in addition to general content related to service delivery, administration, and research, an in-depth knowledge of at least one field (its policies, programs, fiscal mechanisms, and social work practice) should be required.

The School of Social Work at the University of Pennsylvania, which is currently redesigning its master's degree curriculum, can serve as an illustration of one pattern of the proposed MSW. The program is designed for advanced practice, and consequently admission is based on educational background (social work undergraduate programs) and/or experience in direct practice roles in social work. The following discussion in part reflects the plans for the new program and in part reflects the authors' philosophy.

The curriculum offers four specializations from which the student can select his preferred field. The four selected at Pennsylvania, which reflect the unique competencies within the school and university, are presented for illustrative purposes only; they include health, corrections, the urban family, and education.

While the field placement for this two-year program is in the student's area of specialization, the academic course work offers both general content (administration and supervision) and specialized content (legislation, programs, practice issues). The general content areas are handled during the first and fourth semesters; specialization occurs during the second and third. An independent project of the student's choice provides an opportunity for an independent in-depth study in the field of specialization in the third and fourth semesters.

As the figure below indicates, the general and specialized contents are seen as overlapping and continuous rather than as discrete and separate areas.

Figure 2. An MSW Curriculum

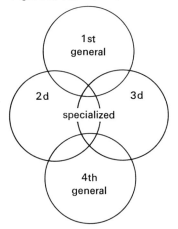

As are degrees at the earlier levels, the MSW can be a terminal degree for specific practice roles in the field or it can serve as the basis for continuing on to the doctorate in social work. However, with more sophisticated and vigorous training at the MSW level, this degree should indeed serve as a sound base for practice at advanced levels in the field.

The Doctorate in Social Work. This level requires careful consideration in view of the legitimation of the BSW and the advanced specification of the MSW. What objectives are uniquely served at this level? Three can be clearly specified: teaching, research, policy-planning—all three unique in their level of expertise and technical competence. The teaching role would serve all the other levels of education, from the training of teachers for AA programs to faculty for graduate departments; the research role would be one of initiating and directing research in social work and social welfare (as opposed to the team participant role of the MSW); the policy and planning role would be in relation to major government and national level programs. Some doctoral programs will probably continue to prepare for "advanced" direct practice roles and award a clinical doctorate.

Criteria for selection must be carefully and flexibly defined to provide the possibility of selecting the best candidates on both academic and professional criteria. While there would be the obvious and direct linkage from the master's program, interest of applicants trained in other disciplines should be encouraged. Entrance into the doctoral level will assume, however, substantial knowledge in social welfare (history and philosophy, practice theory, and so forth). These content areas must be the building blocks either through the MSW or through courses taken upon admission as prerequisites. The doctoral program will then be free to focus on selected areas for academic and professional excellence.

Linkages must thus be carefully examined in order to maximize the utilization of past credits and to minimize duplication. Various patterns are possible, and one which should be given careful consideration is the "en route" master's degree. This is the usual pattern in many fields and may be appropriate in some programs, such as research specialization. The organizing principle of any doctoral program must be its thrust for a disciplined program within the university context of academic excellence.

An interdisciplinary program in social and behavioral sciences can be viewed as fundamental in doctoral level work in that it provides an internal rigor and methodology which can then be applied to the field of social welfare. The selection of social science content would depend on the interests of the student: for example, a student in administration might select sociology (organization theory); a student in policy-planning might select political science.

The emphasis of the remainder of the curriculum will vary according to the mission of the program (teaching, planning, research). Thus, for example, in a school which aims to produce educators, a second major content area would be in the field of education (curriculum design, learning theory). Similarly, the doctoral dissertations would reflect the central thrust of the program in their demonstration of the students' independent and scholarly contribution to their area of competence.

Thus the doctorate is viewed as the degree necessary for the advanced roles to be performed in an increasingly complex environment. The tension between the professional objectives versus the academic expectations is an anachronism in the present reality: both must be viewed as integral parts of a program designed to produce excellence.

Other educational functions. These too must be included in this integrated model. Continuing education, as mentioned above, is a responsibility of the professional school in helping people in the field remain *au courant* with new knowledge and skill in the field. It is particularly important in a society such as ours where rapid technological change creates profound changes in fields of knowledge. This program can be organized through short courses and institutes related to the broader educational objectives of the educational setting, as opposed to in-service training which is agency defined.

The educational model which encompasses six levels of manpower is schematically presented in Table 2.

Conclusions

In the past, the MSW was both the entry and the terminal degree. It was the center and core of professional preparation for social work practice. With the advent of the BSW as the initial mark of legitimacy for professional practice, and preprofessional training for prescribed and delimited performance roles, master's level preparation will inevitably continue to assume new and evolving characteristics.

Table 2. Social Work Level as Related to Qualifications and
Work Tasks

Social Work Level	Qualifications	Work Tasks-Roles (Complexity, Autonomy, Uncertainty)
Preprofessional		
Paraprofessional	Personal	Low
AA	Personal and	
BA	Academic	Moderate
Professional		
BSW	Personal and	
MSW	Academic and	High
DSW	Professional	

At the other end of the continuum, some social work positions have begun to require doctoral level certification. This is increasingly true in university positions in schools of social work and in advanced research and policy-planning roles in national agencies and governmental programs. This suggests that the pivotal role of master's level education may be substantially modified, perhaps in the direction assumed by the field of education.

One can easily anticipate substantial development during the 1970s of educational and training programs at both ends of the educational continuum. Efforts that link early training programs to educational offerings at subsequent levels, and early professional education to master's and doctoral curricula, can be expected to assume the central stage in educational planning. One can expect additional universities with graduate social work education programs to establish undergraduate departments. In the process, faculties will increasingly become integrated, and individual faculty members will become interchangeable in handling BSW, MSW, and advanced degree courses. Students, similarly, can be expected to move between course offerings on more than one level, and share courses with candidates for higher or lower degrees. The urgent task is to develop a realistic and effective system of education which can meet the various needs at the various levels.

References

Alexander, Chauncey A. "Foreword," in Edward E. Schwartz and William C. Sample, *The Midway Office.* New York, National Association of Social Workers, 1972.

Anderson, Claire M., and Thomas Carlsen. "The Midway Project on Organization and Use of Public Assistance Personnel," in Robert L. Barker and Thomas L. Briggs, eds., *Manpower Research on the Utilization of Baccalaureate Social Workers.* Washington, D.C., Veterans Administration, 1971, pp. 17–28.

Barker, Robert L., and Thomas L. Briggs. *Differential Use of Social Work Manpower.* New York, National Association of Social Workers, 1968.

—— *Using Teams to Deliver Social Services.* Syracuse, N.Y., Syracuse University Press, 1969.

Blum, Arthur. "Differential Use of Manpower in Public Welfare," *Social Work,* XI, No. 1 (1966), 16–21.

Brawley, Edward A. *Training Preprofessional Mental Health Workers.* Philadelphia, Community College, 1971.

Briggs, Thomas L. "Needed: Differential Education for Differential Staffing—a Prerequisite for Effectiveness." Paper presented at Annual Program Meeting, Council on Social Work Education, 1973; mimeographed.

Carlsen, Thomas. *Social Work Manpower Utilization in Mental Health Programs; Proceedings of a Workshop.* Syracuse, N.Y., Syracuse University Press, 1969.

Denham, William H., and Eunice O. Shatz, "Impact of the Indigenous Nonprofessional on the Professional's Role," in Willard C. Richan, ed., *Human Services and Social Work Responsibility,* pp. 178–87. New York, National Association of Social Workers, 1969.

Epstein, Laura. "Differential Use of Staff: a Method to Expand Social Services," *Social Work,* VII, No. 4 (1962), 66–72.

Farrar, Marcella, and Mary L. Hemmy. "Use of Nonprofessional Staff in Work with the Aged," *Social Work,* VIII, No. 2 (1963), 44–50.

Fry, John, M.D. *Medicine in Three Societies.* Aylesbury, Bucks, England, Chiltern House, 1969.

Gindy, Aida. "Launching the Second Development Decade: the Challenge to Social Work Education," in *Social Work Education in the Seventies,* XVth Congress of Schools of Social Work, International Association of Schools of Social Work, 1970, pp. 29–44.

Heyman, Margaret M. "A Study of Effective Utilization of Social Workers in a Hospital Setting," *Social Work,* VI, No. 2 (1961), 36–43.

Levitan, Sar A. *The Great Society's Poor Law,* Baltimore, John Hopkins Press, 1969.

Parsons, Talcott. "The Professions and Social Structure," in *Essays in Sociological Theory,* pp. 34–39. New York, Free Press, 1964.

"Proposed Standards for the Evaluation of Undergraduate Programs in Social Work." Council on Social Work Education Document #74-210-1, Jan., 1973.

Reich, Charles A. *The Greening of America.* New York, Bantam Books, Inc., 1971.

Richan, Willard C. "A Theoretical Scheme for Determining Roles of Professional and Nonprofessional Personnel," *Social Work,* VI, No. 4 (1961), 22–28.

——— "Indigenous Paraprofessional Staff," in F. Kaslow, ed., *Issues in Human Services*, pp. 51–71. San Francisco, Jossey-Bass, 1972.

Rivesman, Leonore. "Use of the Social Work Team with Aging Family Service Clients," in Robert L. Barker and Thomas L. Briggs, eds., *Manpower Research on the Utilization of Baccalaureate Social Workers*, pp. 63–76. Washington, D.C. Veterans Administration, 1971.

Roszak, Theodore. *The Making of a Counter Culture.* New York, Doubleday, 1969.

Rosengren, William R., and Mark Lefton. *Organizations and Clients.* Columbus, Ohio, Charles E. Merrill Publishing Co., 1970.

Schwartz, Edward E., and William C. Sample. *The Midway Office.* New York, National Association of Social Workers, 1972.

Scott, W. Richard. "Professional Employees in a Bureaucratic Structure: Social Work," in Amitai Etzioni, ed., *The Semi-Professions and Their Organization*, pp. 82–140. New York, Free Press, 1969.

Sobey, Francine. *The Nonprofessional Revolution in Mental Health*, New York, Columbia University Press, 1970.

——— "Introducing Content on Paraprofessionals in Schools of Social Work: Some Issues and Concerns for Educators," in *Workshop on Preparing Graduate Social Work Students to Work with Paraprofessionals*, pp. 3–8. New York, Council on Social Work Education, 1971.

Thompson, Jane K., and Donald P. Riley. "The Use of Professionals in Public Welfare," *Social Work*, XI, No. 1 (1966), 22–27.

Weed, Verne, and William H. Denham. "Toward More Effective Use of the Nonprofessional Worker: a Recent Experiment," *Social Work*, VI, No. 4 (1961), 29–36.

Wolfe, Corrine H. "Improving Services by Better Utilization of Staff," *Public Welfare*, XIX, No. 2 (1961), 53–57, 80–81.

——— *Use of Personnel without Professional Training in Social Service Departments.* New York, Medical Social Work Section, National Association of Social Workers, 1959.

——— "Strategies, Processes, and Resources for Achieving Needed Change in Education for the Social Professions." Paper presented at Symposium on Higher Education and the Social Professions, University of Kentucky, 1972; mimeographed.